# FOUNDATIONAL STUDIES IN TEACHER EDUCATION

## A Reexamination

STEVEN TOZER
THOMAS H. ANDERSON
BONNIE B. ARMBRUSTER
Editors

Special Issues from the *Teachers College Record*

JONAS F. SOLTIS, Series Editor

Teachers College, Columbia University
New York and London

Published by Teachers College Press, 1234 Amsterdam Avenue
New York, NY 10027

Originally published in *Teachers College Record*, v. 91, no. 3, Spring 1990.

*Library of Congress Cataloging-in-Publication Data*

Foundational studies in teacher education : a reexamination / Steven
   Tozer, Thomas H. Anderson, Bonnie B. Armbruster, editors.
      p.   cm. — (Special issues from the Teachers College Record)
   Includes bibliographical references and index.
   ISBN 0-8077-3059-9 (alk. paper)
   1. Teachers—Training of—United States. 2. Learning, Psychology
of. 3. Educational sociology—United States. 4. Education—United
States—History. 5. Education—Study and teaching—United States.
I. Tozer, Steven. II. Anderson, Thomas H. III. Armbruster, Bonnie
B. IV. Series.
   LB1715.F68   1990
   370'.71'0973—dc20                      90-37230
                                             CIP

# Contents

# Introduction

STEVEN TOZER,
THOMAS H. ANDERSON, AND
BONNIE B. ARMBRUSTER
*University of Illinois at Urbana-Champaign*

The teaching and learning processes in any culture are based in part on beliefs about how people learn and what people should learn. From Revolutionary times through today, educators in the United States have based their educational recommendations on their understandings of human psychology and on the knowledge and values of a particular culture at a particular time. In reading Thomas Jefferson's educational writings, for example, or the Yale Faculty Report of 1828, or Horace Mann's annual reports to the State of Massachusetts in the 1840s, one is struck with the pervasiveness of faculty psychology metaphors as part of the foundation on which these educational ideas were built. The other part of the foundation of their recommendations was not psychological but cultural in a wider sense, consisting of the social institutions, processes, and ideals of the culture for which people were being educated. Jefferson's and Mann's efforts at developing public school systems in their respective states were grounded not just in their beliefs about human learning, but in their views about what young people should learn in their particular cultural circumstances.

The earliest systematic efforts at professional preparation of public school teachers in the United States did not engage teacher candidates in studying these psychological and social foundations of teaching and learning processes. Emphasizing subject-matter content knowledge and standardized methods of teaching, the early two-year normal school curriculum *assumed* these foundations, rather than treating them explicitly — or critically. Near the beginning of the twentieth century, however, as the fields of psychology, sociology, history, and philosophy assumed importance as disciplines for the study of education, educational administrators and, soon after, teachers were expected to study these disciplines to develop understanding of the theory behind the practices of teaching.

At the same time, the two-year normal school curriculum rather quickly expanded to four years as teacher education became a function of colleges and universities. Benefiting from the study and teaching of such scholars as E. L. Thorndike and W. H. Kilpatrick in psychology and philosophy of education, respectively, Teachers College at Columbia University led the nation in developing a theory-based curriculum in teacher education, with teacher candidates expected to take coursework in such foundational disciplines as history, philosophy, sociology, anthropology, and psychology of education. In the 1920s and 1930s, the Foundations Division of Teachers College collapsed these several areas of study into two categories: the psychological foundations, which examined the nature of the human mind and learning processes; and the social foundations, which combined the other foundational areas into a cross-disciplinary approach examining the social institutions, processes, and ideals underlying educational policy and practice.

In creating this separation, the Foundations Division of Teachers College achieved two significant outcomes. First, they identified mind and culture as the twin foundations on which all teaching and learning processes are built; and second, they created a model for the *professional* preparation of teachers that has been adopted to one degree or another by certification agencies in every state in the nation. We underscore "professional" because the Teachers College faculty deliberately sought to reject what they saw as the technical training model of the normal school in favor of preparing practitioners who were as theoretically informed as practitioners in other professions. The Teachers College program envisioned teachers as potentially important decision makers in educational institutions — "educational statesmen," they said, who would apply theory to their practice and who would help formulate educational policy at local and state levels in a rapidly urbanizing, industrializing society with new educational needs — and new needs for the preparation of teachers. Prominent among the universities that followed and further developed the Teachers College foundations model was the University of Illinois at Urbana-Champaign, which formed a foundations division of its own in the 1940s — one that continued to focus on questions of theory and practice in foundations of education.

In the course of developing from discipline-based research on the psychological and cultural roots (or foundations) of educational processes to a legislated component (the foundation) of nearly all teacher education programs in the United States, the term "foundations of education" took on a dual meaning. The consequences of this development have become a point of no small significance today.

## THE ILLINOIS CONFERENCE

The 1980s are again a time of reexamination of society's educational needs and the nature of the professional preparation of teachers. In the context of the current national debate on teacher education, the University of Illinois College of Education, in May 1989, hosted a national conference to re-examine the nature of psychological and social foundations of education in teacher education programs. Leaders in the fields of psychology, sociology, philosophy, and history of education — and one practicing schoolteacher who has published from a social foundations perspective — were invited to present papers on the role and responsibility of foundational studies in teacher education. The purpose of the conference was not to establish a unified or consistent view of foundational studies, nor to propose a new curriculum for foundational studies. Rather, the purpose was to stimulate a national dialogue about foundational studies in teacher education. This book presents the papers from that conference and is thus an instrumental part of what we hope will be a continuing conversation.

Although the conference represented no effort toward a unified perspective, we were struck, as we first listened to the presentations and later prepared the papers for publication, with the prominence of recurrent themes that suggest to us, at least, common perspectives. Our introduction to these papers is thus structured around these themes. Our interpretation of the themes reflects our own perspectives and concerns; it is offered not as a definitive statement about these essays, but as an introduction and an invitation to further exchanges.

## THE FOUNDATIONS METAPHOR

One of the two major themes recurrent in the chapters of this book is a questioning of the foundations metaphor itself. Recognizing that the predominant understanding of this architectural metaphor today implies a primary place for the study of mind and culture in the teacher education enterprise, three of the four plenary-session presenters (Peterson, Soltis, and Shulman) at the Illinois conference questioned that application of the metaphor. While it might make sense to think in terms of mind and culture as the twin foundations of educational processes in any society, the view that study of mind and culture should be the foundation of teacher education programs is severely challenged in these chapters. These scholars appear wholeheartedly to endorse two views that emerged from the Teachers College efforts early in the century: first, that if we as theorists fail to study human psychology and human culture, we will never adequately understand teaching and learning processes (and the corollary, that teaching and learning processes can be employed as a text for understanding psychology and culture); and second, that teachers should be equipped with our best understanding of psychology and culture if they are adequately and professionally to understand their practice in schools.

Peterson, Soltis, and Shulman argue, however, that this does *not* mean that study of mind and culture must be the foundation of teacher candidates' programs. Each of them calls for a different metaphor for the study of mind and culture in teacher education — one that assumes not a primary but instead a complementary role for the study of mind and culture. Peterson, for example, suggests that the proper metaphor might be a "web" of understandings that integrate theory and practice, or a "dialogue" that suggests the relational processes of understanding theory and practice. Soltis suggests a notion of "professional literacy" that would provide a more accurate portrait of the professional importance and relative placement of the study of mind and culture in teacher education than the foundations metaphor provides. Shulman argues that such understandings should provide not a foundation but a "scaffolding" that integrates with other professional knowledge essential to the teaching enterprise.

All of these educators join with the others in this volume in arguing that we continue to need deeper understandings and greater research in the psychological and cultural foundations of teaching and learning processes. The question they go on to address, all from their own disciplinary perspectives, is how those understandings can best serve the education of teachers. This question raises the second of the recurrent conference themes.

## INTEGRATION: AIMS, CONTENT, METHODS, AND THE CONTEXTS OF EDUCATION

Many of the authors explicitly criticize contemporary practices in foundations of education for their persistently inadequate integration of foundational theory and knowledge into teacher education programs. While the research into mind and culture is voluminous and persuasive, teacher education programs, they charge, have failed to present that knowledge in ways that provide teachers with the benefits of that research. Nearly every chapter in this volume responds to that perceived inadequacy by arguing for attention to the practical contexts of teaching as a guide to integration of research knowledge and theory into the teacher education curriculum.

This attention to context is focused in ways that vary with the disciplines of the authors. Violas, for example, argues that teaching and learning take place in historical context, and that teachers need to understand that historical context if they are to make informed judgments with regard to selection of aims and methods in their practice. He illustrates how even seemingly remote European educational history can help raise critical questions challenging contemporary justifications for educational practice in the United States.

Trent argues that the changing sociological context of schooling, marked by growing percentages of minority students whom schools have served least effectively, necessitates new sociological understandings and new practical approaches for teachers. Leck argues that the contexts of gender and patriarchy have distinctively negative consequences for teaching and learning outcomes, and that patriarchal language and habits of thought present obstacles to exploring alternative aims and methods of schooling. Leck seeks to show that teacher educators and teachers alike need to understand those negative consequences and alternative approaches if schools are to serve the development of boys and girls adequately.

From a psychological foundations perspective, Doyle argues that research into classroom processes should provide the very foundation of teacher education, and Ames argues that classroom contexts should guide the selection of theoretical and research findings on the nature of motivation. Similarly, Linn argues that not all that we know about measurement theory is necessary for teachers to learn in the limited program space available, but that certain theoretical and practical understandings in the area of assessment are essential for the classroom teacher. The context of learning and, hence, of instruction is an important theme in Anderson and Armbruster as well.

All of this seems to say that while research in the psychological and cultural foundations of education might (and probably must) stray far afield from classroom contexts and forseeable classroom applications, the contexts of classrooms in our society, as they provide sites for practical applications of such research, should guide the selection of what teachers should be taught in teacher education programs. A reciprocal implication, stated explicitly in some chapters, is that research focused on classroom processes will reveal much of general significance about mind and culture.

One theoretical issue that crosses the boundaries of psychological and social foundations of education is the nature of the social and psychological construction of knowledge itself. In separate but complementary ways, Peterson, Leck, Soltis, Linn, and Anderson and Armbruster argue for recognition that knowledge cannot be delivered in a whole package to half-vacant minds, but must be constructed in a substantive dialogue between teacher and learner. One consequence of this view is that the learner's knowledge, values, and theory base must be taken seriously as an essential ingredient in the dialogical learning process. From the perspective of a practicing classroom teacher, Bigelow provides an account of how classroom dialogue can affirm the knowledge and values of the learner while at the same time employing that knowledge and value base to construct new and different understandings. A problem confronting the classroom teacher, then, is how to integrate the knowledge and perspectives of the learner with the new knowledge and perspectives to be achieved in a way that is educative for all students, not merely those who "take well" to traditional educational processes.

Peterson, Anderson and Armbruster, and Leck, in different ways, remind us that this problem of integration through dialogue is a problem that foundations educators must confront in their own classroom efforts to teach prospective teachers. Such an aim is a part of the intent to provide for prospective teachers — or better, to construct *with* prospective teachers — theory and knowledge in the form of tools they can use in practice.

This suggests a second major dimension of the theme of integration: classroom method. Several authors in this volume address the problem of how to integrate foundational perspectives with classroom methodology. A common response — one made explicit in Anderson and Armbruster, Leck, Bigelow, and Ames, for example — is that foundations professors should "teach as we would have them teach," as Soltis says. This integration of aims, methods, and content can be a model that serves to equip teachers to select intelligently and critically from available aims and methods of education. Many of our contributors agree with Doyle that such an insight is essential to the development of a profession of teachers who understand and can apply theoretical understanding to their practice.

A third dimension of the integration theme, discussed by Shulman, Peterson, Soltis, Doyle, Anderson and Armbruster, and most elaborately Broudy, is the role that case study can play in the professional preparation of teachers. Broudy argues that the failure of teacher education to develop and employ an appropriate method of case study is one of the major obstacles to the integration of research knowledge into professional preparation. Broudy describes how case study in other professions helps stabilize a "consensus of the learned" as cases mark the most important and recurring problems these professions address in their research and in their training of new professionals. While it is likely that different authors in this volume have different conceptions of case study in mind, their recurrent mention of this potential component of teacher education suggests a fruitful theoretical and practical problem for teacher educators in the foundations and elsewhere in the professional program.

## CONCLUSION

We hope these essays will contribute meaningfully to the current dialogue on teacher education and on the role of psychological and social foundations in that enterprise. The struggle with the foundations metaphor itself, for example, appears promising to us. Just as we expect our foundational studies to help equip teachers to be self-critical in their practice, so should we, our contributors advise, become more self-critical about our practice as teacher educators. To question the application of the foundations metaphor to teacher education curricula is not to diminish in any way the fundamental meaning of psychological and social foundations as bases on which teaching and

learning processes must inevitably rest. Nor should it diminish our disciplinary efforts to understand those processes. Clearly, however, further work
must be done if we are to develop ways in which foundational questions and
understandings are integrated potently into the full range of teacher education experiences.

We also find encouraging the prominent place of "dialogue" in these
chapters. Our understanding of dialogue as a method for helping students
in schools discover their own capacities—and for helping us as educators
more effectively equip prospective teachers to do so—remains a promising
area for theory, research, and classroom practice. In particular, the recurrent references to case study suggest an approach in which classroom
dialogue in teacher education can bring student experience and research
knowledge together into rich interpretations of problems in professional
practice.

# FOUNDATIONAL STUDIES IN TEACHER EDUCATION

A Reexamination

# Reconnecting Foundations to the Substance of Teacher Education

LEE S. SHULMAN
*Stanford University*

*After briefly reviewing the history of the idea of foundations in the education of profession-als, Lee Shulman explores a more integrated view of what psychologists and philosophers have to offer teachers in training. He offers an alternative metaphor to foundations that connects foundational disciplinary perspectives to the subject matter that teachers teach.*

Part of the education reform effort in the United States in the 1980s has been directed at improving teacher education and the activity of teaching itself. Traditionally, foundational studies have been given an essential role to play in preparing teachers by providing them with professionally relevant philo-sophical, psychological, sociological, and historical knowledge. On this firm but separate base, the edifice of an informed craft of teaching is supposed to be built. Is this way of thinking about foundations for teacher education the best way? Where did this idea of a discipline-based foundation for profes-sional training come from? Would not a more integrated view better serve to reconnect foundations with the substance of teacher education? What might such an integrated view look like? These are the themes I will explore in this chapter.

## HISTORICAL PERSPECTIVE

In 1908/1909, Abraham Flexner spent eighteen months on a grand tour that brought him to nearly every medical school in the United States and Canada. The report he wrote on those medical schools was so scathing, so uncompromising, it would make the most veteran observer blush. He found medicine practiced and taught in filthy storefronts, diplomas given to the in-competent, and no uniformity of curriculum or standards even in the better

*I wish to thank Jonas Soltis, who performed editorial magic in transforming the tapescript of my address to the conference into readable prose. I take full responsibility for its content and the relative informality of its style.*

2

schools. More than half of the medical schools in the United States closed within the decade after this report was published.

Flexner's report produced such powerful results because he had a normative image of what the ideal medical school ought to look like, which he used as a template to judge the adequacy of the medical schools he visited. His normative image of what constituted a sound medical education grew out of the German university model as instituted at the Johns Hopkins University Medical School in the United States.

Flexner was not a physician. He was an educator, the former headmaster of a preparatory school. However, he had helped his brother, Simon, complete medical school at Johns Hopkins. Flexner was mightily impressed by the Hopkins curriculum. It was built on the model of physicians being trained as scientists. It also was based on the idea that a proper medical education should be provided by a professional school at a university.

At this time, most who attended medical schools in the United States did so right out of high school. Medical schooling was more often apprenticeship rather than education. After the Flexner report, the norm steadily became acquiring a college education prior to admission to a medical school — a college education heavily invested in the sciences. Flexner argued that physicians had to be taught the foundations first. In fact, ten years after the Flexner report, the University of Rochester Medical School was founded on Flexner's model and, to this day, the standard medical school program is still called the Flexner curriculum. It requires two years of basic science done discipline by discipline before any clinical work is permitted.

This clearly is an early instance of the idea of foundations in professional education, but Flexner was not its inventor. The development of the university in the United States in the last half of the nineteenth century created a set of educational problems, one of which was the proper place and form for professional education. The answer was to put it in the university and provide an academic foundation for practice.

Listen to John Burgess of Columbia University in 1884 wrestle with the problem. Columbia was changing from a college to a university and Burgess was seeking to make sense of professional education in the new context.

> The philosophy faculty [i.e., arts and sciences] is the life and glory of the university. It is the foundation for everything further. Without it theology becomes a dreary dogmatism, law a withering letter and medicine a dangerous empiricism. [Technical, practical training in theology, law, or medicine is not education] for the simple reason that there is no philosophical faculty connected with them to furnish the broad basis of psychology, logic, history, literature, and philology . . . to give it the life and energy for an ever continuing development.[1]

Here in 1884, a quarter century before Flexner, we have an argument for the importance of foundations in professional education. Many thought, however, that the technical preparation of practitioners was not the proper mission of the new university. In Burgess's own time, Columbia did not accept its Teachers College as a professional school. Teachers College had to get its own charter, its own trustees, its own endowment, and negotiate a working relationship with the university. It remains independent to this day, and, some would say, not fully accepted by the arts and science faculty. Nevertheless, professional schools did find a place in many universities and foundations was their link to the academic community.

## THE FLEXNER LEGACY

Flexner did not invent something new in 1909. He participated in a tradition developing in the late nineteenth century that was trying to define and legitimate the education of professionals, and he made a major contribution to the improvement of medical education in the United States. Nevertheless, I remember vividly and lividly that when I became a medical educator at Michigan State in the mid-1960s and we tried to create a new form of medical education, the single most significant impediment to the improvement of the curriculum was Flexner! The foundations were disconnected, disintegrated, unrelated to practice. Each represented the agenda of the respective discipline and the concerns were not with the preparation of medical students for the practice and doing of medicine. Yet when we tried to revise the curriculum we met incredible resistance from those who saw the Flexner curriculum as the solution, not the problem.

This is not an isolated instance. You can look at the recent history of most reform attempts in medical education as attempts to overcome the discipline-bound conception of foundations in the Flexner curriculum. Some thirty years ago at Case Western Reserve University, for example, an organ systems curriculum was designed in which the circulatory system, the nervous system, the digestive system, the genito-urinary system, and so forth, were studied in interdisciplinary fashion. In a similar antifoundational manner, at Michigan State we designed a problems-based curriculum in which we used clinical cases as the organizing units. We came very close to being denied accreditation on grounds that our nondisciplinary-based curriculum did not meet the standard.

Given this difficult situation I began to look for a model of curriculum that would contrast with and provide a counter-example to the Flexner curriculum. I found it in Larry Cremin's *The Transformation of the School.*[2] This is a history of progressivism and progressive education in the United States. In it is an extraordinary account of the creation of a very special school at Teachers College, Columbia University, called the Lincoln School. The Lincoln School was created to exemplify the principle that there is something far more important than the classic disciplines for constructing curriculum;

that the curriculum ought to be constructed around real events, real problems, real tasks, real projects that students could engage in. There are two facing pages in *The Transformation of the School* that summarize the year-long curriculum on "boats" from the Lincoln School in which everything—the mathematics, the history, the geography, the science, the reading—was organized around the topic of boats. These pages vividly exemplify an interesting little irony about the Lincoln School, this extraordinary antithesis to the Flexner curriculum in medicine. The irony is that the creation of this school was inspired by the thinking of one particular educator, Abraham Flexner.

His monograph *A Modern School* was written in 1916, the same year in which Dewey published *Democracy and Education* and seven years after the publication of the Flexner report.[3] These two professional tracts provided the basic architecture for the Lincoln School. The apparent inconsistency between the medical Flexner and the elementary-school Flexner is understandable when one looks at the historical context: Each is offered as a solution to real, albeit distinctively different, problems. In 1909, for medical education the problem clearly was a lack of a core of basic scientific foundations, but in 1969, the same curricular solution—foundations through basic sciences—had become the medical curriculum's problem. In education at the turn of the century, the curriculum was the disciplines. The problem, as both Flexner and Dewey saw it, was how to make knowledge meaningful to young people who were not on the academic track to college; how to overcome the isolation and separateness of disciplinary knowledge. Unfortunately, the Lincoln School solution never became a problem because no one ever really accepted it as a solution.

## A DEWEYAN VIEW OF FOUNDATIONS

Interestingly, Dewey began to think institutionally about the problem when William Rainey Harper, the first president of the newly established University of Chicago, invited him to join the faculty and create a school of pedagogy in 1896. Like Burgess, Dewey understood that a professional school had to prove itself worthy of living in a university. He did not choose the foundations-first path, however. He took a more integrated view of the knowledge base for teacher education. In the school of pedagogy the "scholastic side" would be developed in historical and theoretical phases. The "historical development of ideas concerning education" is "an organic part of the record of the intellectual development of humanity," as the history of educational institutions is of humanity's "institutional development." The theoretical study required a generalization of this history into an account of the "various systems of pedagogy which have emerged," together with "a thorough discussion of psychology and sociology, in their bearings upon the selection, arrangement, and sequence of the studies of the curriculum and the methods required to give them their full efficiency."[4]

Dewey was talking here about the teaching of foundations in a manner that was integrated with the teaching of curriculum and the teaching of pedagogy. Teacher education would not be limited to methods required in a teaching subject; it would include but also integrate foundations. Regarding methods, Dewey went on to say that "the question of methods is impossible of divorce from that of subject matter; it is simply a question of the relation one subject bears to another and bears to the human mind."[5]

Method is something you do to subject matter and subject matter is what it is because it was arranged in its current form by a particular method. The abstractness of a disciplinary subject is convenient for the purposes of its own study, which is what the scholar in the university does. However, professional practitioners must see concrete connections of subject matter and method with the rest of the world of knowledge and culture and with the life of real people in society. In this way, Dewey argued for the melding of foundations with pedagogical practice and of pedagogical practice with content understanding. It is no accident that he called the school that he put on the University of Chicago campus a laboratory school and not a training school, which is what the normal schools for teacher training called themselves. The students in Dewey's school were not only to be trained as teachers there. This laboratory was a place in which future teachers and educational scholars experimented together. It is a very different, highly integrated model of teacher education.

### FOUNDATIONS: EXAMPLES OF ALTERNATIVES

In the rest of this article, I argue for reconstruction of a Deweyan kind of integrated foundations model. I fear this means that I will not make many friends, because I am going to argue for a withering away of the field of educational foundations as we now know it as separate, disconnected studies in psychology, history, sociology, and philosophy of education. In my view, foundations must be seen as an integral part of the connective tissue that gives shape and meaning to the education of teachers—as the framework for connecting and integrating the knowledge acquired in the liberal arts and sciences with the practice of pedagogy.

I will flesh out this idea with a few examples, some personal and some from research. The first example grows out of the Foundations of Learning for Teaching course that the philosopher Denis Phillips and I teach together at Stanford to secondary teacher education candidates. Our students are concurrently interning as teachers, and so have actual classroom experience to draw on. We wish to link the content of the school curriculum with the foundations for teaching that content and to connect the foundations for teaching with the actual methods for teaching in context. Much of what Phillips and I do in that course therefore begins with pieces of school text. We sit with our students and examine pieces of textbooks or readings that they are using in their everyday teaching activities. We ask questions about these, such as: What makes this hard to learn? What do your students think about this sort of thing before they even come to school? How many of you tried teaching this? How does it work? How do you know if the students know anything? We start thinking together, not about general learning theories, but about the very specific problems of learning particular things. A major theme in cognitive psychology today concerns the extraordinary power of what students already know. At the point in our course where the theme of prior knowledge becomes central, we read from the following important foundational text:

> Two households, both alike in dignity,
>     In fair Verona, where we lay our scene,
> From ancient grudge break to new mutiny,
>     Where civil blood makes civil hands unclean.
> From forth the fatal loins of these two foes
>     A pair of star-cross'd lovers take their life;
> Whose misadventur'd piteous overthrows
>     Do with their death bury their parents' strife.
> The fearful passage of their death-mark'd love,
>     And the continuance of their parents' rage,
> Which but their children's end nought could remove,
>     Is now the two hours' traffic of our stage;
> The which, if you with patient ears attend,
> What here shall miss our toil shall strive to mend.[6]

Exit stage right, at which point we begin Act 1, Scene 1 of *Romeo and Juliet*.
   We ask the students, only a quarter of whom are preparing to teach English, what is difficult about this text and what there is to be learned. Of course the first thing they say is that the words are very hard and the syntax is alien. We talk about the difficulty of the language and I suggest that we get past the language and figure out what Shakespeare is doing here. As far as I know, this is the only one of his plays that has a prologue. When high school students perceive that in this prologue Shakespeare reveals the plot of the play, they react with disbelief. They are convinced that a play or movie is good only if you do not know how it is going to end. Why would Shakespeare give away the whole plot at the very beginning? We begin to work on this.
   As we move into a discussion of tragedy, someone is likely to comment on the phrase "star-cross'd lovers." This phrase indicates that Shakespeare believed in the role of fate in human affairs. We explore possible problems that

the students' prior knowledge or expectations with regard to what constitutes a good play might create in learning this text. In particular, we consider the difficulties caused in prior knowledge in reading this very special kind of play, in which the tragic ending is clear from the beginning. We begin to explore what it is about tragedy that makes it compelling and emotionally wrenching even though you know how it is going to turn out.

After this discussion about the nature of the subject matter, we talk about such matters as advance organizers, schemata, and the ways in which certain kinds of frameworks for looking at a text connect what you already know with what is going to come later. In our class at Stanford, this very small piece of text — a text some of the students had already taught or were going to teach — became the basis for a fairly elaborate discussion not only of what was involved in learning about tragedy but also about the cognitive psychology of learning such things. This learning about general principles of learning was embedded in a piece of real school text. We try to use that kind of embedding whenever possible. We use excerpts from texts on human evolution, the American Revolution, and the quadratic formula. It puts more pressure on us, because we cannot use existing psychological or philosophical foundations textbooks, since there are no textbooks that conduct business in quite this way. We have to study particular subject matters. On the other hand, it encourages the students to start bringing in their own examples of texts they are actually teaching or planning to teach as exemplifications of some of what I will call foundational problems of pedagogy. This helps the students overcome the perennial question asked of foundations courses: What does this have to do with what we are doing in classrooms?

## FOUNDATIONS AND THE COMPREHENSION OF TEXT

Let me offer another example. One of the problems in teaching a kind of disembodied cognitive psychology is a tendency to assume that all learning from texts is alike. We have very powerful models of information processing and text processing. Very often, however, they distort rather than illuminate what is really learned in schools if they ignore the discipline-specific character of the particular kinds of texts being processed. Wineburg is currently studying the learning and teaching of history. The question he is asking is what it means to learn to read a piece of historical text.[7]

To answer that question Wineburg assembled a group of experienced historians, some of them scholars in American history and some who knew almost nothing about American history except what they learned in high school. He gave them a set of materials that we had earlier used in designing one of our assessment prototypes for history teachers.[8] These comprised original source documents dealing with the battles of Concord and Lexington, which included depositions taken from participants in the battle on both sides. These documents include paintings that were done at points ranging from a year or two after the battle to a century later, and some secondary sources, one of which was a piece of history and one of which was part of a novel by Howard Fast. Wineburg asked the historians to work through and make sense of these documents. At the same time, he got a group of very smart high school seniors who were taking an advanced-placement history course and asked them to do the same.

It was fascinating. The high school students began "text processing." Given materials they were supposed to learn, they started trying to "learn the materials." They knew that their job was to use active, constructive, strategic, comprehension processes to dig out the information in the text, and this was not very considerate text, which made their job even harder.

The historians did not expect the text to be considerate. In almost every case the first thing they did when they looked at a document was to find out who wrote it. For the high school students the text was faceless. It was a piece of text. For the historians, there was someone who had written this text, an author behind the text. They needed to identify the author to decide how much credibility to give him or her and the degree of reliability of the text. Wineburg had them thinking aloud as they were doing it. They began engaging in an active conversation with those texts, sometimes even arguing with them. Those texts were not seen as passive media for active teachers.

Wineburg claims that when you take the subject matter domain (in this case history) as the starting point, rather than the psychology of information processing, you end up with a very different model of what it means to make sense of a text. This represents a real challenge to the hegemony of a certain kind of information-processing model in accounting for human cognition. Different texts from different disciplines call for quite different forms of reading. We do not learn that from psychology; we learn it from the discipline itself. It is then our job as psychologists to discover how our general theories need to be modified so they are faithful to the preparation of teachers for particular content areas.

In this example of the doing of a foundational discipline, we see the necessity of turning things upside down. We put the content first and then ask the foundational discipline, in this case psychology, to adapt to the subject matter, rather than what we psychologists have tended to do in the past. Following this line of thinking, if I am to be honest about what is truly foundational, I have to conclude that the true foundation disciplines are not what we call foundations. The true foundation disciplines are the arts and sciences themselves. It is where the students of pedagogy learn the understandings, the skills, the dispositions, the forms of knowledge and of manner, that they in turn are expected to transform and teach to their students. Those are the real foundational disciplines. One of the things we have to analyze is how we would reformulate the arts and sciences and their teaching if we had the power to do so and if we had it in mind to teach them so that our students would be better future teachers.

## FOUNDATIONS AND CASES

One idea that many are exploring these days is to use the case method to teach what we would normally treat in foundations as declarative or propositional knowledge.[9] Looking for earlier examples of case-based teaching, I rediscovered a wonderful book, James Conant's *On Understanding Science*.[10] Conant argues that if you want students to understand science — and I am going to borrow terms from my late teacher Joseph Schwab — not as a rhetoric of conclusions but as a narrative of inquiry, as human events and human constructions rooted in human contexts, the only way to teach that kind of science is through case studies of doing science.

One example Conant gives is Galileo's work on pumps.[11] In the sixteenth century, it was widely known that there was an anomaly about pumps: A pump would only work as long as the well was no more than thirty-four feet deep, but no one knew why. Galileo attempted to solve the problem. He reasoned that when the pump stretches the water to a height of thirty-four feet, the weight of the column reaches the limit of what it can bear and the water falls back. The metaphor he used was of the water as a coiled spring, which the pump stretches upward.

Using that metaphor he failed abysmally to solve the problem. He was the captive of his own metaphor that pumps were pulling water up, even though he knew enough physics to know that fundamentally the problem was one of pressing down, not pulling up. This extraordinary scholar was so captured by his coiled-spring metaphor, however, that he could not solve the problem. Conant remarks wisely that the hardest job in the world is to reformulate your own metaphor. A generation later, two far less gifted scientists solved the problem, unencumbered by the weight of a misleading preconception.

I use this case in our course at Stanford to teach the content, to teach something about the nature of science as a mode of inquiry, and to teach a great deal about both the intellectual and the moral character of pedagogy. The lovely thing about such cases is that they offer not only intellectual lessons but also moral lessons. Galileo failed to solve the problem not because he was dumb, but because smart people can be captured by their own preconceptions as easily as and sometimes more easily than people who are not so smart. Teachers need to be aware of the fact that they themselves are often the source of students' preconceptions. In trying to simplify something, we often provide such a powerful analogy that it washes out everything that comes afterward.[12]

## FOUNDATIONS RECONSTRUCTED

I have tried to suggest some of the features of a reconstructed, integrated view of foundations. There is much more to be worked out. In closing I will offer five principles that will be essential to enacting the kind of program I have in mind.

1.  We must teach foundations in a way that is bound up with the content of instruction. It does not make sense to separate the content from the pedagogy now any more than it did for Dewey in 1896.

2.  The best way to think about the foundations is as that set of ideas and experiences through which we forge connections between what students learned in the arts and sciences and the pedagogy that they are going to be learning with us.

3.  Cases should become an important tool for teaching foundations. Cases can be selected, crafted, sequenced. If we can learn to make them more vivid and interactive, we can derive all of the virtues of their situatedness and their connectedness, and have the opportunity to add the moral to the intellectual in the teaching of pedagogy.

4.  We must use what we call the foundations to create vivid, compelling images of the possible in education, images of the long-term moral as well as intellectual possibilities of being an educated person in a good society.

5.  Our foundations work should continually present students with the opportunity to test the correspondence between their own thinking and doing and these images of the possible that they generate.

To help consolidate the import of these principles and my reconstructed image of foundations, I would like to propose a new metaphor. The old metaphor of foundations, of course, comes from the world of construction, where the bigger the building you want to build, the more solid and firm the foundation you must first provide. However, a little more than one hundred years ago, in Illinois, one of the great inventions in the history of construction occurred. In 1884 and 1885 the Home Insurance Company skyscraper, all ten stories of it, was built in Chicago. What was remarkable about it was that this ten-story skyscraper did not rest on a firm foundation. The architects invented a new form of support. Instead of heavy foundations and bearing walls, they built a steel skeleton, a scaffolding that was internal to the building. They first erected that scaffolding, and then on that skeleton they effectively hung the skyscraper. That system of girders and skeletal scaffolding remains to this day the technology for building skyscrapers. It is much more powerful than a solid foundation because it is integral to the structure. It weaves itself through it; it becomes part of the very structure it is trying to support. This new metaphor suggests that we in psychology, history, philosophy, anthropology, and sociology of education should not think of ourselves as foundations but, if you will, as scaffoldings, as the framework for pedagogy. This will free us to give up the notion that we are separate and autonomous, sitting there at the bottom holding everything up. We will have to find ways to integrate ourselves functionally, as well as intellectually, into the agenda of teacher education as it seeks to develop teaching as a true profession.

## Notes

1    John W. Burgess, *The American University, When Shall It Be? Where Shall It Be? What Shall It Be?* (Boston: Ginn, Heath, 1884), pp. 15–16, reprinted as Appendix 1 in John W. Burgess, *Reminiscences of an American Scholar: The Beginning of Columbia University* (New York: Columbia University Press, 1934), as quoted in Charles Wegener, *Liberal Education and the Modern University* (Chicago: University of Chicago Press, 1978).

2    Lawrence A. Cremin, *The Transformation of the School* (New York: Alfred A. Knopf, 1961), pp. 284–85.

3    Abraham Flexner, *A Modern College and A Modern School* (Garden City, N.Y.: Doubleday, 1923); and John Dewey, *Democracy and Education* (New York: Macmillan, 1916).

4    John Dewey, "Pedagogy as a University Discipline," *University of Chicago Record* 1, as quoted in Wegener, *Liberal Education and the Modern University,* p. 45.

5    Ibid.

6    *The Complete Works of William Shakespeare, Romeo and Juliet* (New York: Avenel Books, 1975), PROLOGUE, Act 1, p. 1011.

7    Samuel Wineburg, "Historical Problem Solving: A Study of the Cognitive Processes Used in the Evaluation of Documentary Evidence" (Ph.D. diss., Stanford University School of Education, 1989).

8    Ibid.

9    I discuss cases at some length in my American Educational Research Association presidential address published as "Those Who Understand: Knowledge Growth in Teaching," *Educational Researcher* 15, no. 2 (1986): 4–14.

10    James B. Conant, *On Understanding Science* (New Haven: Yale University Press, 1947).

11    Ibid., pp. 43–47.

12    The work of Rand Spiro and Paul Feltovich and their colleagues at the University of Illinois Center for the Study of Reading and the Southern Illinois University School of Medicine is particularly helpful in thinking about the role of analogies and cases in the learning of complex ideas. See, for example, Rand J. Spiro et al., "Cognitive Flexibility Theory: Advanced Knowledge Acquisition in Ill-Structured Domains," in *Tenth Annual Conference of the Cognitive Science Society* (Hillsdale, N.J.: Erlbaum, 1988).

# A Reconceptualization of Educational Foundations

JONAS F. SOLTIS

*Teachers College, Columbia University*

*Soltis claims that the members of any profession need a "professional literacy" of concepts and concerns held in common if they are to communicate effectively in debate and cooperative problem-solving. Properly conceived, he argues, social and psychological foundations instruction can provide teachers with a common background of theoretical frameworks, major concepts, alternative models, and historical precedents necessary for shared understanding and communication. Toward this end, Soltis suggests several fundamental educational questions that each prospective teacher should be equipped to reflect upon in informed ways.*

The reconceptualization of foundations of education that I will offer here rests on a basic set of philosophical and normative assumptions. In spirit, they are Deweyan. Dewey's idea of community as a form of associative living, as a sharing of common language, concepts, and interests, as the free interaction among different groups and the using of collective intelligence in the solution of common problems, is very basic to my view of what a community of professional educators should be. So too is Dewey's pragmatic view of knowledge.

Many think in shorthand terms of pragmatism as a view of knowledge as that which is useful and of truth as that which works. This way of characterizing Dewey's view of knowledge may contain an ounce of accuracy, but it also conveys a pound of distortion. The key to understanding Dewey's view of knowledge-in-use is his conception of educative experience and education as growth. Previous experience that enters into present experience to inform it, organize it, transform it, and reconstruct it is not just useful knowledge in the technical sense of knowing how to do something. It is useful in the richer and broader sense of being able to use one's past experience to orient oneself in a new situation, to interpret its manifold dimensions, to analyze its components, to guess at or anticipate its future, and to bring one's purposes to bear on the ongoing interaction of self and situation. This richer view of knowledge-in-use is basic to the view of foundational knowledge that I want to put before you, but I am getting ahead of myself. Let me start at the beginning.

## THE FOUNDATIONS METAPHOR

We are here today at a very crucial time in the history of the education of teachers to reconsider the idea of the foundations of education. Although only a half century old, foundations is a venerable idea in teacher education. Even those who doubt its potency for practice still tend to treat it with respect. There is something magic and majestic in the root metaphor of foundations. It suggests something solid, sound, basic, fundamental, and supportive of the whole superstructure of educational practice. Nevertheless, in the teacher education community today, there are serious doubts about the efficacy and essentiality of foundations.

The foundations metaphor is problematic. It suggests a false logical necessity. We all know that people can teach and even teach well without ever having studied foundations; yet we act as if that were not so. When foundations is claimed to be the essential theoretical knowledge base for educational practice, the lie is cast in indefensible form. Just as knowledge of oceanography is not a prerequisite for skillful fishing and there are superb mountain climbers who have not studied geology, so too there is a lack of necessary connection between foundations and teaching. No matter how natural and appealing this interpretation of the root metaphor is, it is just plain wrongheaded and our belief in the importance of foundations suffers from this misinterpretation, however understandable it may be.

Of course we could remedy this situation by replacing the metaphor of foundations with a new metaphor. That would not be an easy bill to fill, however. A new metaphor would have to be as elegantly suggestive of the power and value of foundational studies as the old. It would have to fit comfortably into the space left in college catalogs when all the references to foundations are removed. Or failing to find a new metaphor, we could change the name of foundations departments or submerge foundations people in other less metaphorically suggestive departments called policy studies, administration, or curriculum and theory as some institutions already have done. But what would happen to the powerfully suggestive idea of the basic importance of educational foundations if we all did so? Would the sense of something being fundamental to teacher education disappear? Would we lose something important to the proper normative conception of the educating profession? If a "foundation" for teaching is not logically necessary, might having one be professionally or morally desirable? Is there any way to conceive of foundations that remains true to the force of the powerful original root metaphor and yet avoids a mistaken view of the relationship between theory and practice, knowledge and use?

I think so and that is what I am here to offer you today. I would like to recast the argument for foundations-as-basic from one that is directly practical and technical to one more philosophical, cultural, and normative in form. I would like to expand the concept of knowledge-in-use beyond the technical sense of application to include the interpretive, perspectival, creative, imaginative, sensitive, normative, critical, and formative uses of knowledge. I would like to offer a reconceptualization of foundations for educators that befits the profession of teaching; a profession not in the sociological sense of having or seeking elevated status, but in the human service sense of intelligent and sensitive practitioners talking, thinking, and debating about good practice as they engage in it; a profession that cares about what it does and constantly strives to do it better.

## THE ARGUMENTS FOR FOUNDATIONS RECONSIDERED

There are two very popular recent scholarly books about education that have surprised their publishers, drawn much scorn as well as support from the academic community, and received a great deal of attention from the media and the public. They are so strident in their recommendations for education that nearly everyone has strong feelings pro and con about them. I cite them today not to join the controversy, but because they seem to speak to fundamental issues regarding education that the American public is concerned about. They are Bloom's *Closing of the American Mind: How Higher Education Has Failed American Democracy and Corrupted the Souls of Today's Students* and Hirsch's *Cultural Literacy: What Every American Needs to Know.*[1]

Forget for the moment your personal reactions to these controversial works. Consider instead what each tries to do. Think with me for a moment about the central arguments in Bloom and Hirsch that the public finds so appealing. Let us see if we can use the themes of these arguments to sketch a parallel direction for a more philosophical and cultural argument for the role foundations of education in teacher education can take.

Bloom claims that our conception of the educated person has become too relativistic, too narrow, and too technical. We need, he says, to reinstitute the idea that the educated person is one who has been asked in his or her college education to seriously consider the fundamental questions of life. He takes these to be: What is the nature of man (*sic*)? What is truth? What is beauty? He sees the college experience as the only time when these fundamental questions of human existence can be raised in a supportive environment and their gnawing persistence injected into the consciousness of the students being educated so that, forevermore, they will wrestle with being human no matter what else they do with their lives.

With a little extrapolation, I think we can argue (and many have) that there also are persistent and perennial educational questions that are equally fundamental to the education of educators and that well-educated educators need to meet and wrestle with them and incorporate them into their consciousness throughout their whole careers if they are to be truly educated professionals. Some of these questions are: What are the aims of education? How do human beings learn? What is the relation of school to society? What knowledge is of most worth? For those charged with the education of our young, these are no less fundamental questions than are questions about the meaning of life, truth, and beauty.

We have here an old, yet seemingly timeless philosophical argument for raising the fundamental questions of education in the minds of all teachers. In today's climate of reform, the serious raising of these questions takes on a new urgency. If reform is to be more bottom-up than in the past, teachers themselves must raise and answer these fundamental questions in their own situations. It is time for us to reaffirm this kind of philosophical argument for the importance of foundational studies, which urges question-asking rather than misleadingly promising technical knowledge essential for practice. We need to raise the consciousness of each new generation of teachers to what is eternally problematic in their profession and in need of their persistent critical and creative attention.

When we turn to Hirsch, we find the cultural strand for our reconsidered argument. Hirsch bemoans the fact that in our society we lack cultural literacy. By cultural literacy he means a set of concepts, ideas, and common knowledge that gives us as members of a common culture the requisite background to engage in public dialogue, to understand each other, and to engage in meaningful debate. Just as people who know no quantum physics or microeconomic theory cannot engage in dialogue about such subjects, he argues, so too those of us whose educations did not produce a common core of our culture's shared concepts cannot fully understand each other or communicate effectively as members of our society.

I do not think the answer to this problem lies in Hirsch's lists-of-words approach or in his dictionary, but that is beside the point. He is correct about the need for a community to share a set of common concepts and knowledge as a background against which they can speak to each other meaningfully and without which not only is understanding of the everyday written and spoken word very difficult, but meaningful and responsible debate is impossible. The same is true in education.

Professionals in any field need to communicate effectively if responsible debate and problem solving are to be achieved. As a community of professionals, educators, too, need to achieve a high level of intragroup literacy. They need to acquire the language and concepts of education, the background history, basic theoretical frameworks, central ideas, and common knowledge and traditions that give them the associative conceptual background that permits serious communication, dialogue, and debate as professionals. Much of this will come from various education courses, of course, but without foundations, the broad historical, social, psychological, and philosophical dimensions of professional literacy will be haphazardly treated if at all and our teachers will be merely literate technicians rather than broadly educated and morally sensitive literate professionals.

## A SPECIFICATION OF EDUCATIONAL FOUNDATIONS

Superficially, it would seem that we already have the wherewithal for providing professional cultural literacy in our current foundations courses and requirements. Yet we all know that across and even within institutions, very few if any basic foundations courses contain the same common elements and students often are allowed to choose among a variety of courses. To say that students can take any courses they wish to meet the foundations requirements and to openly admit that we all do very different things in teaching foundations is to reveal an appalling truth about our lack of agreement about what we believe we should be doing in common, and what we believe is culturally and normatively essential to teacher education. Our contentless agreement that foundations should provide interpretive, normative, and critical perspectives[2] notwithstanding, I do not think that we have been specific enough about the core of common content essential to the education of the literate professional. Nevertheless, I also believe that a highly specific list of such things would be as bad a solution to this problem as is our current, overly broad description of foundations requirements and purposes.

What I think is needed is a middle-range specification of what should be core and common. It should specify the key fundamental questions in education and include a set of theoretical frameworks, major concepts, alternative models, competing arguments, and historical precedents sufficient to provide an appropriate cultural and professional literacy. Such a literacy could serve all educators throughout their careers as background with which they can communicate and understand each other as they puzzle over the major perennial, persistent, and profound educational questions that arise in each new generation in different guises and in unanticipated forms.

Let me illustrate the kind of specificity I have in mind by way of a concrete example. A few years ago I designed and coauthored a set of five textbooks called the Thinking about Education series.[3] Utilizing a case-studies approach, the series offers a version of this mid-range specification of core concepts, of shared background knowledge, and the questions fundamental to education. I cite it here only as an illustration of what I am arguing for. It is one version, only a first effort, but it points in the direction I believe we need to go if we are to provide a common core of foundational cultural literacy for educators. The fundamental questions that are raised and the current conceptual frameworks for dealing with them that I and my coauthors have explored in our five short textbooks are sketched below.

I will start with *Approaches to Teaching* because I think that the question of how to approach teaching is one of the most fundamental questions a teacher can ask. It is akin to asking how to lead one's life. In order to provide the professional background literacy needed to be able to think about and discuss this question, Gary Fenstermacher and I offered three possibilities drawn from the current forms that teaching practice actually takes. We called them the executive approach, the therapist approach, and the liberationist approach. The executive teacher is one who is committed to using the best knowledge available from educational research to effectively manage the classroom and achieve the goal of maximizing learning. A teacher using the therapist approach views each student as unique and in need of nurturing to achieve innate potential. Self-concept and personal growth are the goals so that an autonomous, capable person emerges at the end of the process. The liberationist teacher works toward the goal of freeing the mind. In the liberal arts tradition, this teacher models the moral and intellectual virtues while initiating students into the disciplinary forms of knowledge of liberal learning. These conceptions give teachers a way to think and talk about approaches to teaching that stress very different yet legitimate goals and values, a way to think about what kind of teacher one should be and how to lead their lives as teachers.

Related to the question of what approach to teaching one should take is a second question: How do human beings learn? The shared literacy needed to begin to struggle with this question is rooted in the different theories of learning that have been produced from Plato and Locke to the present array of competing theories including behaviorism, Gestalt, discovery learning, information processing, and artificial intelligence. Denis Phillips and I argued that each of these theories lacks universal adequacy. We illustrated this using clear cases in which at least one theoretical explanation failed. We showed how different theories explained the same phenomenon. We also tried to show that each of them, even the classical ones, offers helpful insights into the multiple and complex situations that define a teacher's struggle to help people learn. In this way teachers see that learning theories provide perspectives on teaching — and ways to think about how to nurture it in different settings — rather than providing single-minded directives for practice.

The third question our series proposes is: What should be the aims of education? Two corollary questions are: What constitutes being an educated person? What should the curriculum be? The history of human thought includes a great tradition of answers to these questions from Plato, Rousseau, and Dewey to the progressive and traditionalist debates early in this century to the current discussions of educational reform. Decker Walker and I sketched these and also dealt with the dominant Tylerian form of curriculum rationalization, different ways to conceive of subject matter, and the politics of determining aims in a pluralistic society. We argued that after thinking and weighing different views on teaching and learning, curriculum questions become personally more meaningful to teachers and are not just exercises in grand theory. Constructing curriculum can then become a personally engaging activity, sometimes in debate with others, and not just something done *by* others and given *to* the teacher to execute with skill but without much deliberative thought.

The fourth question we propose is: In what ways does the school as a social institution serve our ideals of nurturing and developing educated persons and in what ways does our social structure constrain us? Walter Feinberg and I saw the needed literacy to deal with this question along three dimensions. We saw the dominant form of interpretation of the role of school and society to be the functionalist view represented by positivist researchers and we contrasted that with the conflict theorist's and neo-Marxist's critical views of social reproduction. The third perspective was an interpretativist view of the newer ethnographic and qualitative researcher bent on studying how people negotiate their socially constructed world. We argued that these three broad conceptualizations provide the perspective needed for professionals—including teachers—to begin to analyze schooling and make sense of the school as a social institution.

Finally, the fifth question: What moral obligations do teachers share with their colleagues as educators, and its corollary, how can one be an ethical professional? Ken Strike and I tried to lay out the options along consequentialist and nonconsequentialist views of ethics using realistic case studies in which the ethical issues of education arise on a day-to-day basis. Our emphasis, recognizing the pervasiveness of relativism today, was on the principles of benefit maximization and respect for persons and on a rational, objective approach to ethical thinking for educators. We argued that education is a moral enterprise and that foundations has the obligation to help professionals see *their* obligations—in part by learning to share a language and a mind set for identifying and dealing with ethical issues in an objective and rational way.

These may not be the best ways to specify the basic philosophical questions of education and to supply the alternative concepts and theoretical frameworks we currently have available to us to think about and debate our answers to them, but I do believe that this is the kind of middle-range specification we need to have and the format it should take. As for the fundamental aspects of education that the series treats, that is, curriculum and aims, teaching, learning, the school as a social institution, and the ethical obligations of educators, I can think of no others that we need to add that are equally or more essential to understanding the nature of education as a human enterprise. These, in my judgment, constitute the basic core of foundational topic areas.

Even if you were to grant that I have the philosophical questions and cultural literacy topics and arguments right, the reconceptualization of foundations that I promised you when I started has only just begun. We need to explore and understand more fully the normative nature of a community of practitioners and make more explicit the range of uses to which fundamental professional knowledge can be put. I have talked so far only about what might be the core *content* of foundations. It is time to reconceptualize the role of foundational knowledge as it is used in a professional community.

## A COMMUNITY OF PRACTICE

A genuine community of practice is not just an aggregate group of practitioners. It is a community with a past, a present, and a future. It exists by virtue of the older practitioners' transmitting the skills and guiding traditions of the practice to the initiates and instilling in them a commitment to the overarching purpose of the practice and a normative desire to practice well.

Dewey displays these ideas of community, transmission, and solidarity quite nicely in *Democracy and Education* when he talks about the nature of social groups in general. I quote him at length because he gives depth to the idea of foundations that I am trying to develop here. His normative view of social living gives us not only a way to think about a kind of foundation that provides a common base of knowledge to be used in practice, but a foundation of philosophical questions and theoretical frameworks to be infused and diffused in the dialogues of practitioners.

> [A social group] not only continues to exist *by* transmission, *by* communication, but it may fairly be said to exist *in* transmission, *in* communication. There is more than a verbal tie between the words common, community, and communication. Men live in a community in virtue of the things which they have in common; and communication is the way in which they come to possess things in common. What they must have in common in order to form a community or society are aims, beliefs, aspirations, knowledge — a common understanding — a like-mindedness as the sociologists say. . . . The communication which insures participation in a common understanding is one which secures similar emotional and intellectual dispositions — like ways of responding to expectations and requirements. . . . Individuals do not even compose a social group because they all work for a common end. The parts of a machine work with a maximum of cooperativeness for a common result, but they do not form a community. If, however, they were all cognizant of the common end and all interested in it so that they regulated their specific activity in view of it, then they would form a community. But this would involve communication. Each would have to know what the other was about and would have to have some way of keeping the other informed as to his own purposes and progress. Consensus demands communica-

tion. . . . Not only is social life identical with communication, but all communication (and hence all genuine social life) is educative.[4]

The facilitation of professional communication and consensus on the deepest level possible is what the study of foundations must be about. Of course, consensus and communication can also be secured by indoctrination into a single, pervasive point of view. That is why foundations must create a genuine quest for answers to perennial questions with the recognition that our answers may not converge and may have to change over time in response to new problems, new insights, and new social contexts. It is why foundations needs to help people see the alternatives available for making sense of curriculum and aims, teaching and learning, schooling and society, and professional ethics.

Competing conceptions open up the minds and conversations of practitioners. Their conversations should be aimed at securing what is of mutual interest and benefit. Without common basic questions (shared interests) and shared understandings of the best available answers (alternative conceptualizations), the educational community would have little to think with or about. They might be good, effective, hard-working parts of the educational machine, but they would not be professionals who were able to be thoughtfully responsible for the well-being of the learners in our society.

A professional community's normative dimension is even more complex than I have suggested thus far. It is normatively both conservative and progressive; it looks to the past as well as to the future. It is conservative in that it is based on a tradition of practice with time-tested standards of excellence built into it. It is conservative because it is based on historically shared values and interests and on favored ways to organize and communicate knowledge. Its members share a traditional canon of literature in which high ideals, goals, aspirations, and images of good practice both collective and individual are enshrined.

While a community with a tradition is thus conservative, it can also be progressive. Built into the tradition of educational theory and practice are fundamental questions that motivate a seeking of the good, the right, the better, and the best. By continually seeking better answers to questions about curriculum and aims, teaching and learning, and the school and society, we display our progressive and melioristic tendency. Through our own practice and through our ongoing dialogue and debate in the community of practitioners, we seek the improvement of practice and of education. Foundational knowledge serves this progressive normative cause not in a how-to fashion, but by raising the basic philosophical questions of practice, by supplying the needed basic conceptual and theoretical literacy, by instilling the desire to improve practice, and by sensitizing educators to the ethical and normative dimensions of their practice.

## PROFESSIONAL KNOWLEDGE-IN-USE

In this sketch of education as a community of practice, I have suggested that knowledge, especially that of the sort we teach about in foundations, can be variously used. Some, like knowledge of learning theories, for example, may be directly applied in practice. Thus far, however, I have argued for two basic, yet not so direct, uses of foundational knowledge among professionals. The philosophical questions of education are to be used, in this view, to create a hunger for understanding and improving education as a human enterprise. The cultural literacy core is used as the medium for professional dialogue, discussion, and debate, and the location and resolution of common issues and problems. Both of these "uses" provide perspective and interpretive power. Such knowledge is useful in "seeing," in making sense of what is going on and critically seeking its improvement rather than as knowledge of how to do something in particular.

Our dominant technical sense of knowledge-in-use as how-to knowledge is much too narrow a view for a profession to take, however necessary it may be to the transmission of sophisticated skills and well-meaning directives for establishing good practice. Knowledge-in-use is a much richer concept when viewed from a broader context outside of being told what to do and how to do it.

One of the most dynamic and richest conceptions of knowledge-in-use that I know of is also to be found in Dewey.[5] His model of experience leading to growth fits very well with what I am trying to convey here. One component of his model is *funded* experience, and that means knowledge that is meaningful for the individual because of its connection with past experience. What we know enters into a present situation both because it was meaningful to us in the past and because it is meaningfully useful to us in the present. The possible uses of knowledge in any particular situation, however, are multiple. It might be used to express our interests or our purposes. It might suggest possible actions or desirable ends. It might be used to assess the means at our disposal to act in the situation. It might be used in the form of executive to secure our ends-in-view. It might be used as a standard of judgment applied to the results of our actions. It might generate alternative hypotheses for action. I could go on. If not endless, the uses of knowledge, on Dewey's view, are many and expansive. Still, this is only the start for understanding his view of knowledge-in-use.

The activity that one is engaged in when using knowledge should also be an occasion for the reconstruction, reorganization, and transformation of one's fund of knowledge. We build on what we know. In the process of using our knowledge we often find that it needs modification or is added to by present experience. Such transformation and reorganization of our knowledge gives us added power to project into and anticipate the future forms that experience might take. There is a dynamic, creative, transactive, and continuous quality to the growth of personal knowledge and our ability to act effectively in the world in the pursuit of our purposes. This kind of knowledge-in-use is cumulative not in some simple additive way, but organically and transformationally.

Moreover, this Deweyan view of educative experience and education as growth is applicable not only to the individual psyche, but also to a social group as a whole. Foundational knowledge not only provides the individual with empowering perspectives, but also makes possible a community of practitioners who share a fundamental set of interests in improving teaching, learning, schooling, curriculum, aims, and the ethics of their craft. By using their collective experience in making sense of education and developing new meanings and new ways to address future education problems and situations, as a professional community they also grow and progress. This broader view of foundational knowledge-in-use coupled with the concept of a core of literacy provides the glue that holds the community of educators together and moves them forward. The foundations metaphor works if only we reconceptualize it this way. In fact, I would argue that the conception of foundations that I have sketched here is what education in general is and should be about. It provides a model for the effective teaching and learning of any subject. We should teach our teachers as we would have them teach.

## Notes

1   Allan B. Bloom, *Closing of the American Mind: How Higher Education Has Failed American Democracy and Corrupted the Souls of Today's Students* (New York: Simon & Schuster, 1987); and E. D. Hirsch, *Cultural Literacy: What Every American Needs to Know* (Boston: Houghton Mifflin, 1987).

2   Council of Learned Sciences in Education, *Standards for Academic and Professional Instruction in Foundations of Education, Educational Studies, and Educational Policy Studies* (Ann Arbor, Mich.: Prakken Publications, 1986).

3   Gary D. Fenstermacher and Jonas F. Soltis, *Approaches to Teaching* (New York: Teachers College Press, 1986); D. C. Phillips and Jonas F. Soltis, *Perspectives on Learning* (New York: Teachers College Press, 1985); Decker F. Walker and Jonas F. Soltis, *Curriculum and Aims* (New York: Teachers College Press, 1986); Walter Feinberg and Jonas F. Soltis, *School and Society* (New York: Teachers College Press, 1985); and Kenneth A. Strike and Jonas F. Soltis, *The Ethics of Teaching* (New York: Teachers College Press, 1985).

4   John Dewey, *Democracy and Education* (New York: Macmillan, 1961), pp. 4-5. Emphasis in original.

5   Ibid.

# Educational Psychology as a Foundation in Teacher Education: Reforming an Old Notion

PENELOPE L. PETERSON,
CHRISTOPHER M. CLARK, AND
W. PATRICK DICKSON
Michigan State University

*In this article, the authors raise questions about the place and form of educational psychology in the larger conversation about the thoughtful preparation of teachers. Recent research and theory in cognition and instruction suggest alternatives to traditional concepts of the learner, the teacher, and classroom learning. This research has implications for the reconsideration of the content, curriculum, and methods of teaching educational psychology and also for the ways in which teacher educators learn to teach the adults who will become tomorrow's teachers.*

The way in which teachers are educated and supported to meet the challenges of the twenty-first century has become an issue of contention. In raising alarm, criticizing the status quo, and making recommendations, various study groups and blue-ribbon panels have focused on economic issues, equity and excellence, the need for more rigorous subject-matter preparation, and the restructuring of incentives and the career ladder for teachers. Although considerable agreement exists about the need for improvement in teacher education and professional development, wide differences of opinion are apparent about where to concentrate limited resources. These difficulties of opinion will probably persist as the recommendations and mandates of the 1980s become the legislation, regulations, and redesigned teacher preparation programs of the 1990s. Whatever programs and designs emerge from the present period of scrutiny, research, and revision in teacher education, we are confident that each route to certification will include substantial attention to learners, learning, and human development. For, in the broadest sense, the roles and purposes of teachers will continue to focus on the facilitation of learning and development by each student, to the practical limits of teachers' abilities. Consider what one portrait of future teachers implies about their knowledge of learning and development. Such teachers would

> possess broad and deep understanding of children, the subjects they teach, the nature of learning and schooling, and the world around them. They exemplify the critical thinking they strive to develop in students, combining tough-minded instruction with a penchant for inquiry. . . . Competent teachers are careful not to bore, confuse, or demean students, pushing them instead to interact with important knowledge and skill. Such teachers interpret the understandings that students bring to and develop during lessons; they identify students' misconceptions, and question their surface responses that mask true learning.[1]

This quotation portrays a teacher who has deep knowledge of the psychology of learning, development, and instruction; who is able to apply and draw on this psychological knowledge in his or her own teaching; who is able to transform this knowledge when necessary to adapt to new learning situations and learners; and who is continuously adding to and developing psychological knowledge through informal inquiry, as well as through formal education. Thus, knowledge of the domain of educational psychology is central to the teaching enterprise and to the preparation of teachers.

It was almost a century ago that William James, in his *Talks to Teachers,* made the argument for including psychology in the preparation of teachers. At that time, psychology was an infant science with only the sketchiest understanding of the human learner and human cognition. Since then, educational psychologists have filled in much detail in the explanation of human cognition that James put forth:

> The gist of the matter is that: Every impression that comes in from without, be it a sentence which we hear, an object of vision, or an effluvium which assails our nose, no sooner enters our consciousness than it is drafted off in some determinate direction or other, making connection with the other materials already there, and finally producing what we call our reaction. . . . The impression arouses its old associates; they go out to meet it; it is received by them, recognized by the mind. . . . It is the fate of every impression thus to fall into a mind preoccupied with memories, ideas, and interests, and by these it is taken in. This way of taking in the object is the process of apperception. . . . The apperceived impression is engulfed in this, and the result is a new field of consciousness, of which one part (and often a very small part) comes from the outer world, and another part (sometimes, by far the largest) comes from the previous contents of the mind.[2]

Although James's vision of the learner anticipated much of the work by contemporary educational psychologists on cognition and instruction, today educational psychologists have more to contribute to the teaching-learning enterprise than they did a century ago. For example, in the last decade research on learning has revealed a great deal about students' conceptions and misconceptions and has shown how the knowledge that students bring to the teaching-learning situation affects substantially what and how students learn.[3] William James's broad and general claims about learning have been supported and elaborated by subject matter — specific research on teaching and school learning.

Although one prominent source of proposals for reform of teacher preparation, the Holmes Group, drew significantly on recent theory and research in the psychology of learning and teaching in portraying the ideal teacher, their report left the reformulation of educational psychology as a course of study undefined. The group's only caveat was that "professional courses of study in education should meet the standards of the core disciplines from which they derive; that is, educational psychology must be sound psychology."[4] Now that many institutions are attempting to build on such general recommendations to reform their teacher education programs, faculty need to begin to explicate, more specifically, the learning and teaching of educational psychology in the preparation of teachers for the twenty-first century.

## RETHINKING EDUCATIONAL PSYCHOLOGY

How should educational psychology be conceptualized in the new teacher preparation programs being developed in the United States and elsewhere? As we reflected on this question, we found that we drew heavily on the recent scholarly writing and theorizing of educational psychologists in the area of cognition and instruction. Moreover, we sense a growing awareness among educational psychologists of the need to reexamine their own discipline.[5] Such a reexamination needs to focus not only on the learning and teaching of educational psychology but also on understanding how educational psychology as a course of study influences the knowledge of candidates in teacher preparation. The content and methods of educational psychology courses seem to be determined largely by the scope and sequence of educational psychology textbooks, which seem to reflect a static conception of educational psychology as a "foundation" in teacher education. Our reading of recent research and theory in cognition and instruction led us to begin to question this unexamined metaphor.

## DILEMMAS IN THE LEARNING AND TEACHING OF EDUCATIONAL PSYCHOLOGY

We found that what emerged was not a new "scope and sequence chart" for teaching educational psychology, but rather several interconnected questions and problems that might provoke our thinking and that of our colleagues as we begin to consider how educational psychology should be incorporated into revised teacher education programs. Each suggests inherent dilemmas for the learning and teaching of educational psychology. Some of these dilemmas may be resolved or managed by appeal to empirical research on teaching and learning. Others may yield to practical constraints or to local traditions, norms, and preferences. In any case, the time is upon us, as educational psychologists, to engage in thoughtful dialogue about what knowledge our field has to offer to future teachers and how that knowledge might be taught well.

Our questions confront both educational psychologists and teacher educators with four persisting problems of practice in preparing professionals for a changing profession: the problem of transfer or application of psychological knowledge, the problem of balance between general and content-specific knowledge about learning; the need to consider the knowledge and beliefs of prospective teachers; and the challenge of applying knowledge about teachers' learning to the teaching and learning of educational psychology. In short, the curriculum and the instructional approaches appropriate for creating an educational psychology for teachers in tomorrow's schools need examination in light of recent research on teaching and learning. In what follows, we use these problems to frame a discussion of issues to be considered in rethinking educational psychology as a foundation in teacher education.

## THE PROBLEM OF TRANSFER

Educational psychology is taught as a foundations course in most teacher education programs, and at least one course on the psychology of human learning is typically required for teacher certification by most states. Typically, in most colleges and universities teacher education majors take a course or courses in the psychology of learning, development, and instruction prior to taking their methods courses and practicum experiences, and prior to doing their actual teaching in schools. The pattern, sequencing, and methods of teaching educational psychology make implicit assumptions about teachers' knowledge of learners and learning. An underlying rationale for the timing and format of educational psychology courses is that teacher education majors need the basic factual information and conceptual knowledge of the psychology of learning, development, and instruction to be able to apply this knowledge in their clinical teaching experiences, in their methods courses, and, eventually, in their classroom teaching. Thus, the teaching of educational psychology as a foundation in teacher education has rested on certain classic but typically unquestioned psychological assumptions about the learning of the prospective teacher and the transfer of that learning to teaching.

## UNQUESTIONED ASSUMPTIONS UNDERLYING PSYCHOLOGY AS A FOUNDATION

From early attempts to extrapolate laws of learning from laboratory studies of animal learning to the present writers of contemporary educational psychology textbooks who still hark back to some "rather obvious principles known since the beginning of this century," educational psychologists have framed the problem as one of transfer of learning from one situation to another, or from in school to out of school.[6] Gagne introduced the concepts of vertical transfer and horizontal transfer—two concepts that have affected significantly the content and methods of teaching educational psychology for the past two decades. In his theory of vertical transfer, Gagne posited the idea that learning lower-level skills in a learning hierarchy facilitates learning higher-level skills in the hierarchy because they serve as prerequisites for those higher-level skills as follows:

> In *vertical transfer,* intellectual skills exhibit transfer to "higher-level" skills, that is, to skills which are more complex. . . . The intellectual skill of multiplying whole numbers, for example, is a part of the more complex skills of dividing, adding, and multiplying fractions, finding square roots, solving proportions, and many others. Transfer to the learning of these more complex skills is dependent primarily on the *prior learning* of the simpler skills. The more basic skills must be "mastered," in the sense that they can be readily retrieved, in order for transfer to take place to the learning of the more complex intellectual skills. This principle is illustrated by the learning hierarchy.[7]

While Gagne's description of vertical transfer seems to pertain more to the learner's procedural knowledge, Bloom et al.'s *Taxonomy of Educational Objectives* sets forth a similar hierarchical model with the application of factual knowledge being dependent on prior learning of propositional knowledge and factual information.[8] Thus, in an educational psychology course the prospective teacher might be taught the "definition of learning" prior to being taught the "principle of learning" on the assumption that the propositional knowledge—the definition—is necessary to learn the principle.

Gagne identified a second kind of transfer as lateral or horizontal transfer. He defined lateral transfer as generalization by the learner of what is learned in one situation to a new situation that differs from the situation in which the learning occurred. An example of lateral transfer in teaching would be learning a principle of child development in an educational psychology course and then applying that principle in teaching practice. Gagne argued that "there is evidently some advantage to having the learner practice the application of the skill to a *variety* of situations or problem contexts."[9] By implication there must exist a knowledge base in educational psychology, including psychological facts, principles, and theories of learning, development, and learners that the teacher education student would learn and then would be able to apply and transfer to the actual teaching situation.

In some ways, this dilemma is similar to that posed in the design of curricula for learning and teaching of reading and mathematics in elementary schools (e.g., should students memorize and learn basic number facts before they learn to use the number facts to solve real mathematics problems?). To illustrate, and to illuminate the choices faced by educational psychologists, we discuss briefly the learning and teaching of elementary reading and mathematics.

## RETHINKING THE NOTIONS OF LEARNING HIERARCHIES AND TRANSFER

In the past, most teaching in elementary reading and mathematics has rested on the assumption, derived primarily from task analyses and behavioral psychology, that students must learn lower-order facts and skills before going on to master higher-order problem solving and application skills. In contrast, recent theory and research from cognitive psychology call this idea into question:

> This assumption—that there is a sequence from lower level activities that do not require much independent thinking or judgment to higher level ones that do—colors much educational theory and practice. Implicitly at least, it justifies long years of drill on the "basics" before thinking and problem solving are demanded. Cognitive research on the nature of basic skills such as reading and mathematics provides a fundamental challenge to this assumption.[10]

For example, computational skills may not exist as lower-order prerequisites for higher-order mathematical problem solving, but rather may be learned in relation to, and as part of, the problem-solving activity.[11] Ample evidence also exists that both top-down and bottom-up processes are involved in reading.[12]

An important point is that new information to be learned and taught needs to be related in a meaningful way to knowledge and information that the learner already has. Thus, instructional content and practices ought to relate new knowledge in a meaningful way to the knowledge that students have already developed. This means, for example, that reading should be taught with a basis in meaning and that mathematics computation should be taught in the context of problem solving.[13] What does this rethinking of elementary reading and arithmetic teaching and learning imply about educational psychology for prospective teachers? If learning involves both top-down and bottom-up processes, then a hierarchical model in which educational psychology is a prerequisite or a foundation in teacher education is inconsistent with the best psychological research and theory.

Researchers are also questioning the notion of horizontal transfer and the relationship of in-school and out-of-school learning. For example, researchers have discovered instances where students have learned and can perform complicated mathematical procedures with understanding in an out-of-school setting. On the other hand, mathematical procedures that students learn in school often do not transfer to the out-of-school setting. This notion of knowledge as contextually situated calls into question the basic notions of how to facilitate learning in school being used and applied later by the student in real-life situations.[14]

Although concepts of vertical and horizontal transfer have affected the teaching of educational psychology as a foundation for at least two decades, we need to reconsider them as well as the content and methods of educational psychology in light of several alternative framing assumptions that have emerged from recent research on cognition and instruction. These include the notions that *thinking and cognition are situated* in physical and social contexts, that thinking and learning are situated within the contexts of *personal and social epistemologies, beliefs, and understandings*; and that learners have "strong potential capabilities for cognitive growth that enable complex and subtle *processes of construction of knowledge and thinking skills.*"[15] These alternative framing assumptions are related not only to the substance of what is traditionally taught and learned, but also to the methods by which learning is presumed to take place. Given these alternative framing assumptions, researchers have begun to think differently about knowledge and about the thinking and learning of children and youth in school and out.

Just as we are beginning to think differently about the development of children's knowledge and about the learning and thinking of children, we may also need to begin to think differently about the development of teachers' knowledge about learners, learning, and development and about how we facilitate the learning and thinking of teachers through teacher education. In doing so, we need to consider how these alternative framing assumptions fit with our developing understanding of the psychology of teachers' knowledge and thinking and the contextualized nature of that knowledge and thinking.

## TEACHERS' GENERAL VERSUS SUBJECT-MATTER-EMBEDDED KNOWLEDGE OF LEARNING

An important beginning question is how to think about teachers' knowledge of the principles and theories of learning and development that define much of the domain of knowledge in educational psychology relevant to teachers. Such knowledge is what comprises most of the texts currently used in educational psychology courses for teachers. As described by Carpenter and his colleagues, this knowledge includes what Shulman has referred to as knowledge of learners and their characteristics — as well as aspects of what he has identified as pedagogical content knowledge:

the conceptual and procedural knowledge that students bring to the learning of a topic, the misconceptions about the topic they may have developed, and the stages of understanding that they are likely to pass through in moving from a state of having little understanding of the topic to mastery of it. It also includes knowledge of techniques for assessing students' understandings and diagnosing their misconceptions.[16]

Such knowledge clearly concerns the psychology of learning even though it is embedded within a specific subject or content area. Relevant knowledge also includes teachers' content-specific cognitional knowledge or teachers' awareness of the mental processes or cognitions by which learners acquire subject-specific knowledge through classroom learning.[17]

To illustrate a possible way in which educational psychologists might think differently about the knowledge that teachers need to develop about the psychology of learning, we use an example from a study that Peterson conducted with her colleagues Thomas Carpenter and Elizabeth Fennema at the University of Wisconsin–Madison. In this study we tried to make accessible to teachers some knowledge from psychological research on children's learning of addition and subtraction. Because recent research had shown the importance of initial knowledge, we began by asking to what extent teachers already have this knowledge: (a) What do teachers know about the distinctions that young learners naturally make between addition and subtraction problems types? and (b) What do teachers know about the strategies that children use to solve different addition and subtraction word problems? We assessed teachers' knowledge through questionnaries and an interview. We found that, in general, most of the forty first-grade teachers were able to identify many of the critical distinctions between addition and subtraction word problems and the primary strategies that children use to solve such problems. However, teachers' knowledge generally was not organized into a coherent network that related distinctions between problems, children's strategies, children's solutions, and problem difficulty. Given that it took many years of research for psychologists to arrive at such knowledge, perhaps it is not surprising that teachers did not have this in-depth and coherent network of knowledge of young childrens' learning of addition and subtraction.[18]

In a subsequent experimental portion of the study we showed that when we worked with these teachers and gave them access to recent research knowledge on childrens' thinking processes in learning addition and subtraction, the teachers' knowledge base was enhanced.[19] Rather than teaching addition and subtraction facts and computations, experimental teachers taught addition and subtraction within the context of story problems. Experimental group teachers were more knowledgeable about childrens' learning processes than control teachers who had not participated in the workshop. By observing these teachers in their classrooms during the following year, we found that experimental teachers were able to use this knowledge to assess their childrens' thinking and to modify their instruction in addition and subtraction. Children in experimental teachers' classes were better at solving complex addition and subtraction story problems than were children in control teachers' classes and were more confident of their ability to do so. Children in experimental teachers' classes also knew the addition and subtraction facts as well as did children in control teachers' classes.

*Implications*

These research findings have three implications for our present discussion of the knowledge of educational psychology that is relevant to teachers. First, the research demonstrates that there is new, emerging knowledge of the psychology of children's learning of mathematics. By being given access to this knowledge, teachers modified their knowledge and understanding of children's mathematics learning, changed their classroom instruction, and improved their childrens' mathematics problem solving and learning of number facts. The research demonstrates the importance of contextualized or situated knowledge of the psychology of childrens' learning to the continuing education of teachers who are then able to facilitate the meaningful learning, understanding, and problem solving of their students. Left for further thought and discussion is the question of how to provide such integrated knowledge and practice in the education of prospective teachers, who typically do not have daily access to teaching young learners and who typically do not learn educational psychology within the context of their actual teaching.

Second, the findings suggest a possible evolution in the boundaries of the domain of educational psychology that is relevant to teachers. According to this conception, educational psychology would include subject-matter-embedded knowledge of the psychology of learning and development, as well as more general knowledge of theories of learning and development. A related implication is that in teaching educational psychology, educational psychologists need to work more closely with subject-matter specialists, just as they have in the development of this knowledge through research.[20] Although the above discussion refers to the psychology of learning mathematics, the same argument might be applied to other subject areas, for example, reading[21] and science.[22]

Third, our research was based on the idea that children's learning of addition and subtraction is a process of active construction of knowledge. In working with the teachers we took the same view of teachers' learning as a process of active construction of knowledge. As we shall see, such a view presents an interesting dilemma for educational psychologists, who have often used a lecture approach to teach constructivist theories of learning.

## TEACHERS' LEARNING AS THE ACTIVE CONSTRUCTION OF KNOWLEDGE

Over the past decade, educational psychologists studying children's learning and cognition have provided extensive evidence that "problem solving, comprehension, and learning are based on knowledge, and that people continually try to understand and think about the new in terms of what they already know."[23] More and more psychologists are viewing learning as a process of active construction of knowledge by the learner.[24] Such a constructivist view of learning stands in sharp contrast to the passive reception or absorption psychological models of learning that have dominated educational practice for decades.

Most of this research on knowledge has focused on young learners and has dealt with the specific content areas of reading, science, or mathematics, such as childrens' learning of arithmetic.[25] Although researchers have done some cognitive analyses of the subject-matter knowledge of teachers, they have not yet done similar cognitive analyses of the prior knowledge and learning of educational psychology by teachers. Such research might be conducted to understand how students in teacher education come to actively construct knowledge in the domain of educational psychology.

### BELIEFS ABOUT KNOWLEDGE AND UNDERSTANDING

In addition to the assumption of learning as active construction of knowledge, psychologists have proposed, as a framing assumption, that thinking and learning are situated in contexts of beliefs and understandings about cognition.[26] Thus, for example, teachers' learning is situated within the context of their beliefs and understandings of what they consider knowledge and understanding to be.

We return to an example from our own research to illustrate one way in which psychological knowledge might be connected to teaching through teachers' active construction of knowledge. Our example also illustrates how teachers' learning and thinking were situated within the context of their beliefs about children's knowledge and their own beliefs about what knowledge and understanding are. Although others have attempted or are attempting similar endeavors,[27] we provide this example because it is one of which we have personal knowledge.

In the year-long activity described above, Elizabeth Fennema, Thomas Carpenter, and Penelope Peterson worked with a group of first-grade teachers to change their practice of mathematics teaching in addition and subtraction in ways compatible with recent findings from psychology. From clinical interviews with children, psychologists have found that before young children enter school they have significant knowledge and abilities to solve many simple word problems by using counting strategies that they have already developed. Although we worked with teachers through a traditional mechanism — a staff-development workshop during the summer — the staff-development activity itself was unusual because we focused the workshop on giving teachers access to knowledge about a wide variety of word problems and the informal knowledge and strategies that young children possess to solve these problems. Teachers were then encouraged to use the knowledge, think about it, construct their own knowledge, and plan and change their first-grade mathematics instruction based on this knowledge. The research findings that we shared with teachers were rather precise — a taxonomy for thinking about types of word problems that reflects both psychologists' and children's thinking about these problems, as well as examples of strategies that children use to solve these problems. We did not prescribe precisely the way in which teachers would take this knowledge and construct their own classroom instruction.

In this work with first-grade teachers, we viewed the staff-development workshop as only the beginning of a process of knowledge construction and learning for the teachers. During the workshop, teachers viewed videotapes of children thinking aloud while solving problems in addition and subtraction. Then each teacher interviewed a child, gave the child different types of word problems, and asked the child how he or she solved the problem. Thus, beginning in the workshop, the teachers gathered evidence and tested for themselves to ascertain that children entering first grade *do* have knowledge and strategies for solving word problems. When teachers began teaching addition and subtraction to their own classes, they further tested these ideas with their own students. During the summer when viewing the videotapes, many teachers regarded some of the videotaped children as exceptional and were skeptical about children's informal knowledge and abilities to solve certain kinds of problems. However, when teachers began posing problems to their own classes in the fall and, listening carefully, seeing for themselves their own students' abilities to solve problems, they found that the children they had seen on the videotapes during the workshop were not exceptional and that *their own students* had knowledge and strategies for solving many types of word problems. Teachers came to see that children can solve different problems by counting or modeling the quantities and relationships between the quantities and the problem with physical objects. This knowledge then served as a "hook" to expand teachers' understanding of children's informal and formal mathematical knowledge and thinking. Teachers' beliefs about children's knowledge changed most fundamentally as a result of asking their students to solve word problems aloud during class and then listening to the strategies children used to solve those problems.

The teachers who became most knowledgeable about their own students' mathematics knowledge and strategies in solving word problems and who also held most constructively oriented beliefs about children's knowledge tended to adopt a personal and active constructivist view of the learning process and of children's mathematics understanding. An example is Ms. Jennings, who seemed to redefine her work as a teacher "to include on-the-spot clinical research into the way a learner thinks about something."[28] In an interview, Ms. Jennings gave a description of the knowledge of a particular first-grade child in her class:

> I was working with Cheryl the other day, and she had 12 cubes in her hand. The problem was Ms. Riva had 12 carrots, and she made three carrot cakes. She needed to divide them equally into each cake. And you know, Cheryl had these cubes, and go, go, go — she snapped it off real quick. I said, "How did you get that so quickly?" And she goes, "Oh, you know the numbers, you know, — first there were three. If you put three cakes, three carrots in each cake, and then I had nine. But if I add one more, that would be four." So they [the children] are thinking. It's just so sophisticated. It just seems to come together for them.

Teachers who experienced the workshop differed in the extent to which they knew and believed that children enter first grade with useful problem-solving knowledge. Some teachers clearly knew and believed that children have their own knowledge. For example, Ms. Pruitt referred specifically to children's knowledge "as their own," and Ms. Jennings described the sophistication of children's knowledge. Ms. Donaldson noted how questioning, listening to, and observing children's problem-solving strategies made her "realize how many children can do these things [problem solving] in different ways" and that "we were trying to mold them into one of way of doing that. It's exciting to see what they [children] can do without us molding." However, in a very real sense, the best of these teachers began engaging in psychological research into their own children's mathematical thinking.

Even the five teachers who were the highest among the twenty workshop teachers in having cognitively based or constructivist-oriented beliefs about children's knowledge varied in the extent to which they were constructivist in classroom process.[29] We did find that these five teachers were significantly higher than the other teachers in the amount of time they spent listening to processes that their students were using to solve problems. Ms. Jennings, the most constructivist teacher in her classroom practice, clearly listened to determine the knowledge of mathematics that her children had, and then she used that information to decide what to teach, given where the child was in his or her thinking. The following excerpt from an interview captures Ms. Jennings' approach.

> Some first-graders don't need to be introduced to addition. I think teachers do kids injustice when they drill on things that kids already

know, because kids get bored. I found my kids a lot more exciting. I was more excited, and I tried to give things to them and really listen to them . . . before the holidays one kid said, "five times five is twenty-five, take away twenty is five," and my mouth dropped open. And I said, "Oh, they are ready for multiplication." And not everybody was, but some kids were, and so then it became my challenge to find out which kids were ready for it.

Providing an insight into how very personal and experiential this knowledge is, Ms. Jennings also illustrates clearly how her own thinking about children's knowledge is situated within the context of her beliefs about what it means to understand mathematics. Before the workshop, when asked what kinds of problems she had her first-graders solve, Ms. Jennings said only that she had her students work problems that could be solved by answering the question, "How many do you have altogether?" In order to solve these problems, she said that she would teach the children to focus on the word "altogether" and what that means. Interestingly, psychologists as well as mathematics educators have sharply criticized this "key-word approach" because it focuses on a mindless or rote approach to problem solving rather than on conceptual understanding of the problem. When asked why she had the children learn that kind of word problem in addition and subtraction, Ms. Jennings replied, "Because I didn't learn how to solve them; and word problems were always hard for me. It was like, 'how do you even attack a problem like this?' "

A year later, at the end of this study, Ms. Jennings was once again asked, "Are there certain kinds of word problems that you deal with in addition and you believe all children should learn to solve?" In response she replied with feeling, "I would like all my kids to be able to, if I throw out any problem, say, 'OK, I'm going to tackle it.' You know, and *not* throw up their hands and say, 'I can't do it.' " In a follow-up question, we asked her why she decided that these kinds of word problems were important for all children in her class to learn to solve. In a revealing statement she admitted, "I think going through the workshop last summer helped, because I'd never done these kinds of problems in my life, and again, it was exposure in what kids could do with it."

The kinds of thinking in which teachers engaged are similar to the kinds of examples that Donald Schön provided in describing teachers' reflection-in-action.[30] Eleanor Duckworth and Magdalene Lampert reported similar insights into teachers' thinking and on-the-spot clinical research into the way a learner thinks about something. They described the thinking, beliefs, and understandings of teachers engaged in the Teacher Development Project at the Massachusetts Institute of Technology, organized around the concept of teacher as psychological researcher.[31] In this project — another example of an

alternative approach to connecting psychological knowledge to teaching—
two cognitive psychologists, Jeanne Bamberger and Eleanor Duckworth, en-
deavored to make Piaget's theories and research accessible to teachers. They
constructed musical, mathematical, and physical tasks for the teachers (for
example, keeping track of the changing phases of the moon) that were meant
to make teachers more conscious of the usefulness of their own intuitive
knowledge. They demonstrated clinical research methods with children, and
they led discussions with teachers in the use of these methods in their
classrooms.

One of the important similarities between the projects is that teachers
came to understand a constructivist viewpoint *not* through being lectured to
about Piagetian or constructivist learning theory. Rather, teachers' learning
was situated within the context of specific activities and tasks. Often teachers
worked on these activities together in groups. In both projects teachers began
to ask questions intended to illuminate how their students were thinking; to
ask questions that would help them as teachers understand how students
were interpreting a problem and to capitalize on the knowledge that students
have; and to think of students' questions as a way of gaining insight into how
a student was making sense of an experience or situation. In both projects
the emphasis was on understanding children's conceptions, *not* misconceptions. This may be an important difference between these projects and
others, which focus on changing students' misconceptions. For example,
Monk and Stimpson found that teachers' focus on students' *mis*conceptions
rather than students' conceptions tended to be related to teachers' desire to
"teach" or "tell." They noted, as did Lampert in describing the Teacher
Development Project teachers, that teachers found it difficult to assume the
role of researcher as one of diagnosing or understanding students' intuitive
knowledge and how the students were making sense of something. Teachers
often felt a need to assume the role of teacher, which they construed as telling
formal knowledge or as alleviating students' misconceptions.[32]

These examples demonstrate how teachers' learning was situated within
the context of their own personal epistemologies. In these projects, what
teachers were learning in psychology was inseparable from how they were
learning and was connected inextricably to their insights into their own
learning. The growth of teachers' knowledge in these projects demonstrates
the development of thoughtful teaching of the kind advocated in recent
reform reports.

KNOWLEDGE OF THE PSYCHOLOGY OF TEACHERS' LEARNING

In their recommendations for reform in teaching and teacher education,
both the Carnegie Forum Task Force and the Holmes Group portray the

new vision of thoughtful teachers as ones who are engaged continuously in the process of learning; who are "able to learn all the time"; and who view learning and development as a lifelong process for themselves and their students.[33] Just as the field of educational psychology has been affected by advances in cognitive psychology, the field of developmental psychology has been transformed in recent years by a life-span developmental perspective that argues for a view of teachers as professionals who continue to learn and develop throughout their teaching careers.

In developing this capacity for continuous learning, teachers may benefit not only by knowing something about how other teachers learn, but also by reflecting on their own processes of learning.[34] If teachers are to become thoughtful professionals, they need to have both meta-cognitive knowledge for classroom learning and meta-cognitive knowledge for classroom teaching. The former involves learners' self-awareness of their own cognitions through which they acquire information, gain understanding, and learn in the classroom. Meta-cognitive knowledge for classroom teaching includes self-awareness and the ability to reflect on one's own knowledge for classroom learning, as well as ability to reflect on knowledge about classroom teaching. Although little research has been done on such meta-cognitive knowledge of teachers, many researchers, including educational psychologists, are now suggesting that teachers' self-awareness and deliberate action are important aspects of teaching expertise that need to be studied.[35]

This discussion illustrates the centrality of knowledge of the psychology of teachers' learning. In reflecting on this topic, we propose three related points for consideration: first, that the psychology of teachers' learning constitutes an important new domain of knowledge in educational psychology; second, that the knowledge of theories and research findings on the psychology of teachers' learning may be meaningful and important for students in teacher education and, further, may enhance their teaching practice; and finally that knowledge of the psychology of teachers' learning may enhance the ability of faculty to teach educational psychology more effectively in teacher preparation programs.

## TEACHERS' LEARNING AND THINKING AS A NEW DOMAIN IN EDUCATIONAL PSYCHOLOGY

Both our discussion and several current research endeavors suggest the emergence of a new domain of knowledge in educational psychology—the psychology of teachers' learning. Although the subject of teachers' learning was the focus of some early studies by educational psychologists more than a decade ago,[36] educational psychologists have tended not to focus on teachers' learning as an important area of study. Only in the past decade have educational psychologists turned their attention from the study of teachers' behavior to the study of teachers' thinking, cognitions, and knowledge.[37] The studies by Putnam and Leinhardt (of networks of teachers' knowledge and script theory) and Lampert (on the role of teachers' understanding of subject matter and interpretation of what students mean) are most salient.[38] One can begin to see in that research why and how teachers come to behave as they do. This literature and that of other researchers on teacher thinking have explored the many ways in which teachers think, plan, and decide, and how teachers' work is constrained by the world in which they operate.[39] Using psychology to understand the teacher in this way might make contact with teachers in powerful ways. Such psychological windows into teachers' thinking or psychological lenses for examining teaching also open up new possibilities for metaphors that convey new ways of thinking about how to connect psychology to teacher education.

Researchers studying teachers' thinking and teachers' knowledge have typically used cross-sectional rather than longitudinal approaches and thus have not examined teachers' learning or the development of teachers' thinking over time. More recently, educational psychologists and teacher educators have begun working together to conduct a longitudinal study of how teachers learn to teach.[40] They are studying the development of teachers' knowledge, skills, and dispositions related to teaching writing and mathematics in eleven different teacher education programs over a three-year period. They are also examining teachers' beliefs, including their conceptions of knowledge. This research represents an ambitious new effort and the methods as well as the findings may be useful to educational psychologists who want to study the learning of students in their own teacher education programs. Because both research on teachers' thinking and research on teachers' learning is relatively recent, not much of the content and findings from this work has appeared in contemporary educational psychology textbooks. Still, these topics may constitute an important content domain that should be learned and taught in educational psychology in teacher preparation programs.

Knowledge of the psychology of teachers' learning might contribute to the effective teaching of educational psychology in two ways. First, such knowledge would be useful as educational psychologists begin the process of conceptualizing the learning and teaching of educational psychology in the preparation of teachers for the twenty-first century. Second, such knowledge would be particularly informative as educational psychologists think about the possibility of adapting the content and methods of educational psychology to the individual learner.

## ADAPTATION OF THE CONTENT AND METHODS OF EDUCATIONAL PSYCHOLOGY

A final question concerns how to adapt the content and methods of educational psychology to the individual learner—the teacher—to facilitate the meaningful learning and application of that learning to teaching practice. Here we revisit the problem of transfer because it is central to this discussion.

Although some deeply entrenched notions of transfer have dominated the teaching of educational psychology for two decades, recent research on cognition and instruction suggests the need to think differently about it. For example, if cognitive research suggests that first-graders come to know and understand addition and subtraction best within the context of a real-world story problem relevant to their lives, then the teacher should begin with the story problem to teach the addition/subtraction number facts and problem solving. The student is simultaneously learning number facts (what would have been called a lower-order skill) while solving a story problem (what would have been called a higher-order skill). Similarly, the story or problem (which would have previously been conceptualized as a transfer or application activity) serves as the context for learning computation and problem solving (which would previously have been thought of as the in-school skill).

The use of word problems as the context for children's learning of addition and subtraction has come from years of comprehensive research on children's learning of addition and subtraction. Unfortunately, similar research has not yet been done on *teachers'* meaningful learning and application of educational psychology. Recent work on everyday learning, learning outside of school, and the contextualization of cognitive tasks has demonstrated the importance of context in affecting meaningful learning, task performance, and application to a work environment.[41] Thus, we can only speculate and propose the following for consideration: Just as childrens' meaningful learning and application of mathematics skills is facilitated by teaching-learning within the context of real-life mathematics problems, teachers' meaningful learning and application of knowledge and theories in educational psychology may be facilitated by teaching and learning educational psychology within the context of real-life teaching-learning problems or cases. Recently, some educational psychologists have suggested that the study of cases may serve as a basis for meaningful learning and teaching in teacher education.[42] Cases have long been used effectively in the education of lawyers as well as physicians.[43]

## THE CASE FOR CASES

In the context of the learning and teaching of educational psychology, a case might represent a realistic learning-teaching problem in a classroom. Thus, such cases for teachers in educational psychology would be similar to the real-life story-problem experience of the first-grader learning addition and subtraction (or of the medical student or law student learning to solve problems in a complex, uncertain task environment). Cases might take the form of print, text, video, or audio recordings, jointly witnessed field experiences, or role-played simulations of a learning-teaching problem. Although the advocates for use of cases are increasing in number, some scholars are more cautious and are urging systematic study and analyses of how to facilitate students' knowledge growth and learning from cases.[44]

One such systematic study was completed by Karen Stoiber at the University of Wisconsin–Madison, who taught educational psychology to preservice teacher education majors using written and videotaped cases depicting dilemmas in classroom management.[45] She assigned preservice teachers in educational psychology randomly to one of several approaches to teaching classroom management. At the beginning and end of the course, she assessed preservice teachers' knowledge, beliefs, and thinking using interviews and questionnaires. She found that the use of cases was particularly effective in the context of the learning and teaching of strategies aimed at reflective decision making. In this approach preservice teachers were encouraged to develop their own teaching schemata or representations for classroom management. Self-questions, inner-directed speech, and examples of reflective processes were provided to scaffold the teachers' development of their own representations of classroom management. Cases were used in two ways. First, cases were used in the context of decision-making training. In this situation class members worked in pairs, and each pair member read a vignette about a classroom management situation that ended as a problem or dilemma. One member was instructed to act as a reflective decision maker who reported decision-making thought processes while the other acted as observer who critiqued his or her partner's reflective processing. Cases were also used by the instructor to lead discussions aimed at guiding participants to use specified reflective decision-making processes to analyze a depicted teacher's handling of a classroom management event. In another approach (the technical-skills approach), cases were used to teach and illustrate technical principles of classroom management derived from research by educational psychologists.

Stoiber's findings are provocative. Although teachers who experienced reflective decision making were not *taught* technical principles, they *knew* these principles of classroom management by the end of the course as well as did students in the technical-principle group. In contrast to students in the technical-skills approach, students in the reflective approach showed better understanding and processing of classroom situations when confronted with a videotaped case that posed a real classroom management dilemma. Stoiber concluded that the learning and teaching orientation in the reflective-deci-

sion-making approach did more to facilitate sophisticated cognitive processing and thinking by the preservice teachers than did the learning and teaching orientation in the technical-skills approach.

Although we have little research to go on, we are encouraged by Stoiber's
research, by our own teaching experiences, and by the work of others to believe that cases may provide a meaningful context within which the student
in educational psychology might learn and apply educational psychological
knowledge. Cases provide a mechanism for shared thinking and construction
of knowledge in a group situation. Each student in educational psychology
will see the same case differently because each brings different knowledge
and beliefs to the experience. Thus, students in educational psychology, even
when viewing or reading the same case, will construe the case or think about
it in terms of their past and current teaching-learning experiences. Sharing
of individuals' thinking about cases and arguing and justifying different interpretations may be particularly powerful ways of promoting thinking and
reflection in prospective teachers. Moreover, individual cases might be selected and tailored to individual students of educational psychology. Although adaptation to the individual learner has long been advocated by educational psychologists, the development and use of educational psychological
knowledge, by students in teacher education may depend on educational
psychologists' listening to their own advice.

## THE PROBLEM OF ADAPTATION

Facilitation of transfer is often a reason for adapting content and methods
of educational psychology to the individual learner. If the content and methods of educational psychology were adapted completely to the needs of the
individual student in teacher education, the student would have little work
to do to transfer or transform the information and content of educational
psychology in order to learn and apply educational psychology to teaching.
A relevant question becomes, "To what extent should the content and methods of educational psychology differ significantly for the elementary teacher
who is going to teach first grade compared with the high school teacher who
is going to teach mathematics to ninth-graders?" As we have seen, cognitive
research has demonstrated that specific subject-matter knowledge plays an
important role in learning and thinking. Thus, for the ninth-grade mathematics teacher, at least part of the content and methods of educational psychology needs to focus on learning and teaching of mathematics in ninth
grade. However, the ninth-grade math teacher also needs to understand
more general issues of learning and development.

In teaching educational psychology, educational psychologists are faced
with a fundamental dilemma: whether to offer an educational psychology

that is primarily concerned with prospective teachers' own learning and development, or one that is primarily concerned with the learning and development of schoolchildren. Prospective teachers are adult learners and should be taught as adults, but they need to learn and know theories of learning and development relevant to the children and youth they will teach. A teacher-as-adult-learner approach to educational psychology would have educational psychologists teach in ways consistent with the learning and teaching processes that beginning teachers themselves should use in their classrooms. Possibly, even if teaching and learning are situated or domain-specific, teachers will deduce some principles from their adult learning experiences and will apply these principles to the actual situation in which they would teach. As we have noted, many constructivist approaches to working with teachers begin by having the in-service or preservice teachers work on learning tasks or solve problems themselves.[46] Out of these experiences and insights into their own thinking and learning, teachers develop beliefs and understandings about cognition that may carry over to the way they think about the knowledge and understanding of the children as they teach. Alternatively, a psychology-of-young-learners approach suggests that students of educational psychology should study content and methods dealing primarily with specific children and school situations to be later encountered on the job. This second approach runs the risk of missing the mark when teachers find themselves working with students and in situations that differ in important ways from those of the teacher preparation period.

In sum, the problem of transfer and adaptation to the individual learner and teaching situation remains a fundamental dilemma that faculty need to consider as they conceptualize educational psychology in the new teacher-preparation programs. We suggest that one possible technique that might be considered is the use of cases as described earlier. As faculty begin to design and use new techniques and methods, such as the case method, we hope that they also conduct research and collect data on the learning of teachers in these innovative educational psychology courses.

CONCLUSION: UNANSWERED QUESTIONS AND THE CHALLENGE

We have raised only a handful of issues that we hope will provoke thought and dialogue among our colleagues as they begin to consider how educational psychology should be conceptualized in the new teacher-preparation programs. As we have seen, each of these issues poses dilemmas for the learning and teaching of educational psychology. Although recent research findings in cognition and instruction suggest some new conceptions and alternative framing assumptions, educational psychologists will still need to interpret, analyze, and use this knowledge in their own ways in teaching educational psychology. Thus, as educational psychologists, we face the same curricular and instructional puzzles that teachers face daily in their classrooms.

We have described some possibilities suggested by recent research, as well as some troubling dilemmas. As individual faculty in the teacher-preparation institutions begin to create new educational psychology courses and field experiences, they will face many learning and curriculum design challenges. For example, how should educational psychology faculty think about teachers' motivation and social learning as they begin to develop the content and methods of educational psychology in the new teacher education programs? Teaching educational psychology to cohorts of students in teacher education might facilitate the development of shared knowledge and experiences related to educational psychology by students in the cohort. In addition, this cohort structure might encourage social interaction of the type that has been found to be effective in developing critical thinking strategies and problem solving in children.[47]

Theory and research suggest that meaningful learning and application of educational psychology might be facilita.ed by closer collaboration among educational psychologists, teacher educators, and subject-matter researchers. The reward structure for faculty in research universities will need to change both to promote closer collaboration between these educators and researchers and to encourage faculty to spend time and effort to design innovative approaches to teaching educational psychology in the context of teacher education within real classrooms and schools.

If we are to advance our knowledge of the learning of educational psychology as a discipline, then we need to apply methods similar to those used to study childrens' knowledge and cognition to the study of learning by students in teacher education. Researchers might determine, for example, what knowledge of and beliefs about learning and development learners hold when they begin their study of educational psychology. Certainly, by the time students in teacher education reach college, they have developed their own informal notions and theories of learning as a result of having been learners themselves for a number of years.[48] In addition, researchers might ask, "How are teachers' general and subject-matter-embedded theories of learning related to their meaningful understanding and application of knowledge in educational psychology?" "How do teachers' knowledge and theories change through a course of study of educational psychology?" and "How is teachers' psychological knowledge—subject-matter-specific and general—related to their classroom practice and teaching?" As educators of learners, as well as researchers on learners, we may face the same dilemma noted by Monk and Stimpson and Lampert. Like the teachers in their studies, we as teachers may find it difficult to focus on understanding our teacher education students' conceptions and informal knowledge, rather than on alleviating their misconceptions and on teaching formal knowledge related to educational psychology, even though, as researchers, we are able to assume the stance of diagnosing and understanding teacher education students' knowledge and conceptions.

New metaphors are needed for the learning and teaching of educational psychology in teacher education. The metaphors must convey the way that psychological knowledge is viewed and the way in which psychological knowledge can be connected to teaching. For example, the metaphor might convey the view that knowledge of basic facts and general principles of learning and their application to the problems of teaching are interactive and interdependent and that meaningful learning depends on relating the new knowledge from educational psychology with the teacher's already existing knowledge. Attention must be paid to the conceptualization of both the knowledge that the teacher-education student brings to the learning situation and to the changes expected in the teacher's knowledge as a result of studying and learning educational psychology. A *web,* a *network,* a *dialogue,* and a *lens* are possible metaphors to consider in thinking about the learning and teaching of educational psychology.

The traditional boundaries, the text, and the materials for teaching educational psychology ought also to be questioned. The day of the self-contained, lecture-and-discussion, text-and-test course in educational psychology may be over. Team teaching, psychological reflection on field experiences, case analyses in learning and teaching, integration of the logic of instructional design with the real constraints and opportunities of public school life, attention to students' and teachers' learning in groups, to teachers' knowledge development across many years, and to construction of particular knowledge involved in learning different school subjects — all these should be part of the larger conversation about teacher education reform. One thing seems certain: Teacher preparation is changing. If educational psychologists seize the moment as an opportunity to revitalize the field, the changes and the profession will be better for it.

## Notes

1  Holmes Group, *Tomorrow's Teachers: A Report of the Holmes Group* (East Lansing, Mich.: The Holmes Group Incorporated, 1986), pp. 28–29.

2  W. James, *Talks to Teachers and Students* (New York: Holt, 1899), pp. 157–58.

3  See, for example, R. Glaser, "Education and Thinking: The Role of Knowledge," *American Psychologist* 39 (1984): 93–104; L. B. Resnick, "Cognition and Instruction: Recent Theories of Human Competence," in *Master Lecture Series: Psychology and Learning,* no. 4, ed. B. L. Hammonds (Washington, D.C.: American Psychological Association, 1985), pp. 123–86; and T. J. Shuell, "Cognitive Conceptions of Learning," *Review of Educational Research* 56 (1986): 411–36.

4  Holmes Group, *Tomorrow's Teachers,* p. 216.

5    See, for example, R. Calfee, "The View from the Editor's Desk: Comments on the Discipline of Educational Psychology in 1988" (Paper presented at the convention of the American Psychological Association, Atlanta, Georgia, August 1988). With David Berliner, Calfee has proposed the writing of an edited volume or "handbook" in educational psychology to develop an image of the field of educational psychology. See also H. J. Klausmeier, "The Future of Educational Psychology and the Content of the Graduate Program in Educational Psychology," *Educational Psychologist* 23 (1988): 203-19.

6    R. E. Slavin, *Educational Psychology: Theory into Practice* (Englewood Cliffs, N.J.: Prentice-Hall, 1988), p. 2.

7    R. M. Gagne, *The Conditions of Learning,* 2nd ed. (New York: Holt, Rinehart & Winston, 1970).

8    B. Bloom et al., *Taxonomy of Educational Objectives: The Classification of Educational Goals: Handbook I: Cognitive Domain* (New York: Longmans Green, 1956).

9    R. M. Gagne, *Essentials of Learning for Instruction* (Hillsdale, Ill.: Dryden Press, 1975), p. 84.

10    L. B. Resnick, *Education and Learning to Think* (Washington, D.C.: National Academy Press, 1987), p. 8.

11    L. B. Resnick and W. W. Ford, *The Psychology of Mathematics for Instruction* (Hillsdale, N.J.: Lawrence Erlbaum, 1981).

12    I. Beck and P. Carpenter, "Cognitive Approaches to Understanding Reading: Implications for Instructional Practice," *American Psychologist* 41 (1986): 1098-105; and R. C. Anderson et al., *Becoming a Nation of Readers: The Report of the Commission on Reading* (Washington, D.C.: The National Institute of Education, U.S. Department of Education, 1985).

13    For example, Anderson et al., *Becoming a Nation of Readers;* Resnick, "Cognition and Instruction"; and E. Fennema, T. P. Carpenter, and P. L. Peterson, "Learning Mathematics with Understanding," in *Advances in Research on Teaching, Volume 1,* ed. J. Brophy (Greenwich, Conn.: JAI Press, Inc., 1989).

14    L. B. Resnick, "Learning in School and Out," *Educational Researcher* 16, no. 9 (1987): 13-20.

15    J. G. Greeno, "A Perspective on Thinking," *American Psychologist* 44 (1989): 135 (emphasis added); see also J. S. Brown, A. Collins, and Paul Duguid, "Situated Cognition and the Culture of Learning," *Educational Researcher* 18, no. 1 (1989): 32-42.

16    Thomas P. Carpenter et al., "Teachers' Pedagogical Content Knowledge of Students' Problem Solving in Elementary Arithmetic," *Journal for Research in Mathematics Education* 19, no. 5 (1988): 386; and L. S. Shulman, "Knowledge and Teaching: Foundations of the New Reform," *Harvard Educational Review* 57, no. 1 (1987): 1-22.

17    P. L. Peterson, "Teachers' and Students' Cognitional Knowledge for Classroom Teaching and Learning," *Educational Researcher* 17, no. 5 (1988): 5-14.

18    For a complete description of this study, see T. Carpenter et al., "Teachers' Pedagogical Content Knowledge of Students' Problem Solving in Elementary Arithmetic," *Journal for Research in Mathematics Education* 19 (1989): 385-401. For psychologists' descriptions of this knowledge, see M. S. Riley, J. G. Greeno, and J. I. Heller, "Development of Children's Problem-solving Ability in Arithmetic," in *The Development of Mathematical Thinking,* ed. H. Ginsburg (New York: Academic Press, 1983), pp. 153-200; T. P. Carpenter and J. M. Moser, "The Acquisition of Addition and Subtraction Concepts," in *The Acquisition of Mathematics Concepts and Processes,* ed. R. Lesh and M. Landau (New York: Academic Press, 1983); and M. S. Riley and J. Greeno, "Developmental Analysis of Understanding Language about Quantities and of Solving Problems," *Cognition and Instruction* 5, no. 1 (1988): 49-101.

19    For a complete description of this study, see T. C. Carpenter et al., "Using Knowledge of Children's Mathematics Thinking in Classroom Teaching: An Experimental Study," *American Educational Research Journal* (forthcoming).

20    For example, Riley, Greeno, and Heller, "Development of Children's Problem-Solving Ability in Arithmetic"; and Carpenter and Moser, "The Acquisition of Addition and Subtraction Concepts." Interestingly, in the Preface to *Cognitive Science and Mathematics Education,* Alan Schoenfeld lists as four "essential contributors to progress in mathematics instruction" cognitive scientists, mathematics educators, mathematics teachers, and mathematicians. Educational psychologists are not mentioned ("Preface," *Cognitive Science and Mathematics Education,* ed. Alan Schoenfeld [Hillsdale, N.J.: Lawrence Erlbaum, 1987], pp. 1–32).

21    For example, Beck and Carpenter, "Cognitive Approaches to Understanding Reading"; and Anderson et al., *Becoming a Nation of Readers.*

22    A. B. Champagne and L. E. Klopfer, "Research in Science Education: The Cognitive Psychology Perspective," in *Research within Reach: Science Education,* ed. P. B. Ludz and D. Holdzkom (Washington, D.C.: National Science Teachers Association, 1984); S. Carey, "Cognitive Science and Science Education," *American Psychologist* 41 (1986): 1123–30; and C. Anderson and K. Roth, "Teaching for Meaningful and Self-regulated Learning of Science," in *Advances in Research on Teaching, Volume 1.*

23    R. Glaser, "Education and Thinking: The Role of Knowledge," *American Psychologist* 39 (1984): 100; see also idem and R. Takanishi, "Creating a Knowledge Base for Education: Psychology's Contributions and Prospects," *American Psychologist* 41 (1986): 1025–28.

24    For example, L. B. Resnick, "Developing Mathematical Knowledge," *American Psychologist* 44 (1989): 162–69.

25    For example, L. B. Resnick and S. F. Omanson, "Learning to Understand Arithmetic," in *Advances in Instructional Psychology,* vol. 3, ed. R. Glaser (Hillsdale, N.J.: Lawrence Erlbaum, 1986), pp. 41–95; and Riley, Greeno, and Heller, "Development of Children's Problem-Solving Ability in Arithmetic."

26    Greeno, "A Perspective on Thinking."

27    See, for example, M. Lampert, "School/University Collaboration in Developing Mathematical Pedagogy" (Paper presented at the annual meeting of the American Educational Research Association, New Orleans, April 1988); P. Cobb, E. Yackel, and T. Wood, "Curriculum and Teacher Development: Psychological and Anthropological Perspectives," in *Integrating Research on Teaching and Learning Mathematics,* ed. E. Fennema, T. Carpenter, and S. Lammon (Madison: Wisconsin Center for Education Research, University of Wisconsin-Madison, 1988); G. S. Monk and V. C. Stimpson, "Mathematics Teachers' Constructions of Revised Pedagogical Approaches" (Paper presented at the annual meeting of the American Educational Research Association, San Francisco, March 1989); and M. A. Simon, "The Impact of Intensive Classroom Follow-up in a Constructivist Mathematics Teacher Education Program" (Paper presented at the annual meeting of the American Educational Research Association, San Francisco, March 1989).

28    Even though the words "on-the-spot clinical research into the way a learner thinks about something" were not used by Jennings, they aptly describe her thinking. This phrase was coined by Magdalene Lampert in "Teaching and Thinking and Thinking about Teaching," *Journal of Curriculum Studies* 16 (1984): 1.

29    In an earlier study, we defined what we mean by cognitively based or constructivist-oriented beliefs. We used the same conceptualization in the experimental study. See P. L. Peterson et al., "Teachers' Pedagogical Content Beliefs in Mathematics," *Cognition and Instruction* 6, no. 1 (1989): 1–40.

30    D. Schön, *The Reflective Practitioner: How Teachers Think* (New York: Basic Books, 1983).

31    E. Duckworth, *"The Having of Wonderful Ideas" and Other Essays on Teaching and Learning* (New York: Teachers College Press, 1987); and Lampert, "Teaching about Thinking," pp. 1–18.

32    Monk and Stimpson, "Mathematics Teachers' Constructions"; and Lampert, "Teaching about Thinking," p. 15.

33    Carnegie Forum, *A Nation Prepared: Teachers for the 21st Century* (New York: Carnegie Forum on Education and the Economy, 1986), p. 25; Holmes Group, *Tomorrow's Teachers;* and J. Lanier, "The Holmes Group and Professional Development Schools" (Address given at the Second National Holmes Group Meeting, Washington, D.C., January 1988).

34    P. L. Peterson, "Teachers' and Students' Cognitional Knowledge for Classroom Teaching and Learning," *Educational Researcher* 17, no. 5 (1988): 5–14.

35    See, for example, K. M. Zeichner and D. P. Liston, "Teaching Student Teachers to Reflect," *Harvard Educational Review* 57 (1987): 23–48; D. A. Schön, *Educating the Reflective Practitioner* (San Francisco: Jossey-Bass, 1987); and C. M. Clark and P. L. Peterson, "Teachers' Thought Processes," in *Handbook of Research on Teaching,* 3rd ed., ed. M. C. Wittrock (New York: Macmillan, 1986), pp. 255–95.

36    C. M. Clark, R. E. Snow, and R. J. Shavelson, "Three Experiments on Learning to Teach," *Journal of Teacher Education* 27, no. 2 (1976): 174–80.

37    See Clark and Peterson, "Teachers' Thought Processes"; and R. Shavelson and P. Stern, "Research on Teachers' Pedagogical Thoughts, Judgments, Decisions, and Behavior," *Review of Educational Research* 51 (1981): 455–98.

38    R. T. Putnam and G. Leinhardt, "Curriculum Scripts and Adjustment of Content to Lessons" (Paper presented to the annual meeting of the American Educational Research Association, San Francisco, April 1986); G. Leinhardt and D. A. Smith, "Expertise in Mathematics Instruction: Subject Matter Knowledge," *Journal of Educational Psychology* 77 (1985): 247–71; and M. Lampert, "Connecting Mathematical Thinking and Learning," in *Integrating Research on Teaching and Learning Mathematics,* pp. 132–65.

39    See J. Calderhead, *Exploring Teachers' Thinking* (London: Cassell, 1987).

40    See M. Kennedy, R. Floden, and S. Feiman-Nemser, *Technical Proposal for the Work of the National Center for Research on Teacher Education* (East Lansing: Michigan State University, 1987).

41    M. C. Cole and P. Griffin, *Contextual Factors in Education* (Madison: Wisconsin Center for Education Research, 1987); and Resnick, "Learning in School and Out."

42    See, for example, Shulman, "Knowledge and Teaching: Foundations of the New Reform."

43    M. Kennedy, "Inexact Sciences: Professional Education and the Development of Expertise," *Review of Research in Education,* vol. 14, ed. E. Z. Rothkopf (Washington, D.C.: American Educational Research Association, 1988), pp. 133–67; and C. R. Christensen and A. J. Hansen, *Teaching and the Case Method* (Boston: Harvard Business School, 1987).

44    For example, Gary Sykes describes the problems and pitfalls he faced in his beginning attempts to use cases in courses such as School and Society and Practice and Problems in Educational Administration ("Learning to Teach with Cases," *Colloquy,* Spring 1989, pp. 7–13).

45    K. C. Stoiber, "Effects of Technical Principle, Reflective Decision-Making, and Integrated Instruction in Classroom Management on Teachers' Knowledge and Thinking" (Ph.D. diss., University of Wisconsin–Madison, 1988).

46    See, for example, Lampert, "School/University Collaboration in Developing Mathematical Pedagogy"; Cobb, Yackel, and Wood, "Curriculum and Teacher Development"; Monk and Stimpson, "Mathematics Teachers' Constructions"; Simon, "The Impact of Intensive Classroom Follow-Up in a Constructivist Mathematics Teacher Education Program"; Duckworth, *"The Having of Wonderful Ideas"*; and Lampert, "Teaching about Thinking."

47    Resnick, *Education and Learning to Think*; and A. S. Palincsar, D. D. Stevens, and J. R. Gavelek, "Collaborating with Teachers in the Interest of Student Collaboration," *International Journal of Educational Research* 13, no. 1 (1989): 41–53.

48    See, for example, D. Ball, "Unlearning to Teach Mathematics," *For the Learning of Mathematics* 8, no. 1 (1988): 40–48; and R. Floden, "What Teachers Need to Know about Learning" (Paper presented at the National Center for Research on Teacher Education seminar for Education Policymakers, Washington, D.C., February 1989.)

# Classroom Knowledge as a Foundation for Teaching

WALTER DOYLE

*University of Arizona*

*Classroom knowledge provides a framework for understanding how classroom systems work and how curriculum can be represented and enacted in these environments. It also provides a framework for inventing practices grounded in the realities of school settings. Doyle argues that classroom knowledge is the core foundation for teacher research and practice.*

Although a literature on teaching has been accumulating for centuries, investigators have only recently begun to examine systematically the knowledge structures and comprehension processes that teachers use daily to interpret classroom events, reflect on the many dilemmas of teaching, and navigate the complex task environments in which they work.[1] As one might expect, this emphasis on teachers' classroom knowledge is beginning to have important repercussions for conceptions of both the content and the pedagogy of teacher education. In particular, the explication of classroom knowledge is forcing a reconceptualization of what is thought of as technical knowledge for teaching and, indeed, of the nature of technique itself. As conceptions of technique change, so also do conceptions of what is foundational knowledge for teachers.

The major purpose of the present discussion is to clarify the concept of "classroom knowledge" and define its place within the larger arena of knowledge domains in teacher education. To this end, I first survey conventional approaches to defining knowledge for teaching. This background is essential for appreciating the distinctive contributions of classroom knowledge to teacher education curriculum. I then turn to classroom knowledge itself to

*The author is grateful to Kathy Carter, Tom Good, Mary Rohrkemper, Jill Keller, Stefinee Pinnegar, Barbara Morgan, and Paul Heckman for help in clarifying many of the ideas presented here but accepts full responsibility for all opinions and errors.*

examine its origins and character. Finally, I discuss the implications of this analysis of classroom knowledge for understanding the role of foundational studies in teaching.

## CONCEPTIONS OF KNOWLEDGE FOR TEACHING

Proximal knowledge for teaching has traditionally fallen under the purview of methods. The label "methods" refers to at least three categories of knowledge. The first includes historic exemplars devised by such figures as Socrates, Comenius, Froebel, Pestalozzi, Herbart, and Montessori, and, more recently, frameworks such as whole language teaching and discovery or inquiry methods. These frameworks are essentially integrated systems of teaching practices derived from conceptions of the broad purposes of education, the nature of the content to be taught, and how the content is learned. These integrated systems reflect the philosophical, curricular, and psychological foundations of educational thought and practice.[2] The second category includes quite specific teaching procedures or practices such as lecture, discussion, questioning, and group work. More elaborate versions of these methods include mastery designs and cooperative learning. This category reflects a narrow psychologizing of method into generic treatments that are often stripped of philosophical and curricular dimensions.[3] Finally, recent applications of cognitive psychology to teaching have resulted in the design of methods or strategies tailored to specific outcomes such as reading comprehension. Reciprocal teaching is a good example of this emerging category of method.[4]

### KNOWLEDGE AS PRESCRIPTIONS FOR IMPROVEMENT

At least three basic ideas or themes have shaped the field of methods. First, it is usually assumed that knowledge about method is derivative or applied. That is, methods have their origins in basic disciplines outside the field of education — traditionally philosophy and psychology. Second, method is thought to consist of prescriptive rather than descriptive content.[5] That is, a method is largely a set of specifications for how practice should be carried out. Finally, methods are developed under the banner of improvement — that is, methods are intended to replace existing practices, which are assumed not to be as good as they ought to be.

These themes have led to a neglect, if not devaluing, of both context and the common forms of schooling in building a body of knowledge about teaching. If classroom practice is best guided by knowledge derived from external domains, there is little need to study existing practices or understand how classrooms work. Rather, the problem is, as Richardson has pointed out, basically one of implementation, that is, how to get teachers to do what external change agents want them to do.[6]

The devaluing of existing practice has resulted in a curious tension between teacher education and the teaching profession. In a recent study of methods courses, McDiarmid provides data suggesting that methods instructors typically advocated a specific model for teaching their content field, in this case language arts. The pedagogy in methods classes typically consisted of a vigorous espousal of the model in an effort to establish a strong commitment among teacher education students to use the model when they got to the classroom. Methods instructors feared student teaching and the school environment as the great eradicators of the practices they advocated, so they argued for their methods with fervor and often expressed a siege mentality in warning students about the perils to be found in schools.[7] Theory was translated into practice, in other words, through emotionality in an effort to inoculate prospective teachers against the dangers of contamination in school settings. Perhaps this is why Weinstein found that prospective student teachers did not expect to learn much from experienced practitioners.[8] Moreover, the inoculation view of preservice teacher education undermines the relationship between colleges of education and schools. If the university's primary purpose is to subvert what schools do, then partnership among institutions, which is essential for educating teachers, is unlikely to develop. Indeed, one of the reasons it is so difficult to discuss the curriculum of teacher education openly may well be an implicit sense that it is fundamentally a subversive instrument.

EFFECTIVENESS AND THE REMOTE CONTROL OF TEACHING

By far the most influential theme shaping methods in teaching, however, is effectiveness.[9] On the surface, a concern for effectiveness seems quite natural and praiseworthy. Who could be against an effective education for all children? In practice, however, this idea has been most often expressed as a preoccupation with the remote control of quality in teaching, that is, a search for indicators of the best teachers or the best way to teach and a use of these indicators to control teaching from the outside. From a quality-control perspective, teachers are viewed as instruments or tools in the production of school achievement. These tools can be controlled remotely by employing a common set of indicators to evaluate performance or by imposing uniform practices on all teachers. Research serves schooling, in turn, by generating lists of effectiveness indicators or classroom practices that reliably predict achievement test scores. In other words, "It is the task of research to replace faulty remedies with effective treatments."[10]

The consequences of this emphasis on the remote control of quality in teaching are, I think, unfortunate. The search for effectiveness indicators and uniform practices lifts teaching from its particulars and strips it of context and, therefore, meaning. Extracting indicators from descriptions of classroom practices inexorably fractionates and trivializes teaching and serves to narrow rather than enrich knowledge for teacher education. Indeed, evidence of this narrowing and trivializing is quite clear in recent state proposals to assess specific teaching skills, reduce the amount of preparation needed for entry into the profession, and construct alternative routes to certification that virtually bypass professional content.

## CLASSROOM KNOWLEDGE

Classroom knowledge evolved under a quite different set of themes to address some of the neglected issues in the traditional approaches to building a body of knowledge for teaching. In this section, the origins and basic character of classroom knowledge are described.

### ORIGINS IN CLASSROOM MANAGEMENT

Interest in classroom knowledge originated primarily in the area of classroom management.[11] Traditionally, discussions of classroom management were focused on treatment issues, that is, what to do about disruptive students or disruptive situations. A variety of discipline models have been developed over the years to treat either inappropriate behaviors or the underlying psychodynamics of misbehavior in schools.[12] In part because of the seminal work of Kounin,[13] attention turned to ways of organizing and managing classes to create work involvement and prevent misbehavior. The focus on prevention transformed research and theory in this area.

From the perspective of management, classrooms are crowded and busy places in which groups of students who vary in interests and abilities must be organized and directed. Moreover, these groups assemble regularly for long periods of time to accomplish a wide variety of tasks. Many events occur simultaneously, teachers must react often and immediately to circumstances, and the course of events is frequently unpredictable. Teaching in such settings requires a highly developed ability to manage events.

### ACTIVITIES: THE CORE OF MANAGEMENT

Studies of this management task have focused on the activity as the central unit of classroom order. An activity can be defined as a segment of time in which participants are arranged in a specific fashion and communication follows an identifiable pattern.[14] A segment of classroom time, such as a spelling test, a writing lesson, or a study period, can be described in terms of

(1) its temporal boundaries or duration; (2) the physical milieu—that is, the shape of the site in which it occurs, the number and types of participants, the arrangement of participants in the available space, and the props or objects available to participants; (3) the behavior format or program of action for participants; and (4) the focal content or concern of the segment.

Although considerable attention in management studies has been given to rules, procedures, and routines, the concept of "program of action" is key to understanding classroom order. Each activity defines a distinctive action structure that provides direction for events and "pulls" participants along a particular path at a given pace.[15] In seatwork, for example, students are usually expected to work privately and independently at their desks, attend to a single information source such as a textbook or worksheet, and finish within a specified time. In whole-class discussion, on the other hand, students are expected to speak publicly and monitor information from multiple sources. To say a classroom is orderly, then, means that students are cooperating in the program of action defined by the activity a teacher is attempting to use. Misbehavior, in turn, is any action by students that threatens to disrupt the activity flow or pull the class toward an alternative program of action. If order is not defined in a particular setting, that is, if an activity system is not established and running in a classroom, no amount of discipline will create order.

Studies of classroom activities have shown that types of activities are systematically related to the behavior of students and thus place different classroom management demands on teachers. In a study of third-grade classes Gump found, for instance, that involvement was highest for students in teacher-led small groups and lowest for pupil presentations. Between these extremes, engagement was higher in whole-class recitation, tests, and teacher presentations than in supervised study and independent seatwork.[16] In addition, the physical characteristics of a classroom, including the density of students, the arrangement of desks, and the design of the building (open space vs. self-contained) affect the probability of inappropriate and disruptive behavior as well as the difficulties a teacher encounters in preventing or stopping such behavior.[17] In general, the more loosely structured the setting and the weaker the program of action, the higher the probability that inappropriate behavior will occur. Similarly, the greater the amount of student choice and mobility and the greater the complexity of the social scene, the greater the need for overt managing and controlling actions by the teacher.[18]

## ESTABLISHING AND MAINTAINING ACTIVITIES

Research on how classroom activities are established and maintained has shown that the level of order created during the first few days of school reliably predicts the degree of student engagement and disruption for the rest of the year.[19] Most studies indicate that successful classroom managers rely on three basic strategies to establish order at the beginning of the year: simplicity, familiarity, and routinization. Early activities, in other words, have simple organizational structures that are typically quite familiar to students (e.g., whole-class presentations and seatwork rather than multiple small groups). Teachers then repeat the same activity forms for the first weeks to familiarize students with standard procedures and provide opportunities to rehearse them. This routinizing of activities helps sustain classroom order by making events less susceptible to breakdowns because participants know the normal sequence of action.

Monitoring plays a key role in establishing and maintaining classroom activities. Teachers must be aware of what is going on in a classroom and be able to attend to two or more events at the same time.[20] The content of monitoring — what teachers watch when scanning a room — includes at least three dimensions. First, teachers watch *groups,* that is, they attend to what is happening in the entire room and how well the total activity system is going. Localized attention to individual students must be scheduled within the broader framework of the group activity. Second, teachers watch *conduct or behavior,* with particular attention to discrepancies from the intended program of action. This enables teachers to recognize misbehavior early, stop it before it spreads, and select the appropriate target for intervention. Third, teachers monitor the *pace, rhythm, and duration* of classroom events.[21] Excessive delays in the flow of classroom events or abrupt shifts in direction are often associated with inappropriate or disruptive student behavior.

TASKS AND CURRICULUM ENACTMENT

It soon became clear in management studies that the type of work students were assigned affected classroom order. In other words, academic tasks were a significant component of the programs of action for both teachers and students in classrooms, and are thus implicated in classroom management. As a result, investigators began to examine the academic tasks students accomplished in various subject matter domains.[22]

An academic task can be defined in terms of the following general components: (1) a product, such as words in blanks on a worksheet, answers to a set of test questions, or an original essay; (2) operations to produce the product, for example, remembering words from previous lessons, applying a rule to select appropriate words, or composing a descriptive paragraph; (3) resources, such as notes from lectures, textbook information, conversations with other students, or models of finished products supplied by the teacher; and (4) the significance or "weight" of a task in the accountability systems of a class; for example, a warm-up exercise in math might count as a daily grade whereas a unit text might account for 20 percent of the grade for a term. The concept of "task," in other words, calls attention to four aspects of work in a class: (1) a goal state or end product to be achieved; (2) a problem space or set of conditions and resources available to accomplish the task; (3) the operations involved in assembling and using resources to reach the goal state or generate the product; and (4) the importance of the task in the overall work system of the class.

Studies of academic tasks in classrooms have revealed that when academic work is routinized and familiar to students (e.g., spelling tests or recurring worksheet exercises), the flow of classroom activity is typically smooth and well ordered. When work is problem-centered, that is, students are required to interpret situations and make decisions to accomplish tasks (e.g., word problems or essays), activity flow is frequently slow and bumpy. Moreover, students sometimes respond to the ambiguity and risk involved in problem-centered work by negotiating directly with teachers to increase the explicitness of product specifications or reduce the strictness of grading standards. Teachers sometimes respond to these pressures on work flow by excluding higher-level tasks from the classroom altogether. More often, however, they redefine or simplify task demands and accountability by making product specifications more explicit and emphasizing procedures for completing assignments. When this happens, students' attention shifts from meaning and the underlying operations with content to correct answers and the completion of work. As a result, the basic academic purposes of the curriculum are circumvented. In sum, novel or problem-centered work stretches the limits of classroom management and intensifies the complexity of the teacher's tasks of orchestrating classroom events.

As work on the management of academic tasks evolved, it became evident that the concept of task provided a tool for capturing the curriculum in motion. Tasks, in other words, were soon seen as the means through which the curriculum becomes a concrete event in a classroom. It was now possible to study curriculum as a classroom process! This realization led to an emphasis on curriculum representation and enactment as fundamental dimensions of teaching in classrooms.[23] In the structuring and negotiating of tasks in classrooms, teachers and students define the curriculum they experience.

## EFFECTIVENESS REVISITED

This task perspective sheds light on the issue of effectiveness. Traditionally, effectiveness has been tied to teachers and teaching processes with little attention to the content being taught or tested. A concern for knowledge and curriculum forces us to disentangle effectiveness from teaching processes or behaviors and from achievement testing.

Let me illustrate this point with an example taken from a study by Judith Green and others of the comparative effectiveness of two elementary teachers in an experimental setting.[24] Teachers in this study were asked to teach a story about a fictional tiger by having the pupils read the text and discuss it. For the report, two teachers who differed on a measure of effectiveness were selected for close analysis. The first teacher taught the story, that is, she had the students read passages and asked questions to ensure they understood what they read. The second teacher began by asking the pupils what they knew about animals and then as they read the story continued to focus on what they were now learning about animals that they did not already know. As you might imagine, the sessions differed on process measures. The first class was quite orderly and efficient and comments were text-based; the second class was more ragged and pupils' comments covered a wide range of topics. The achievement measure required pupils to retell the story. You can guess which teacher won. Yet the race itself was flawed because the teachers had quite different theories of the content. The first taught reading as a process of extracting information from text and the second taught reading as a process of updating personal knowledge. Considerable support could easily be garnered for the second theory of reading. However, the theory of the content embedded in the achievement measure favored the first teacher's representation of the content.

The obvious implication of this example is that the measurement of effectiveness is a theoretically embedded curriculum issue. Both reading teachers, it would seem, were effective in teaching their theory of the content. The test, however, measured only one theory. Indeed, it is my suspicion that all teachers are effective in teaching their representation of the content, but that our measures capture only a small range of the available representations.

This point underscores the serious problems involved in attempts to reduce effectiveness to a set of teaching behaviors or practices. We do not know from available process-product studies which of the "less" effective teachers were simply representing content differently from that favored by the achievement measure and which were "truly" using less effective procedures. Moreover, the teachers deemed effective were effective only for the theory of the content embedded in the test. The same can be said for many of the experiments on teaching practices such as mastery learning. In a large number of instances the control groups in these experiments were taught either different content or a different representation of the content.[25]

I would conclude from this line of argument that effectiveness is fundamentally a curriculum rather than a process issue and that achievement is constructed locally by teachers and students under particular circumstances. Generic indicators of effectiveness and isolated classroom practices necessarily embody very specific curriculum theories. Their widespread use for the remote control of teaching quality will inevitably narrow and distort the purposes and achievements of schools.[26]

THE CHARACTER OF CLASSROOM KNOWLEDGE

A focus on curriculum representation and enactment transformed research on classroom management from the study of rules, procedures, and reprimands to a research program that subsumes instruction and curriculum. At the same time, the roots of this framework in management served to sustain a continuing interest in context, that is, in capturing the configurations and demands of classroom environments. The emphasis shifted, that is, from externally derived models for teaching to the construction of knowledge about existing practices and common forms of classroom events. Without knowledge of these forms and practices, it is impossible to understand classrooms.[27]

Although effectiveness has always been a theme in management research, the constructs that developed in this area (e.g., activities, programs of action, tasks, curriculum representation and enactment) cannot be translated easily into simple indicators for the remote control of quality. Indeed, work in this area suggests that teaching in classrooms demands an ability to interpret situations, predict the direction of events, and make decisions rapidly. Teaching is, in other words, fundamentally a cognitive activity based on a knowledge of the probable trajectory of events in classrooms and the way specific actions affect situations. Specific teaching skills are, for all practical purposes, useless without a basic understanding of classrooms.

At the same time, the emerging theoretical and empirical work on curriculum enactment suggests, in broad outline, the substance of what experienced teachers know. Knowledge about classroom structures provides insight into what teachers are required to think about when working in these environments. It is likely, therefore, that knowledge of classrooms will provide an analytical framework for understanding teachers' knowledge structures.[28]

One implication of this perspective is that experienced teachers' knowledge is event-structured. That is, what teachers know about chunks of content, instructional actions, or management strategies is tied to specific events they have experienced in classrooms. At the moment, the boundaries of an event are not altogether clear. I would speculate that most teachers have several types of events in their knowledge structures, ranging from very specific episodes with particular students to memories for classes in a given year. I also suspect that the events of major significance in the organization of teachers' knowledge are curricular, that is, tied to units of content. Teachers organize their thinking during planning and enactment around specific chunks of content and what Putnam has called "curriculum scripts."[29] As Pinnegar suggests, teachers watch for signs that students are "with me" as scripts are carried out in classrooms.[30] This analysis implies that the units of teachers' knowledge are relatively large, at least in comparison with variables traditionally used in research on teaching.

If events are both the units of interpretation or meaning for teachers and the form in which their knowledge is stored, then teachers' knowledge is fundamentally particularistic and situational. Their knowledge is, in other words, case knowledge. Cases in teaching are important, therefore, not simply because they convey the complexity of classroom life, but also because they are probably the form in which teachers' meanings are stored, conveyed, and brought to bear on novel instances in problem solving.

In summary, work under the general rubric of classroom knowledge suggests two interrelated images for understanding teaching. The first image depicts teaching as a process of representing and enacting curriculum in the complex environment of the classroom. The second image captures teaching as problem solving with case knowledge.

## IMPLICATIONS FOR FOUNDATIONAL STUDIES IN TEACHER EDUCATION

The picture of proximal knowledge for teaching depicted here would seem to have important implications for understanding the nature and role of foundational studies in teacher education. I will conclude by highlighting some of these implications related to the paradigmatic and the disciplinary foundations of teaching practice.

### PARADIGMATIC SHIFTS

As indicated, classroom knowledge is of a very different order from that generated for the remote control of quality in teaching. The paradigmatic ideal in research for quality control is the experiment, a design that presumably enables an investigator to determine the reliability and predictive validity of specific treatments. Within this framework, research on all aspects of teaching — knowledge, beliefs, decisions, behaviors, judgments, and reflections — becomes a search for answers to the prediction question, that is, what is the optimal content, choice, or characteristic at each of these levels of teachers' action.

However, if one accepts the view that human behavior is fundamentally indeterminant[31] and that achievement is constructed locally under the difficult conditions that exist in classroom environments, then attention shifts from variables and predictors to knowledge that is descriptive and theoretical, that is, a representation and explanation of the contexts and events that occur in classroom settings. Such knowledge is inherently particularistic, that is, richly imbued with the specifics of the contexts in which teaching occurs. It is case knowledge that empowers teachers to interpret situations and create solutions to classroom problems.

The view of effective teaching as problem solving with case knowledge requires a shift from bureaucratic mechanisms for the remote control of teaching quality to a fundamental reliance on the knowledge that empowers teachers to do their work. This view also suggests that teacher education is far more than an inoculation. Knowledge necessary for teaching requires a long time and a great deal of experience to develop. Effective teachers, by this standard, cannot be produced quickly with a minimum of professional content.

## DISCIPLINARY SHIFTS

Foundational studies in education have typically been dominated by academic psychology.[32] Indeed, as most foundations departments in colleges of education have gradually declined in size and influence over the years, educational psychology has flourished as the repository of conceptual and methodological authority in educational research and as the omnibus discipline for grounding teaching practice.

The psychologizing of teaching, which occurred early in this century, was in several respects reasonable in the pursuit of quality control in teaching. Psychology provided a scientific approach to many of the intractable issues of learning and motivation that were embedded in discussions of methods, and it furnished a powerful set of objective tools in measurement, statistical analysis, and experimental procedure to systematize information about schooling and its effects. Thus, schooling gained a strong intellectual foundation and a set of instruments to ensure its efficacy. In addition, academic discourse about teaching became possible through the language of psychology, with the result that teacher education could, through association with the social and behavioral sciences, enhance its position as a legitimate discipline in academia.

Predictably, however, psychology has cast its own special stamp on conceptions of educational phenomena. In particular, the focus has tended to be on generic operations or processes and on individual behavior in learning and teaching. In this framework, little attention has been given to the nature of subject matter and its form in the school curriculum or to the contexts in which teachers and students operate. Academic psychology has, therefore, been an inadequate resource for the research on classroom structures and processes discussed in this article. To understand academic tasks and curriculum enactment it has been necessary to supplement psychological knowledge with theories and methods borrowed from ecological, linguistic, and curricular sources and to construct an indigenous language to describe how classrooms work.

On quite similar grounds, academic psychology would seem to be a necessary but quite insufficient resource for teaching practice. Methods derived from psychological frameworks lack the curricular and contextual information necessary to use them in classrooms. Moreover, many psychological constructs have quite limited diagnostic or interpretive utility for teaching in classrooms. The term *learning*, for example, carries a great deal of weight in discussions of teaching. We even talk of learning as an outcome of teaching. Learning is, of course, an important process that occurs within individual students in school settings. Yet at the classroom level learning is invisible, a process evidenced by a change in knowledge or performance. In enacting curriculum, knowledge and task performance are much more powerful constructs than the illusive entity of learning for interpreting events and guiding decisions.

## CONCLUSION

The argument advanced here is that classroom knowledge is the core foundation for teaching research and practice. It provides a framework for understanding how classroom systems work and how curriculum can be represented and enacted in these environments. It also provides a framework for inventing practices grounded in the realities of school settings. All other disciplines have utility for teaching as resources in the continuing development of classroom knowledge.

## Notes

1   See Kathy Carter and Walter Doyle, "Teachers' Knowledge Structures and Comprehension Processes," in *Exploring Teachers' Thinking*, ed. James Calderhead (London: Cassell, 1987), pp. 147–60.

2   On methods at this level of discourse, see Harry S. Broudy, "Historical Exemplars of Teaching Method," in *Handbook of Research on Teaching*, ed. N. L. Gage (Chicago: Rand McNally, 1963), pp. 1–43; and Mary L. Seguel, "Conceptualizing Method: A History" (Paper prepared for the Society for the Study of Curriculum History, 1978), pp. 1–4.

3   See David C. Berliner and N. L. Gage, "The Psychology of Teaching Methods," in *The Psychology of Teaching Methods*, Seventy-fifth Yearbook of the National Society for the Study of Education, Part I, ed. N. L. Gage (Chicago: University of Chicago Press), pp. 1–20; James Block and Robert Burns, "Mastery Learning," in *Review of Research in Education*, vol. 4, ed. Lee S. Shulman (Itasca, Ill.: Peacock, 1976), pp. 3–49; and Robert Slavin, *Cooperative Learning* (New York: Longman, 1983), pp. 23–30. Method is not a prominent topic in the contemporary literature on teaching; within the research on teaching community, the term seldom appears (see Merlin C. Wittrock, ed., *Handbook of Research on Teaching*, 3rd ed. [New York: Macmillan, 1986], p. 1004). At the same time, methods courses are a prominent target for teacher education reform, a part of the curriculum many reformers feel is superfluous.

4   Annemarie S. Palinscar and Ann L. Brown, "Reciprocal Teaching of Comprehension-Fostering and Monitoring Activities," *Cognition and Instruction* 1, no. 2 (1984): 117–75.

5   On descriptive and prescriptive theory, see Jerome S. Bruner, "Some Theorems on

Instruction Illustrated with Reference to Mathematics," in *Theories of Learning and Instruction,* Sixty-third Yearbook of the National Society for the Study of Education, Part 1, ed. Ernest R. Hilgard (Chicago: University of Chicago Press, 1964), pp. 306–35.

6  Virginia Richardson, "Practice and the Improvement of Research on Teaching" (Invited address at the annual meeting of the American Educational Research Association, San Francisco, March 27, 1989), pp. 4–9.

7  G. Williamson McDiarmid, "Opportunities for Learning to Teach Writing in a Preservice Teacher Education Program" (Paper presented at the annual meeting of the American Educational Research Association, San Francisco, March 31, 1989), pp. 5–12.

8  Carol S. Weinstein, "Teacher Education Students' Preconceptions of Teaching," *Journal of Teacher Education* 40, no. 2 (March-April, 1989): 53–60.

9  For a more complete discussion of the effectiveness theme in teacher education, see Walter Doyle, "Themes in Teacher Education Research," in *Handbook of Research in Teacher Education,* ed. W. Robert Houston (New York: Macmillan, in press).

10  B. Othanel Smith, "Research Bases for Teacher Education," *Phi Delta Kappan* 66, no. 10 (June 1985): 685.

11  For a comprehensive review of the literature on classroom management, see Walter Doyle, "Classroom Organization and Management," in *Handbook of Research on Teaching,* 3rd ed., ed. Wittrock, pp. 392–431.

12  For descriptions of these discipline models, see C. M. Charles, *Building Classroom Discipline,* 3rd ed. (New York: Longman, 1989), pp. 9–132.

13  Jacob S. Kounin, *Discipline and Group Management in Classrooms* (New York: Holt, Rinehart & Winston, 1970), pp. 74–124.

14  See Paul V. Gump, "Intra-setting Analysis: The Third Grade Classroom as a Special but Instructive Case," in *Naturalistic Viewpoints in Psychological Research,* ed. Edwin Willems and H. Rausch (New York: Holt, Rinehart & Winston, 1969), pp. 202–14. See also Susan S. Stodolsky, *The Subject Matters: Classroom Activity in Math and Social Studies* (Chicago: University of Chicago Press, 1988), pp. 31–74.

15  Paul V. Gump, "School Settings and Their Keeping," in *Helping Teachers Manage Classrooms,* ed. Daniel L. Duke (Alexandria, Va.: Association for Supervision and Curriculum Development, 1982), pp. 98–114.

16  See Gump, "Intra-setting Analysis," pp. 214–16.

17  Gump, "School Settings and Their Keeping," pp. 107–110; and Carol S. Weinstein, "The Physical Environment of the School: A Review of the Research," *Review of Educational Research* 49, no. 4 (Fall 1979): 577–610.

18  Jacob S. Kounin and Paul V. Gump, "Signal Systems of Lesson Settings and the Task Related Behavior of Preschool Children," *Journal of Educational Psychology* 66, no. 4 (August 1974): 554–62.

19  See Edmund T. Emmer, Carolyn M. Evertson, and Linda M. Anderson, "Effective Classroom Management at the Beginning of the School Year," *Elementary School Journal* 80, no. 5 (May 1980): 219–31.

20  Kounin, *Discipline and Group Management in Classrooms,* pp. 74–91.

21  See Marshall Arlin, "Teacher Responses to Student Time Differences in Mastery Learning," *American Journal of Education* 90, no. 4 (August 1982): 334–52; Frederick Erickson and Gerald Mohatt, "Cultural Organization of Participation Structures in Two Classrooms of Indian Students," in *Doing the Ethnography of Schooling,* ed. George Spindler (New York: Holt, Rinehart & Winston, 1982), pp. 132–74; and Gump, "School Settings and Their Keeping," pp. 110–13.

22  See Walter Doyle, "Academic Work," *Review of Educational Research* 53, no. 2 (Summer 1983): 159–99; idem and Kathy Carter, "Academic Tasks in Classrooms," *Curriculum Inquiry*

14, no. 2 (Summer 1984): 129–49; Walter Doyle et al., *Patterns of Academic Work in Junior High School Science, English, and Mathematics Classes: A Final Report,* Research and Development Report No. 6190 (Austin: University of Texas, Research and Development Center for Teacher Education, 1985), pp. 59–80; Catherine Cornbleth and Willard Korth, "Doing the Work: Teacher Perspectives and Meanings of Responsibility" (Paper presented at the annual meeting of the American Educational Research Association, Montreal, April 14, 1983), pp. 1–23; and Frederick Erickson, "Taught Cognitive Learning in its Immediate Environment: A Neglected Topic in the Anthropology of Education," *Anthropology and Education Quarterly* 13, no. 2 (Summer 1982): 149–80.

23   See Walter Doyle, "Content Representation in Teachers' Definitions of Academic Work," *Journal of Curriculum Studies* 18, no. 4 (October-December 1986): 365–379.

24   Judith L. Green, Judith O. Harker, and Joanne M. Golden, "Lesson Construction: Differing Views," in *Schooling in Social Context: Qualitative Studies,* ed. George W. Noblit and William T. Pink (Norwood, N.J.: Ablex, 1987), pp. 46–77.

25   For a review of process-product research, see Jere E. Brophy and Thomas L. Good, "Teacher Behavior and Student Achievement," in *Handbook of Research on Teaching,* 3rd ed., ed. Wittrock, pp. 328–75. On mastery learning research, see Block and Burns, "Mastery Learning."

26   See also Karen K. Zumwalt, "Are We Improving or Undermining Teaching?" in *Critical Issues in Curriculum,* Eighty-seventh Yearbook of the National Society for the Study of Education, Part 1, ed. Laurel N. Tanner (Chicago: University of Chicago Press, 1988), pp. 148–74.

27   Some have argued that classroom knowledge is fundamentally personal knowledge. See, for example, F. Michael Connelly and D. Jean Clandinin, "On Narrative Method, Personal Philosophy, and Narrative Unities in the Story of Teaching," *Journal of Research in Science Teaching* 23, no. 4 (April 1986): 293–310. Pushed to an extreme, this definition precludes the possibility that formal knowledge of teaching can be developed.

28   See Kathy Carter, "Teacher Comprehension of Classroom Processes: An Emerging Direction in Classroom Management Research," *Elementary School Journal,* in press.

29   Ralph T. Putnam, "Structuring and Adjusting Content for Students: A Study of Live and Simulated Tutoring of Addition," *American Educational Research Journal* 24, no. 1 (Spring 1987): 13–48.

30   Stefinee E. Pinnegar, "Learning the Language of Practice from Practicing Teachers: An Exploration into the Term 'With Me'" (Paper presented at the annual meeting of the American Educational Research Association, New Orleans, April 5–9, 1988), pp. 1–28.

31   On the indeterminancy of human behavior, see Gary A. Cziko, "Unpredictability and Indeterminism in Human Behavior: Arguments and Implications for Educational Research," *Educational Researcher* 18, no. 2 (April 1989): 17–25.

32   Gardner distinguishes clearly between academic psychology and the cognitive sciences and describes academic psychology in the following terms: "Working largely in artificial experi-mental settings and relying excessively on findings obtained with laboratory rats and college sophomores, researchers in this field have methodically constructed, brick by brick, an edifice that includes chambers on how people see three-dimensional forms, how they learn to type, how they remember lists of words, and how electrical shocks can influence their behavior, as well as an assortment of other issues that lend themselves to experimental manipulation. Forming the mainstay of teaching in colleges and having a virtual stranglehold on the awarding of doctoral degrees, academic psychology has had little effect on the wider public. . . . Moreover, this neglect may be justified. If traditional academic psychology has first raised and then solved many little puzzles, it has failed to convince many critical observers . . . that its studies are central to an understanding of the mind" (Howard Gardner, "Cognition Comes of Age," in *Language and Learning: The Debate between Jean Piaget and Noam Chomsky,* ed. Massimo Piatelli-Palmarini [Cambridge, Mass.: Harvard University Press, 1980], pp. xxiv–xxv).

# Race and Ethnicity in the Teacher Education Curriculum

WILLIAM TRENT

*University of Illinois at Urbana-Champaign*

*William Trent presents a series of arguments for his proposal that the importance of race and ethnicity in education should become a primary area of study for the prospective teacher. Trent notes recent research showing that blacks and Hispanics are among those groups least well served by schooling in the United States, yet these groups will constitute an ever-increasing proportion of students. The problem is exacerbated, in Trent's view, by the opposite trend in the proportion of minority students who will be teachers, necessitating new understandings and new approaches for majority-population teachers who will be called on to teach increasing numbers of minority youth.*

It seems unnecessary today to write an article addressing the need for the explicit, informed treatment of the issues of race and ethnicity as a part of the curriculum in the preparation of the nation's teachers. We are, after all, thirty-five years beyond the Brown decision, twenty-five years beyond the 1964 Civil Rights Act; we have fair housing laws and we have affirmative action legislation. Time does not heal all wounds, however, nor does time erase centuries or years of lived history, and change has been painfully slow.

It is out of respect for the lived history of minorities in America that I argue for the necessity of including scholarship on race and ethnicity as a core part of the preparation of teachers. There are five compelling reasons that support this recommendation. The first is demographic: We are going to have an increasingly diverse nonwhite student population. Second is an economic incentive: We cannot compete in the modern world if we ignore the educational needs of a third or more of our future labor force. Third is the trend in the composition of the teaching force, which is increasingly female and white. Fourth is the idea of competence; no occupation should lay claim to the title "profession" if its treatments fail for a third of its clients or if the incumbents believe themselves to be unable to treat more than a third of its potential clients. Fifth, and in my estimation most important, is the imperative to protect the human and civil rights of the clients. In this article, I will elaborate these reasons with evidence gathered from a variety of research efforts (my own and those of others) following a few prefatory comments.

## SELECTED FEATURES OF THE SOCIAL CONTEXT

Despite the positive advances of the late sixties and early seventies, which created a very narrow window of opportunity, we have also had benign neglect of minorities: the Bakke and Weber legal decisions, which weakened affirmative action efforts; a declining rate of postsecondary enrollment for blacks; limited advances in enrollment of Hispanics and American Indians; a Justice Department bent on dismantling any efforts aimed at affirming civil rights; the recent demonstrations of overt racism brought to mind by names such as Howard Beach, Willie Horton, and skinheads; and finally a Supreme Court apparently constituted along ideological lines, decisions of which have substantially constrained, if not crippled, affirmative action. The past forty-five years have brought about more school desegregation, but not substantially more societal desegregation and certainly not the pervasive integration that many assumed would occur. Inequality in educational and employment opportunity is still a reality.

In many ways the conditions we confront in examining the nation's minority community are far more complex than was the case when the war on poverty was launched, due to the even more diverse composition of that community. The racial and ethnic composition of the minority community is today more diverse in national and geographic origin, political history, social and cultural history, language, and political and social vision. Each of these sources of diversity is further complicated by past and current conditions of social class and gender unique to each group.

One result of these aspects of social context is an increasing awareness of the embeddedness and pervasiveness of racism. There is also a growing understanding that the differences among and between us require special recognition and treatment. Research illuminating the latter point makes clear the need to prepare teachers differently if they are to handle diversity better.

Research by sociologists modeling the status-attainment process has shown explicit differences among the experiences of blacks, Hispanics, and whites.[1] Results of such studies have consistently revealed that the fairly logical socialization-based, contest-type model (which assumes a meritocratic process) has not held for blacks and Hispanics as it has for whites. Rather, a sponsorship type of explanation seems to best characterize the attainment process for them. For example, socioeconomic status does not have the intergenerational significance among blacks and Hispanics that it does for whites. Nor does the role of significant others. Instead, avoiding disciplinary problems, adopting the right attitudes, and performing well seem to identify blacks for "sponsorship," or selection for upward mobility.[2]

These results, from quantitative studies of attainment, have been made clearer by the qualitative work of Cicourel, Rist, and others pointing to the ways in which teacher-held conceptions of capable students vary by race, ethnicity, and social class.[3] These latter works have heightened our attentiveness to teacher expectations as a critical factor in the educational success of different groups of students. Finally, European social scientists and others have led a sustained challenge to the meritocratic characterization of the educational process in Western, capitalist societies.[4]

The combination, then, of the continuing societal inequalities and the research underscoring the ways in which schooling contributes to their persistence suggests a compelling argument for changing the way teachers are prepared to handle racial, ethnic, and gender diversity. This argument becomes even stronger when demographic, economic, professional, and ethical dimensions of the current situation are made explicit.

## DEMOGRAPHIC CHANGE

If the preceding depiction of inequality and schooling is an accurate one, the demographic realities we confront are cause for major concern. Writing in 1985, Hodgkinson reported that

> today we are a nation of 14.6 million Hispanics and 26.5 million blacks. But by 2020 we will be a nation of 44 million blacks and 47 million Hispanics — even more if Hispanic immigration rates increase. . . . At the moment . . . [Asian Americans] are a much smaller group than Blacks or Hispanics (about 3.7 million in 1980), but their growth potential from immigration is very great for the next decade — they currently represent 44% of all immigrants admitted to the US. However their diversity is very great.[5]

It is not the population mix itself but what it portends for schools that captures our attention. In 1984 there were sixteen states in which minority public school enrollment exceeded 25 percent. Ten of those states had the highest dropout rates during that period, ranging from a high of 43.7 percent to a low of 35.4 percent. Simply put, minority students are now, and seem increasingly likely to be, those who experience the least success in our schools. Failure to prepare teachers responsibly for the existing conditions will at least perpetuate if not exacerbate the current conditions of high dropout rates and low levels of educational attainment or achievement that characterize the minority educational experience.

At the very least, prospective teachers need to understand why the school classroom composition they envisioned is less likely to be available to them now or throughout their careers in teaching. Not just central city urban schools but also suburban schools are increasingly diverse in racial and ethnic terms. In many instances the diversity is more complex due to the added factors of poverty, single-parent female-headed households, and language differences. The content of instruction in teacher education, moreover, must be very clear with regard to the distinctive groups of students, for few generalizations will hold either within or between groups. No single set of assumptions about student learning, and no one instructional approach, will adequately serve the learning needs of all students in our schools. Fundamental to the content of instruction in teacher education will be the knowledge and experience necessary to enable teachers to envision and implement a model of excellence to which all students are entitled.

## ECONOMIC CONSEQUENCES OF AN UNDEREDUCATED POPULATION

Almost without exception, the economic necessity of better preparing a broader group of students follows closely on the heels of the presentation of the demographic realities. It is a return to the theme of enlightened self-interest stated so clearly in *A Nation at Risk,* which, despite its narrow ideological framework, merits our attention.[6] Because of the historical patterns of economic discrimination against minorities, combined with the declining ratio of earners to retirees, we now entertain arguments that make minority human capital a greater resource in constructing the nation's market competitiveness and hence our quality of life. This is not a new condition. It has always been the case that minorities have been a core supply of labor even if only in the tertiary or reserve labor pool.[7] Support for the education of minorities, particularly blacks, has often been cited as a quality-of-life issue for this nation,[8] but only in recent times have the demographic data become so compelling as to require that we address their educational needs from the standpoint of inclusion in the primary labor force. This necessitates examining the adequacy of teacher preparation in equipping teachers for this task. It should be done, however, so as to avoid the traditional mistake of assuming that vocational education is the solution to the educational problems of minority students. If Weisberg is correct in his finding that "general literacy skills are more likely than any other factor to yield success in the labor market,"[9] then the economic imperative, too, suggests that new ways must be found to facilitate all students' learning in communication and computational skills.[10] To teach teachers that high schools are a place for minority students to learn specific job skills in an increasingly service-oriented economy is to divert attention from the basic educational needs that will have the best "pay-off" for all students in the future.

## TRENDS IN THE COMPOSITION OF THE TEACHING FORCE

The third reason for preparing teachers to understand race and ethnicity centers on who our teachers will be, based on studies of the composition of the teaching force, college enrollment, and degree attainment. Schlecty and Noblit are most often cited for their finding that the best and the brightest leave teaching sooner and at a greater rate than their peers. They also reported that the teaching force will increasingly be comprised of young white females.[11] With declining black enrollment in higher education and fairly stable Hispanic and American Indian enrollment, combined with fewer students choosing teaching as a career, it is imperative that nonminority teachers be better prepared to address the educational needs of minority students.

General patterns with regard to degree attainment indicate that bachelor of arts degrees in education have been declining overall, and sharply for selected groups of students:

From 1976 to 1981 the total number of bachelor degrees awarded in education went from approximately 151,000 to 105,000, a 31 percent decline.[12]

Females continue to dominate among education degree recipients both in total number and in percentage across all major fields.[13]

Consistent with the forecast of low numbers of minority teachers by the year 2000, blacks show a greater rate of decline in their concentration in education from 1975 to 1981 compared with whites, and black and Hispanic females show a greater rate of decline during that period compared with white females.[14]

Combining these trends with the renewed emphasis on teacher competency as determined by the National Teacher Examination and state testing procedures, the predictable results are that the teaching force will be both more female and more white than Schlecty and Noblit speculated.

Even without regard to race, ethnicity, or gender, the need for better preparation of the future pool of teacher candidates is clear. Especially because of the disparity between the demographics of students and those of teachers, race and ethnic differences and their consequences for education must receive more explicit treatment in the teacher education curriculum. At the same time, we need to redouble our efforts to increase the supply of minority educators. This should not be taken to mean that the minority educator, male or female, will necessarily be a better teacher without a reformed curriculum and other changes needed in the public schools. Minorities too harbor misconceptions and stereotypes. Thus if the implicit assumption is that minority teachers will "naturally" do better, then I think the evidence for that is less than clear.[15] Nor should it be held that hiring minority educators will absolve others of responsibility for educating minority children, an attitude that in itself reveals the need for a reformed teacher education curriculum.

## PROFESSIONAL COMPETENCE

The fourth reason undergirding the recommendation for change results from ongoing research focusing on problems in the teaching profession and the perceived consequences of selected teaching reform policies for minority educators. A pilot of a recent national survey revealed that teachers report their belief that their competency with blacks and other minorities is limited.[16] Inadequate undergraduate exposure to course content familiarizing them with the experiences of minorities and limited cross-race contact or multicultural experiences in or outside of school were given as primary reasons for this belief. In other research we were able to identify "training in sociocultural understanding" as a major area of need for teachers.[17] Each of these tentative findings underscores the need to improve the sense of competence that teachers bring to their work.

Earlier I introduced the idea that no occupation merited the status of a profession if its practices were unsuccessful for a third of its clients. While such a statement may sound alarmist, the statistics that are regularly cited suggest that it may be an understatement. For example, the following are reported in *Barriers to Excellence: Our Children at Risk:*

> Studies conducted in urban high schools have revealed dropout rates as high as 85 percent for native Americans, and between 70 and 80 percent for Puerto Rican students.

> The national dropout rate for blacks in high school is nearly twice that of whites.

> Black students are more than three times as likely to be in a class for the educable mentally retarded as white students, but only half as likely to be in a class for the gifted and talented.

> At the high school level, blacks are suspended three times as often as whites; while minority students are about 25 percent of the school population, they constitute about 40 percent of all suspended and expelled students.

> In our own research focusing on black male students, we find limited evidence of the "criminalization" of these students, a process whereby

teachers are at least implicitly communicating their fear of black males.[18]

These "educational" experiences of black and other minority students suggest that our current strategies for treating their educational needs consist largely of removing the students from what we would consider an effective learning environment. Paraphrasing the often cited declaration in *A Nation at Risk*, these conditions amount to a declaration of war against minority students. It is clear from these conditions that our current preparation of teachers falls far short of most definitions of adequate.

It is interesting to note that the debate over professionalism seldom addresses the transportability of teaching skills. Most education graduates seem to envision themselves returning to the schools they know, not just to any school where the jobs and need for their services exist. I contend that preparing teachers to apply their skills in a wide range of contexts will both improve their sense of personal competency and reduce the stress related to teaching in racially diverse school contexts.

## THE RIGHTS OF STUDENTS

My fifth and final reason for urging systematic attention to race and ethnicity in teacher education programs is that it is the only way to protect the human and civil rights of the students in our schools. In a recent study I interviewed administrators from my hometown school district in Virginia who reminded me of the mission-like and visionary quality of the teachers in my segregated school system. I have since wondered what it was that sustained their ability to teach us despite the overt racism of the separate but (un)equal system and their ability to inspire us to aspire to and prepare for careers that were effectively closed to us. While I have no evidence to substantiate it, I am increasingly convinced that their knowledge of our circumstance and conditions fueled their hopes and aspirations for us, which shaped how they taught us. In many instances these educators were victims of racism and discrimination and had personally experienced denied opportunity despite having fully prepared themselves for excellence. Their intimate understanding of the community, its strengths and constraints, provided them the insights to student needs and potential out of which they taught and with which they nurtured success. Much has changed in the past thirty years, including many human rights accomplishments. Nonetheless, as one respondent put it, "We don't seem to demand as much from or want as much for our students as we did with your group."[19]

Teachers do have a vision for minority students today but it is not one shaped by an informed and intimate knowledge of the students and their circumstances. If we are to change that vision in a positive way, to one that will nurture and sustain aspirations for and commitment to excellence, we must provide teachers with a far clearer and more intense curricular experience focused on race and ethnicity and their implications for education.

## Notes

1   See, for example, Alan Kerckhoff, "The Status Attainment Process: Socialization or Allocation?" *Social Forces* 55, no. 2 (1976): 368-89; idem and Richard Campbell, "Race and Social Status Differences in the Explanation of Educational Ambitions," *Social Forces* 55 (1977): 701-14; idem, "Black-White Differences in the Educational Attainment Process," *Sociology of Education* 50 (January 1978): 15-27; Alejandro Portes and Cynthia Truelove, "Making Sense of Diversity: Recent Research on Hispanic Minorities in the United States," *Annual Review of Sociology* 13 (1987): 359-85; Alejandro Portes and K. L. Wilson, "Black-White Differences in Educational Attainment," *American Sociological Review* 41 (June 1976): 414-531; W. Tenhouten et al., "School Ethnic Composition, Social Context and Educational Plans of Mexican-Americans and Anglo High School Students," *American Journal of Sociology* 77, no. 1 (1971): 89-107; and G. E. Thomas, "Race and Sex Differences and Similarities in the Process of College Entry," *International Journal of Higher Education* 9 (1980): 179-202.

2   Kerckhoff and Campbell, "Black-White Differences in the Educational Attainment Process."

3   See Aaron V. Cicourel and John I. Kitsuse, "The School as a Mechanism of Social Differentiation," in *Power and Ideology in Education,* ed. J. Karabel and A. Halsey (New York: Oxford University Press, 1977), pp. 282-92; and Ray C. Rist, "On Understanding the Processes of Schooling: The Contributions of Labeling Theory," in ibid., pp. 292-305.

4   See, for example, Michael Apple, Pierre Bourdieu, and Jean-Claude Passeron, *Reproduction in Education, Society, and Culture* (London: Sage Publications, 1977); Samuel Bowles and Herbert Gintis, *Schooling in Capitalist America* (New York: Basic Books, 1976); Henry Giroux, *Theory and Resistance in Education* (South Hadley, Mass.: Bergin and Garvey Publishers, 1983); Paul Willis, *Learning to Labour* (Lexington, Mass.: D.C. Heath, 1977); and Michael F. D. Young, *Knowledge and Control* (London: Collier-Macmillan, 1971).

5   Harold Hodgkinson, *All One System* (Washington, D.C.: Institute for Educational Leadership, Inc. 1985).

6   The National Commission on Excellence in Education, *A Nation at Risk* (Washington, D.C.: U.S. Government Printing Office, 1983).

7   See, for example, William Julius Wilson, "Segregation and the Rise of the White Working Class," in *The Declining Significance of Race* (Chicago: University of Chicago Press, 1978); and James D. Anderson, *The Education of Blacks in the South, 1865-1935* (Chapel Hill: The University of North Carolina Press, 1988), esp. ch. 1.

8   Anderson, *The Education of Blacks,* pp. 27-32.

9   A. Weisberg, "What Research Has to Say about Vocational Education in the High Schools," *Phi Delta Kappan* 64, no. 5 (1983): 59.

10   The National Commission on Excellence in Education, *A Nation at Risk.*

11   Philip C. Schlechty and George W. Noblit, *Policy Research,* Vol. 3 of Research in Sociology of Education and Socialization (Greenwich, Conn.: JAI Press, 1982), pp. 283-306.

12   William T. Trent, "Equity Considerations in Higher Education: Race and Sex Differences in Degree Attainment and Major Field from 1976 through 1981," *American Journal of Education* 92, no. 3 (1984): 280-305.

13   Ibid.

14   Ibid.

15   For an insightful discussion of this point, see Lisa Delpit, "Skills and Other Dilemmas of a Progressive Black Educator," *Harvard Educational Review* 56, no. 4 (1986): 379–85; and idem, "The Silenced Dialogue," *Harvard Educational Review* 58, no. 3 (1988): 280–97.

16   Harry Broudy, Steven Tozer, and William Trent, "The Illinois Project on Professional Knowledge in Teacher Education: A Pilot Study of Core Problems in Teaching" (Unpublished Report, University of Illinois College of Education, Champaign, Ill., 1986).

17   William Trent, "The Implications of Reform for Minority Educators" (A presentation to the American Educational Research Association, Washington, D.C., 1986).

18   *Barriers to Excellence: Our Children at Risk* (Boston: National Coalition of Advocates for Students, 1985); see also Broudy, Tozer, and Trent, "The Illinois Project."

19   Trent, "The Implications of Reform for Minority Educators."

# The Role of History in the
# Education of Teachers

PAUL C. VIOLAS

*University of Illinois at Urbana-Champaign*

*Paul Violas argues that if teachers are to understand the problems they face in professional practice — and make informed judgments about them — they must understand the historical context of schooling. Using two examples from European educational history, Violas shows how history can serve as a text for critically interpreting present-day relations between school and society in two ways: one in which history stands as an informative "substitute" for first-hand experience, and one in which history helps us understand how current conditions came to be. Violas believes such understandings are necessary if teachers are to understand the context and consequences of their own practice, and to think critically about the aims and methods of schooling.*

"Consider the herds that are feeding yonder: they know not the meaning of yesterday and today; they graze and ruminate, move or rest, from morning to night, from day to day." Beasts cannot remember past generations. Man, however, is different, because he "cannot learn to forget, but hangs on to the past: however far or fast he runs, that chain runs with him. . . . A leaf is continually dropping out of the volume of time and fluttering away — and suddenly it flutters back into man's lap."[1] Thus, Nietzsche insightfully captured not only a major distinction between humans and others of the animal kingdom, but the fact that humans cannot escape their history.

Therefore, when we ask whether history can be used in the preparation of teachers we are really asking the wrong question. We should ask how our history can be utilized most intelligently, for history will be a factor whether we teach it well, poorly, or not at all. For one answer to this question we might go to the beginning of recorded history.

Nearly two and a half thousand years ago, the first great historian, Thucydides, in justifying the probable unpopularity of his difficult text, explained: "It will be enough for me, however, if these words of mine are judged useful by those who want to understand clearly the events which happened in the past and which (human nature being what it is) will, at some time or other and in much the same ways, be repeated in the future."[2] Although we have since learned to be more cautious regarding the repeatability of history, Thucydides identified the controlling assumptions of all historical study: (1) Human nature, at its most basic level, remains constant; and (2) this constancy allows us both to investigate past events and to learn from them. If it were the case that human nature was fundamentally different in fifth-century Athens from what it is today, then not only would a history of that time be impossible for us, but we would be unable to comprehend any of its documents or artifacts. The fundamental assumption of history, articulated when Western civilization first began to write history and think historically, is that we in the present can learn from the past.

In a significant way history shares this function with its ancient ancestors poetry and mythology. Werner Jaeger has shown that when the Greeks began to utilize history in their education, it in effect replaced poetry.[3] Greek poetry from Homer to Euripides played much the same function in Hellas as the Covenant and the writings of the Prophets did in Judea. Via myth and metaphor, it conveyed lessons from the past. When history inherited this pedagogic function from poetry and mythology, however, historians, bound by their conception of the nature of their enterprise, renounced allegory and metaphor and pledged a true representation of the past as their pedagogical method.[4] This pedagogic conception of history has undergone countless refinements since Thucydides. Space restraints prohibit me from examining them in detail here. Suffice it to say that at the present we are much more circumspect about what kinds of lessons are available and how we should interpret them.

This article will argue that history has not only an important but a central role in the foundational preparation of prospective teachers because of the understandings students can gain from the study of history. I will consider two kinds of understandings that, while related, are importantly different: (1) those understandings that result from history standing as substitute for experience—that is, how people, individually or collectively, forged their responses to specific realities of their times—which are grounded in our ability to understand how the experiences of the past may be generalized across time and applied to the present; and, (2) the understanding of how certain conditions in our present developed. This understanding can only be gleaned from a study of history and is indispensable to a rational consideration of those conditions, our generation of intelligent responses to them, and our wise choice of the alternatives. We will examine first the idea of history as a substitute for experience.

HISTORY AS SUBSTITUTE FOR EXPERIENCE: AN EXAMPLE

The examination of how individuals and societies in the past responded to their particular circumstances can demonstrate the roles played by a wide variety of human emotions and motives, ethical categories, and, indeed, all that was at one time encompassed by the word *humanitas*. If we successfully account for context—that is, carefully delineate and take into consideration the differences separating our ancestors from us—then we can utilize their experience; history can "stand in" for and enlarge our experience. Their experience becomes a part of our own learning. Moreover, we can use that experience to help us understand our present and ourselves. Perhaps an example would be useful.

Suppose we were to examine the history of Roman education with a class of prospective teachers.[5] They would learn that as the republic came into increasing contact with the Hellenistic world it began to import Greek educational ideals, and that by the time of Cicero the Romans had effected an impressive synthesis of Greek education with Roman traditions. The result was best exemplified in Cicero, the greatest orator of the Roman world, and in the ideal called Ciceronian *Humanitas*.

As the empire replaced the republic, however, subtle but significant changes occurred in Roman education and intellectual life. These changes were directly related to social, political, and economic developments. During the latter stages of the republic distant wars required the frequent and prolonged absence of Roman fathers from their families. This was exacerbated during the empire by wars and the need to "administer" the empire. The absence of fathers had at least two important outcomes: the need to find alternatives for "home education" when the fathers were no longer available to teach their sons, and a significant increase in divorce and the consequent decline of the family as the central institution of society.[6] Further, the influx of wealth tended to weaken the old Roman value of hard work. While these developments were eroding the traditional moral and ethical basis of Roman society, the necessity to govern a far-flung empire demanded "competent" administrators and functionaries. Moreover, the political atmosphere was significantly altered. Emphasis on the individual conscience of the senator and the citizen of the republic was replaced by emphasis on the loyalty of the subject to the empire.

Roman education evolved to reflect the realities and needs of the empire. Elementary schools arose to fulfill the function vacated by absent fathers. These and other schools increasingly came under government purview. As Marrou noted, "The Roman Empire gradually came to pursue an active policy of intervention and support in the matters of schools."[7] When Diocletian later reorganized the imperial bureaucracy, nearly all aspects of education were under imperial control. Moreover, students began to complain of the "unnecessary" difficulty of learning two languages and, slowly but surely, the study of Greek declined until by the time of Augustine, the Roman who knew Greek was indeed a rarity. The teaching of rhetoric became increasingly pedantic and divorced from reality as form superseded function. Student declamations, which earlier had been exercises in the application of rhetoric to realistic and practical problems, degenerated into highly stylized rhetorical exercises with absurdly unreal subjects: the Roman equivalent of the Medieval scholastics' debating the space requirement for angels dancing on the head of a pin.

The earlier Ciceronian aim for the education of the orator had been to produce the statesman who would be the protector of society. The education of the orator would introduce him to all the knowledge (as differentiated from facts) associated with humanity and human life. This knowledge, Cicero believed, made it possible for the orator to reach his highest potential as a human. The very safety of society required no less. Soon thereafter, however, as early as Quintilian, subtle changes in the ambience of education were occurring. Quintilian was not a scholar/humanist/literai who could be compared favorably with Cicero. Cicero's concerns centered on philosophy, politics, the good society, and the nature of man. Quintilian's concern, in contrast, centered on educational method. Cicero is remembered as a philosopher and statesman as well as an educator. Quintilian, however, while he still represents much of the Ciceronian ideal, is best remembered for his great work, the *Institutio Oratoria*. While this is undoubtedly the best single work in the field of methodology, it is still methodology; it lacks the nobility of aim and the intellectual depth of Cicero's *de Oratore*. Quintilian stands in a similar relation to Cicero in education as does Gorgias to Protagoras, or Pliny to Cicero in literature.[8]

By the time we reach the age of Diocletian the change in educational goals is well apparent. The aim of imperial education is to create the imperial subject, the administrator, the functionary. Loyalty, efficiency, clarity, in sum, "usefulness"—not the attainment of "full human potential"—is the desired result. It will not be a surprise to our students that there was a corresponding deterioration in the general quality of Roman intellectual life.

What "lessons" can prospective teachers glean from such an examination of Roman educational history (which I have here only sketched)? First, they will be able to begin to understand that intimate relationships exist between the sociopolitical conditions of a society and its educational structures and goals. Second, with appropriate allowances for differences in historic eras, they will note the relationship between political ideals and the potential for "free reign" of the intellect and its resulting impact on the quality of intellectual life. Third, again with due caution against overgeneralization, they will begin to note that social conditions have significant impact on the family and on its role in education. Fourth, our students will not fail to notice the impact of bureaucratic centralization on the vitality of education. Last, will any one be able to miss the importance of prevailing political thought on the aims of education and the resulting impact on the nature of education? Thus, if we carefully delineate the contextual differences between the historical era under study and the present, students can develop important understandings about how humans and human institutions in that era responded to specific realities, which will be useful to us as we consider our present circumstances. What is perhaps more important, students can learn how to think about educational aims and processes as situated in wider social-political contexts.

## THE DEVELOPMENT OF PRESENT REALITY: AN EXAMPLE

A second kind of historical understanding that is necessary for an intelligent response to our current reality is the understanding of how the present reality developed. Without this understanding we cannot rationally comprehend our present or intelligently conceive potential alternatives to the problems we currently face. Again, an example may be instructive.

One of the central policy problems facing American educators and statesmen is the appropriate role of "vocational" education, especially at the secondary level. Crucial to the question is the unhistorical claim made by defenders of vocational education that vocational education represents democracy in education and that any diminution of vocational education will represent a corresponding denigration of democratic education. This claim rests on the tacit assumption that historically education in the *artes liberale*[9] was the exclusive preserve of the aristocracy, and children of the "common" people entered the educational arena only when democratically minded reformers understood the aristocratic nature of this "traditional" education and developed a people's curriculum — vocational education — that was both "practical" for and comprehensible to these children. This, it is respectfully submitted, is a gross misreading of educational history and an example of the muddled thinking that results when educational history is misread, ignored, or invented. A more correct reading will allow a more intelligent generation of, and selection among, alternatives. The alternative interpretation, it will be argued, is important not just for policymakers to understand, but for teachers as well.

The first thing we must note is the vast contextual difference between the past and the present with regard to "productivity." At no time in the history of the West (and probably of all of human history) did the productive capacity of society begin to approximate that of the present. To put it simply, during most of history it was absolutely necessary for the vast majority of humans to begin work at a very early age and continue throughout life in order to produce the necessities of life. Only a tiny majority had the "leisure" for education beyond rudimentary literacy. To ignore the social, philosophical, and educational implications of the great agricultural and industrial revolutions of the past three centuries is an example of unhistorical thinking that can lead to erroneous consequences.

Thus, we can "apply" lessons garnered from the education of the aristocracy during fifth-century Athens, the Renaissance, or eighteenth-century France to our present only with great circumspection. If we wish to apply such lessons it is necessary to translate and interpret the contextual differences. It is simply poor reasoning to say that because Isocrates, Cicero, or Guarino De Varona worked with children of the aristocracy, then their notions of education, ipso facto, apply only to the special few in any society. They were educating and, in their writings, referring to the education of those who were going to have not only power in society but also responsibility for the welfare of all society. Therefore, their students had to have the kind of education that purportedly would allow them to reach their fullest potential as humans. Only so educated could they intelligently bear their responsibilities. If we wish to make "use" of these educational insights we must translate them into our current vernacular (i.e., our present reality). The accuracy of this translation will revolve around the question of who in a democratic society will have input in political decision making, and thus be responsible for social welfare and the health of the state. In a democracy the answer must be: all of the people. They represent the aristocracy of past times, not only because they will have power and responsibility but because the increased leisure that is now available to all provides the material conditions that make mass education as conceivable as our political philosophy makes it necessary.

Second, we must correct the mistaken notion that throughout Western history intellectual education was the exclusive preserve of the aristocracy. This assumption is crucial to the argument that democratically minded reformers at the beginning of the twentieth century concluded that education, especially in the liberal arts, had always been the preserve of the aristocracy and was thus, ipso facto, inappropriate for the lower classes. A careful examination of Western educational history reveals that from the early Middle Ages to the Renaissance, that is, circa seventh century to fifteenth century, the aristocracy were generally unlettered. J. A. Hexter has shown that "ignorance and indifference to letters in the aristocracy was not new in the sixteenth century; what was new and radical was the suggestion that things should be otherwise."[10] In earlier times the education of the nobility had not been neglected, but was chiefly concerned with the vocational training appropriate for a knight. Far from intellectual, it consisted primarily of manual training in the use of arms and behavioral conditioning in social graces. The method was apprenticeship. Changed social and economic conditions were responsible for the new educational attitude.

Conversely, prior to the Renaissance it was not unusual for children of common and often humble parents to attain education in letters, both at grammar schools and at universities. Loren MacKinney's study of Fulbert's career as Bishop of Chartres at the turn of the eleventh century provides some interesting evidence of this. He states: "Fulbert's parents were poor and humble. Like Gilbert of Rheims and many another medieval churchman of ignoble birth, Fulbert rose to a position of prominence through the church schools, which offered ample opportunities for persons of merit and ambition."[11] Further evidence resides in the fact that many of the early gram- mar schools in England were originally founded through the benevolence of a noble or high ecclesiastical official for the expressed purpose of providing education to the sons of the poor.[12] Moreover, the origin of the "college" in the medieval universities was primarily to provide lodging and board for poor scholars who could not afford the expense from their own resources. Phillippe Aries points out that in the medieval universities, "the trend was toward free education."[13] He substantiated the effects of this trend with an examination of the students at the Jesuit college at Chalons-sur-Marne be- tween 1618 and 1736, which revealed that the proportion of artisans' and labourers' sons ranged from 20 to 35 percent of the total — and he estimated that it was probably higher in the Latin schools. Such conditions, however, were about to change: "These colleges full of lower-class pupils were to dis- appear."[14] A "new spirit," which denied access of secondary education to the children of the lower classes, appeared in the eighteenth century. The new spirit was the spawn of the belief that education "unfitted" the children of the poor for manual labor.[15] It should be emphasized that the argument here does not suggest that most or even many of the poor received grammar or university education prior to the fifteenth century — rather, that among the students attending these institutions many were from humble backgrounds.

Thus, our students, when exposed to the history of Western education, will be equipped to reject as spurious and unhistorical the assumption that vocational education is democratic because in the long history of Western education children of laborers were absent from schools and universities until the appearance of vocational education, which alone made their education possible. From the early Middle Ages until they were expelled — gradually, in the seventeenth and eighteenth centuries, and systematically in the nine- teenth — lower-class children were an integral part of the schools and univer- sities of the West. It is their absence, not their presence, that is "new."

A third factor concerning the appropriateness of vocational education that history can help us to clarify concerns the motives of the "democratic" re- formers who were responsible for the introduction of contemporary voca- tional education. Considerations of space and time preclude an extended re- hearsal of the details of the educational histories dealing with this issue in the past decade. It is possible, however, to summarize these findings. Most responsible scholars now can probably agree that these motives have been well documented by recent educational historians. The reformers were motivated primarily by considerations concerning the welfare of the national economy, especially with American industry's ability to compete successfully with the Germans and the British. Most of the reformers wanted to develop an "adequate" work force. Additionally, many were concerned with maintaining social stability and avoiding militant social protest and conflict. Businessmen, industrialists, intellectuals, reformers, and educators generally agreed that vocational education would address these problems. Further, the histories show that the concern for and debate about a differentiated curriculum that included vocational education did not occur before the entrance of working-class children into the public schools. Rather, it occurred after considerable numbers of the immigrant working-class children had inundated the urban schools. Thus, it is clear that the reformers were not paving the way for an education for these children equal to that of middle- and upper-class children. Their reforms were a response to the perceived problems of industrial efficiency, social stability, and the invasion of the schools by working-class children.[16] The argument that vocational education was introduced as a democratic reform will not withstand historical analysis.

How our prospective students might utilize these historical understandings regarding the way the existential present developed gives rise to the question "What is the appropriate role for vocational education in American education, especially at the secondary level?" Most obviously, they will be able to see that two major arguments supporting the continuation of vocational education are based on historically unfounded assumptions. The ideas that liberal education is historically the preserve of the aristocracy (the elite, or economically "advantaged" in modern terms) and that vocational education developed as a democratic reform to enable working-class children to gain access to secondary education are inaccurate. Does this mean that they should conclude that, therefore, there is no place for vocational education? No, the necessity of such a conclusion cannot be supported from historical study. Our historical understandings should lead us to conclude that some of the arguments supporting vocational education are not sound and that we need to carefully examine other potential arguments for and against contemporary vocational education. There may be good arguments for vocational education. To base our educational decisions on historically inaccurate arguments, however, is as intelligent as to base space exploration decisions on the Ptolemaic theory of the universe.

## CONCLUSION

We have examined two kinds of understandings that can be acquired through sound historical study: (1) those resulting from history standing as a substitute for experience, and (2) the understanding of how our existential present was constructed. The former allows us to learn from the achievements and errors of our predecessors. It allows us to escape the necessity of rediscovering fire every generation. The latter makes possible a better understanding of how our present came to be. It makes intelligible the origins of our problematics and lays bare the assumptions undergirding various proposed alternative solutions to those problems — that is, it is necessary for the application of intelligence in our world. The study of educational history is essential in an intelligently planned course of study for prospective teachers because it provides the student with a sense of history, which is necessary for an intelligent understanding of the existential present.

George Logan has analyzed the idea of the sense of history in a way that highlights many of the points I have tried to make. He begins by considering "what it means not to have a sense of history. Where the historical sense is absent, either (or both) of two views of the past is found: (1) the idea that the past is essentially the same as the present (and is itself essentially uniform in character); (2) the idea that the past is qualitatively different from the present." The first leads one to conclude that the past is able "to provide a storehouse of lessons or examples, that can be directly applied" while the second leads to the conclusion that the past has "no real bearing on the present and to be merely a collection of marvelous tales." However,

> where the sense of history is present, the conception appears that, the past and the present have some common elements, the past can be used, but, since there are also pervasive discontinuities between past and present, its valid use is extremely delicate business, not simply a matter of imitation or duplication. At the heart of the sense of history is the realization that context affects significance.

Logan concludes that the sense of history "encourages a large, comparative view of cultures, [and] also encourages a precise, detailed view of individual segments of past and present."[17]

History continually intrudes on the present. We are constantly affected by the achievements and failures of our ancestors (both recent and distant). Any approach to learning that ignores this reality does so at its own peril. Building on this idea, José Ortega y Gasset insightfully observed that historical sense

> grants to man the farthest distance he can travel away from himself, while at the same time, as by rebound, with the closest understanding an individual can gain of himself. For when, in his effort to understand former generations, he comes upon the suppositions under which they lived, and that means upon their limitations, he will by the same token, realize what are the implied conditions under which he lives himself and which circumscribe his own existence. By the detour called history he will become aware of his own bounds, and that is the one and only way open to man by which to transcend them.[18]

It has been suggested that at this point some readers may say: "The argument is interesting, but what does it have to do with teachers? These understandings may seem appropriate for curriculum designers and administrators, but why for teachers? Remember we have a very limited time for the preparation of teachers. Will it not be better spent with courses in methods, or discipline, or computers, or parent/community relations?"

The response to such questions must make at least three points. First, certainly the above-mentioned areas are important and constitute a significant aspect of teachers' technical training. Nevertheless, these technical competences can be utilized most effectively when the teacher has a sound understanding of educational history. Historical understanding allows the teacher to better comprehend a specific technology, and its appropriate use and relation to other technologies, because he or she will know its evolution and the relative strengths of similar techniques. The teacher who knows educational history, for instance, will be better equipped to differentiate educational gimmicks, which are "old wine in new bottles," from genuine innovations. Is it possible to conceive of a teacher who would not be better equipped to understand and sensitively utilize the techniques learned in an audiovisual methods class as a result of studying John Amos Comenius, Johann Heinrich Pestalozzi, and Robert Owens? Will not the teacher who has studied Plato's *Republic* and the Jesuit Port Royal Schools profit more from a methods course in early childhood education than if he or she had been historically ignorant? There is an almost endless array of examples illustrating how understanding educational history facilitates a more effective utilization of educational technique.

Second, there is an important sense in which the history of education also contributes to the teacher's technical competence, but, of course only if we have a noble enough conception of a teacher. If we conceive of teachers simply as technicians who should only "teach" the curricula they have been given by a superior, then, of course, they do not need historical understandings to evaluate curricula or educational goals. If, on the other hand, we conceive of teachers as professionals who participate in the generation of curricula and educational goals and, because of that participation, have much more sophisticated command of their teaching, then these historical understandings are an essential component of their technical competence as teachers.

Third, beyond the technical competence, do we want teachers with a limited sense of their profession, themselves, and the educational enterprise? Or should we demand teachers whose horizons reach beyond their home town, their tribal group, and the temporal boundaries of today? The extended horizon available through the study of history will help teachers better to understand the constraints and opportunities that exist in their existential present. The answer to the suggested questions then depends largely on what kind of teachers we want, what minimum level we are willing to accept.

Quintilian once urged teachers to "let us suppose, then, that Alexander were committed to me, and laid in my lap . . . ."[19] How would they teach if, like Aristotle, they had been called by Phillip to teach the young Alexander? Quintilian implied that all teachers should consider all of their students as future Alexanders. We can all agree that the minimum acceptable for the teacher of a future Alexander, or our own children and grandchildren, should be set high. Must we not echo Quintilian and require the education of all children be given the same highest priority? If we do, then the relevance of history of education in the preparation of teachers becomes apparent.

We should note that when we say the study of history can yield these insights and understandings, not all study called "history" is sufficient. Only the careful, precise, and sensitive study of history can yield a sense of history. There are adequate and inadequate approaches to history — and this is an important distinction that deserves extended and scholarly attention — but that is a story for another time.

*Notes*

1   Frederich Nietzsche, *The Use and Abuse of History* (Indianapolis: The Library of Liberal Arts, 1957), p. 5.

2   Thucydides, *History of the Peloponnesian War* (Baltimore: Penguin Books, 1966), p. 24.

3   Werner Jaeger, *Paideia* (New York: Oxford University Press, 1968), pp. 100-03, 311.

4   The questions regarding how accurate or "objective" historians can actually be in their histories is much too large a topic to be investigated here. Nevertheless, most historians hold the requirement of telling the truth about the past, as best as it can be ascertained, as a professional ideal.

5   Readings might include H. I. Marrou, *A History of Education in Antiquity* (Madison: University of Wisconsin Press, 1982); M. L. Clark, *Rhetoric at Rome* (London: n.p., 1953); W. Wade Fowler, *Social Life at Rome in the Age of Cicero* (London: Macmillan & Co., 1965); M. L. Clark, *The Roman Mind* (New York: The Norton Library, 1968); Aubrey Gwynn, *Roman Education from Cicero to Quintilian* (New York: Teachers College Press, 1966); Moses Hadas, *The Basic Works of Cicero* (New York: The Modern Library, 1951); and Frederick M. Wheelock, *Quintilian as Educator* (New York: Twayne Publisher, 1974).

6   See Marrou, *History of Education in Antiquity,* pp. 229-55; Clark, *Roman Mind,* pp. 135-46; and Fowler, *Social Life at Rome,* pp. 135-67.

7   Marrou, *History of Education in Antiquity,* p. 301.

8   See Jaeger, *Paideia,* vol. I, pp. 107-60; and Clark, *Roman Mind,* p. 142.

9   The defenders of vocational education will usually refer to this as "traditional" or "intellectual" education.

10   J. A. Hexter, "The Education of the Aristocracy in the Renaissance," *The Journal of Modern History* 22, no. 1 (March 1950): 4.

11   Loren C. MacKinney, "Bishop Fulbert and Education at the School of Chartres," in *Texts and Studies in the History of Mediaeval Education,* ed. A. L. Gabriel and J. N. Garvin (Notre Dame, Ind.: The Mediaeval Institute, University of Notre Dame, 1957), pp. 5-6. For example, Rugby and Harrow had been established "to provide a free education for the children of the inhabitants of the parishes concerned" while Winchester, Eaton, Westminster, and Charterhouse all had a specified number of places (ranging from 40 to 70) designated to provide free board and education for the poor (Brian Simon, *The Two Nations and the Educational*

*Structure 1780-1870* [London: Lawrence and Wishart, 1981], p. 312): Rosemary O'Day has also examined the question of the social composition of English universities in the seventeenth century and found that even then they were not the exclusive preserve of the gentlemen's sons (*Education and Society 1500-1800* [London: Longman, 1982], esp. ch. 5 and 7).

12    See, for example, Phillippe Aries, *Centuries of Childhood* (New York: Vintage Books, 1960), p. 156.

13    Ibid., p. 308.

14    Ibid.

15    Ibid., p. 311.

16    See James D. Anderson, *The Education of Blacks in the South, 1860-1935* (Chapel Hill: The University of North Carolina Press, 1988); David Cohen and Marvin Lazerson, "Education and the Corporate Order," in *Education in American History,* ed. Michael B. Katz (New York: Praeger, 1973), pp. 318-33; Joseph Cronin, *The Control of Urban Schools* (New York: The Free Press, 1973); Clarence J. Karier, Joel Spring, and Paul Violas, *Roots of Crisis* (Chicago: Rand McNally, 1973); Harvey Kantor and David B. Tyack, eds., *Work, Youth and Schooling* (Stanford: University of Stanford Press, 1982); Edward A. Krug, *The Shaping of the American High School* (Madison: University of Wisconsin Press, 1969); Marvin Lazerson, *Origins of the Urban School* (Cambridge: Harvard University Press, 1971); Joel H. Spring, *Education and the Rise of the Corporate State* (Boston: Beacon Press, 1972); and Paul C. Violas, *Training of the Urban Working-Class* (Chicago: Rand McNally, 1978).

17    George M. Logan, "Substance and Form in Renaissance Humanism," *Journal of Medieval & Renaissance Studies* 7, no. 1 (Spring 1977): 18.

18    José Ortega y Gasset, *Concord and Liberty* (New York: The Norton Library, 1946), pp. 95-96.

19    Marcus Fabius Quintilian, *Institutes of Oratory: or Education of an Orator* (London: Bell & Daldy, 1873), p. 14.

# Examining Gender as a Foundation within Foundational Studies

GLORIANNE M. LECK

*Youngstown State University*

*Leck asserts that gender relations, particularly the relations of domination and subjugation characteristic of patriarchy, condition our ways of knowing, of teaching, of learning, and even of understanding gender itself. She argues that traditional ways of teaching, learning, and structuring knowledge are inadequate to the task of understanding and challenging oppressive patriarchal relations, and that social foundations instruction should be approached as an opportunity for a "community of learners" to examine relations between society, education, and the formation of selves.*

Gender is not an issue.[1] Gender is a foundational component of our culture. As such, gender represents and serves to maintain patriarchal values in social relations.

While many foundations of education faculty have been including the study of gender-related issues in preservice and in-service courses, it appears that most have not yet risked studying gender as a foundation of education.[2] I wish to call for just such a study as we reexamine the role of foundational studies in teacher education. Many of us have read and shared in discussions of ideas and have begun to examine some of the implications of works by Carol Gilligan, Jane Roland Martin, and Lois Weis, as well as the articles appearing in journals in our field. We have also begun to recognize the implications set forth in works such as *Women's Ways of Knowing*, *Reflections on*

*This article has circulated among a community of learners to whom I am most grateful. To each of the following persons I offer my sincere thanks for sharing in dialogue about this article: Jean Engle, Joan Ellen Organ, Maggie Capel, Jim Pusch, Jane VanGalen, Susan deBlois, Steve Tozer, Averil McClelland, Bill Armaline, Mary Leach, Carolyne White, and Tania Romalho. My most grateful thanks to Peter Baldino, who created institutional time and space for my work on this article and also nurtured its development. A special dedication to Cyndi Tyson, who is educating, doing all this and more with twenty-two co-learners in first grade in a Columbus, Ohio, public school.*

*Gender and Science, Women, History and Theory,* and *The Impact of Feminist Research in the Academy.*[3]

I suspect, in spite of our recent involvement in these discussions, that we are not consciously addressing the fact that we are operating within a patriarchal framework, an ideological system that by definition holds as its central notion that there are two sexes and that male persons and their activities are to be more highly valued than female persons and their activities.

## PATRIARCHY AND THE MAVERICK OF FEMINISM

It is important to know patriarchy in its obviousness as well as in its subversiveness. Patriarchy is so taken for granted it is often invisible. I, the woman, Glorianne, have one name that says who I am. I have another name that says to whom I belong. The surname *Leck* is a symbol of political relation of man over woman, man over child, man over property. In this instance naming is a conveyance of power relations.

In yet another social context, gender status and power are tied to symbols related to appearance. In a two-gender system we have fashions for men and fashions for women. I am expected to appear in public dressed in women's fashions, but precisely because I am a woman and lesser in social value than a man, I may wear men's fashions. To wear men's fashions can be interpreted to mean that I value what men choose to wear. If I were a man, I would not be sanctioned to wear women's fashions; that would be seen as silly. Most importantly, it would display my devaluing my birthright as a male in patriarchy and it would reflect a valuing of what women "choose" to wear.

In *The Second Sex,* Simone De Beauvoir noted that we who are now women were not born women.[4] Persons are identified as either male or female at birth. That sexual identification is a social signal for genderization. Through genderization, persons are socially directed to become masculine or feminine, men or women. These genderizations are socially constructed categories that prescribe and then describe ways of being-in-a-patriarchal-world.[5] To be socialized, to be named, to be dressed, are all genderization processes through which we are taught a group identification and its social value. Genderization is a process through which one may learn to value and demonstrate value of self, others, what is worth knowing, what is worth doing, how things are to be learned, and so forth. Gender studies are investigations and disclosures about those processes.

If we approach gender as a research variable or simply as another issue within schools and we do not analyze genderization as an ideological and thus a foundational process, then we in a very significant way sabotage a serious analysis of the study of foundations of education. I am concerned that most foundations of education classes are being taught in a way that confines gender to the status of variable or issue. If this is true, it appears that few of us seem to be actively acknowledging that patriarchal ideology limits and/

or constructs the ways in which we create meaning for our lives. Patriarchal ideology is served by the institutionalization of reproduction into a hetero-sexualism with its attached theme of dominance and submission, with divisions of labor that ground our assumptions and provide the strict social/sexual orientation through which human relationships are politicized. If we fail to recognize the foundational character of patriarchy and heterosexualism, our confusions and our nonconscious, taken-for-granted ways will make it nearly impossible for us, as learners, to explore the meaning and significance of educational relationships and contexts for learning.

It has been feminism, by definition a maverick within patriarchy, that has created space and audience for voicing views that challenge the central notion of the patriarchal ideology. Feminism argues that the occasion of birth ought not be an event of "birthright" or "birthwrong."[6] Birth category ought not be the preestablished basis for defining an individual's social worth and social prospects for "freedom."[7] Within patriarchy, males are supposed to be genderized into the masculine and through that genderization men are to be more highly valued and have more privilege than those who are genderized as female. While the feminist argument deals specifically with the birthright assignment of males to dominance and contexts for social privilege and the females' birthwrong assignment to contexts for oppression, the feminist argument may also be extended to other birth conditions including race, species, aesthetic appearance, cognitive function, genetic transmission, and so forth.

The feminist argument is not that the feminine should be valued over the masculine.[8] Feminists are arguing that sex and genderization ought not be the basis for assigning social contexts that limit possibilities for social worth. Birth should not determine worth. The feminist critique revolves around concerns about contexts in which worth is defined and around descriptions of the ways in which a sense of worth is learned. It seems to me that we who claim to have an interest in social foundations of education cannot ignore the challenges from and the work of feminist critics. Genderization and the values that it implies are so pervasive and invasive that we cannot go on as we have in an unexamined patriarchal perspective.

## PATRIARCHY AND THE STUDY OF SCHOOLING

If we are serious about getting at what is foundational in the education of teachers, we will have to address this matter of oppression by birth category. Our foundations of education classes, just like the other classes in the professional school, have operated from the view that the masculine experience in patriarchy is the central theme to be heralded and the central perspective from which to view the world. We have allowed masculine viewpoints to define human educational processes and to foster contexts of social worth.

There are two obvious ways in which we have exhibited patriarchal bias in our study of schooling. We have either treated male students with birthright as "insiders" and female students with birthwrong as "outsiders," or, in a move to appear uninvolved in gender matters, we have behaved as if all students are "gender free."

In the first approach it is apparent that insider as male and outsider as female rest on the fundamental dualism that restricts all persons to one or the other sex and then places higher value on the genderization contexts and outcomes for males. In the second approach, wherein we treat all students as gender neutral, we strive to make gender appear to be an irrelevant concept. In doing this we disguise the matter of advantage and disadvantage of genderization processes within a patriarchal system. In either the first or the second approach the use of "neutral" language serves the patriarchal ideology, in which the language selected to be treated as neutral is that which refers to *he, him,* and *mankind.* This choice of the masculine reference to refer to all persons regardless of gender has served to place masculinity at the center of human descriptions, thus making the male viewpoint appear neutral, objective, correct, or superior.

When the masculine serves as the universal reference for all people, it assures that a patriarchal view will hold the central place or central world view from which a collectivity of human beings will generate a legitimized and "objective" description of the world. When mankind refers to all of us, womankind refers to a subset, a part of the group. This maneuver serves to swallow up the viewpoints of women and tell women when and where they are welcome. From the word policemen, I am an outsider; from the word chairman, I am an outsider. When I chair a session I am a chairwoman, a chairperson, or some other awkward formation of that title of privilege and power. When I am called chairman I know I am on man's turf, an exception in their system, a temporary guest. In that I am not a man, to be called a chairman means I am not what I am.

This language allows us to learn that women are deviant from the norm and it is a small step to come to believe that women are problematic to the norming process. As those who would teach teachers about the role of language we must make it clear that *neutral masculine* is an oxymoron. Most foundations scholars, however, are continuing to operate out of this neutral-masculine approach and most are still behaving as if they are trying to get women and minorities an equal place within what is presented as a neutral patriarchal system.

I see *Euro-patriarchy-by privilege* as the controlling definition of social hierarchy in the U.S. schooling system at the present time. The system is not neutral. It is through patriarchal public institutions that the interactive arranging of hierarchies is ritualistically performed. It is through institutions that groups are identified and identify, are labeled and take on labels, and are taught and may learn the characteristics that are to be used by the dominant group in their justification for treating certain groups as inferior to the dominant male group. Studying these genderization processes is foundational to our understanding of schooling as well as to our understanding of other contexts that define teaching/learning processes.

We must challenge each other to look at contexts of learning and at how people are genderized into valuing types of learning, into having certain purposes for learning, into having styles of learning, or into limiting their learning. Turning our attention to an issues-in-schooling approach, "the women's problem," "the African-American problem," or "the special education problem" has tended to draw us into an acceptance of the assumptions of hierarchical ways of viewing human groups and achievement. Our participation in this is signalled by our looking at the characteristics of groups rather than at the patriarchal controls that create conditions for thinking about people in arrangements by group.

I hope we can move quickly toward seeing the absurdity as well as the politics of the way we are being involved in the discussion of such topics as comparative performances on standardized tests by women, men, autonomous minorities, immigrant minorities, involuntary minorities, and underclasses.[9] We can no longer allow ourselves to participate in that discussion without fully examining the foundational patriarchal notion that what one group does in the society should be more highly valued than what another group does. It seems critical that we address concerns about group achievement by looking at the epistemological assumptions within culture that define how we learn what is worth knowing. It is also absolutely necessary to study contexts in which worth is learned and from whom and how we learn our social worth.

To try to encourage women and minorities to struggle for success within patriarchy is to miss the point and challenge of feminist analysis. As Kathy Ferguson has indicated so clearly in *The Feminist Case against Bureaucracy,* we present no significant challenge to partriarchal society by training women to become masculinized school administrators. The feminist question to be addressed is: Are there other than hierarchical ways to organize schools and societies? Ferguson says, "The strength of feminist organizations lies in their ability to demonstrate the potential of feminist discourse to restructure the basic terms of political life."[10] We must ask ourselves about *other ways* and about the *ways of the others.*

Insofar as schooling is masculinized, the perspectives of feminized role-bearing persons are usually invalidated, if not rendered invisible. Women and other *others* are at an acute disadvantage in adapting to and learning to value the knowledge and skills that are valued by men in a patriarchal society. To be coming from an outsider's context while becoming an insider requires a tremendous act of courage, conversion, and/or adaptation. We are constantly reminded that one who has been an other and who becomes an accepted affiliate is an exception and must work twice as hard to convert to and/or to serve the insiders' cause. We have learned of archetypes who converted to the dominant way of being through their acquisition of privilege. Classic examples in our cultural literacy references have been the house slave, the assemblyline supervisor, the woman in charge of the office, the woman athlete, and the house-husband. While successful in their achievements, individuals who sought and attained these cross-over goals have been ridiculed.[11]

What does it mean to come in from the outside? Jane Roland Martin, in reference to the matter of co-education, asks, "What changes were made to accommodate the feminine student?"[12] We did not consider that, to be educated, women had to give up their own ways of experiencing and looking at the world, thus alienating themselves from themselves. To be unalienated they had to choose to remain uneducated.

### "EQUALITY " RECONSIDERED

The word *they* has served as a categorical reference not only to women, but to racial minorities, people with English as a second language, people of different social and economic classes, people with variance ·in their sexual identities and preferences, and people with different learning styles and sense-experience orientation. Feminist analysis calls attention to the fact that equal treatment of those from different contexts of worth does not create equity.

I am sure that if we reexamine so-called equal-opportunity schooling we will discover that even reforms meant to create equality of opportunity have perpetuated a set of conditions that have created a "green-card" system. Those who are not Euro-patriarchal-privileged are necessarily approaching schooling from an outsider's perspective. Outsiders are allowed into the schools under the conditional arrangement that they are either going back to the outside or are willing to convert to the dominant ideology. In such a conversion one learns to use the operating ideology for the maintenance of the system of power by privilege.

Equality, as a concept, is being decoded by the feminist challenge to the patriarchal construct of knowledge. Equality has been an illusive shorthand term used to signal a need among patriarchal institutions for an adjustment in behavior that might assist in maintaining the power relations necessary for male-dominated social conditions. Equality is a justice concept that often disguises deeper conditions of oppression.[13] Who is to be dominated and under what circumstances is a historically situated condition. Discussions that are confined to issues of equal schooling opportunity dissuade us from the necessary fundamental examination of the ideological foundations of *compulsory hierarchy*.

Oppression is not a matter of inequality of opportunity. Oppression is a fluid, integral, and context-specific phenomenon that is woven into cultural activities. Through these activities, oppression maintains the ideological basis of context for privilege. Oppression derives meaning in patriarchy as it serves to maintain conditions of hierarchy. Contextual analysis will allow us to describe specific manifestations of oppression. To refer to the oppression of women, nonheterosexuals, African-Americans, children, and species other than human is to reify the concept of oppression. The circumstances of those characterized are not parallel, although they are significantly interrelated. The ideology of compulsory hierarchy, which is grounded in patriarchy, encourages ranking even and especially among outsider groups. We know all too well the disclaimers, such as, "I may be a female, but at least I'm not poor"; "I may be physically disabled, but at least I'm not learning disabled"; and so forth.

Treating "being different" as a catch-all category is a problem for researchers as well as a problem within our traditional analyses of justice. I suggest that we need to examine traditional attitudes about justice and social adjustment programs on the suspicion that they may be every bit as insidious as was our calling masculine perspective "neutral." By lumping all differences into a polarized category — the oppressed — we will find ourselves actively participating in a socially encoded patriarchal concept of insiders and outsiders. What is not dealt with under an "issues" approach to the study of equality of opportunity in schooling is precisely the matters of contexts and ideological processes.

## CONTEXTS OF OPPRESSION AND CONTEXTS FOR INTERPRETATION

It is necessary to consider the context of meaning for individuals within the time and place of their existential project and in light of their particular survival strategies. We must study the interactive dynamics that create a concept of community around circumstances of oppression.[14]

Mary O'Brien, in *Reproducing the World: Essays in Feminist Theory,* directs our attention to what she finds to be an unacceptable strategy used by contemporary Marxists and ideological structuralists who indiscriminately cluster independently significant oppressed groups. They do so by adding oppressed groups after the concept of class by the insertion of commas so it reads, "class comma race comma gays comma gender comma."[15] She calls this strategy "commatization." O'Brien's idea of commatization might well be expanded in a playful but meaningful way by indicating that those who neglect to consider the context and grounding of oppression in temporal, cultural, and existential circumstances may well be considered to be so entrenched in the invisibility of learned boundaries that they appear to be intellectually "commatose."

If we are to remove ourselves from this "commatose" or nonconscious state and get into a wide-awake gender analysis we will need to pursue scholarship that looks at individuals, contexts, interactions, and ideologies. Part of this process will involve our being more attentive to the way we have studied education and schooling.

Dale Spender, in her very helpful "Education: The Patriarchal Paradigm and the Response to Feminism," advises us that the terms *teacher* and *learner*—as they have been defined by education—are inadequate; while educationalists may wish to divide the world into these two polarized categories, that distinction becomes meaningless in a feminist context, where *all* are teaching and learning.[16] Feminist critics remind us that we who teach teachers about education have much to examine in terms of the entire structure and organization of our ideas regarding human knowledge and knowing processes. We may ask, "If we are embedded in a patriarchal knowledge system, then how, if we can, will we come to know our own particular entanglement? How do we look out from and reflect on our own limitedness?"

It is helpful to recognize that such disciplinary questions as "How do I know if I know something?" and "What is worth knowing?" will reflect our Cartesian limitations and lead us to a dualistic ideology that wraps our query into what seems an inescapable tautology. Patriarchy is a holistic system, a controlling ideology. What constraints does that place on the process of our examination? I am very optimistic and want to suggest that we as members of a community of learners in the foundational studies of education are ready to begin that examination and we are, together, able to reflect on these ideologies, which are grounded in patriarchy. Our combined skills at interpretation and phenomenological description may serve as basic tools for this work.

As we each begin our part of this project we will need to identify our own way of learning. I assume we all have favored starting places and our own contexts for analysis. For my contribution and starting point I turn, for this article, to the work of Eugene Kaelin, one of my teachers and an individual whose scholarship I greatly admire. Here Kaelin articulates a Heideggerian view of beginnings:

> The first "forehaving" for any ontological inquiry is the preontological understanding we already possess. As our implicit knowledge of our own being becomes explicit through the stages of the interpretations we make of our own involvements with our worlds, the results of preceding analyses constitute a new "forehaving" and a new context for further interpretation. Since any human being possesses the necessary preontological understanding of its own being because it is that being, any human being should be able to follow the analyses.[17]

That is the spirit and the approach I would encourage with my co-learners, reminding myself that interpretation begins in contexts, not at such polarized locations as a teacher with the intellectual authority and a student who needs to be evaluated and objectified. The loss of the teacher-student polarity may seem very uncomfortable, perhaps subversive — but subversive to what? John Dewey told us we need not burden ourselves with a quest for certainty; Alan Watts advised us that there is a wisdom of insecurity.[18] Existentialists challenged the contrived institutionalization of a fixed reality. Now feminist critics and critical theorists call us to attend to the ideological constraints that may limit our intellectual directions and outcomes.

As I look for these constraints, or when I accidently encounter limits, I look at them with new forehavings. For example, from within the contexts I had borrowed and built, I long ago decided that learning mathematics was too difficult a task for me. I had also decided that teaching children was easier to do than learning mathematics. Owning my agency and being responsible for my ongoing processing of values, I am now able to reexamine that which I selected to believe about myself, about learning mathematics and about teaching children. In studying patriarchal ideology and its apparent constraints on my perspectives of possibilities for being, I have come to recognize that learning mathematics has been a masculinized context for display of power and labor. Mathematicians have been assigned a high social status within Euro-patriarchy. Teaching children has been contextualized as feminized work and has as such been devalued in Euro-patriarchy. While not fully conscious of it, I did think about math as men's work and teaching as women's work.

When, as a young woman in patriarchy, I came to choose between learning mathematics and learning to teach, I accepted my birthwrong place as one less valued. That particular devaluing of myself served the perception about my inability to learn to do well in mathematics. I did not devalue learning mathematics; I devalued myself as one who could learn mathematics. As with so many others, I found I could become a teacher, and while having a lesser social value, I could be of some value to those who would one day learn mathematics.

Prior to a sturdy, pervasive, and insistent feminist challenge and the related body of work on feminist pedagogy, the assumptions about gender differences and patriarchal dependence on hierarchy have reposed comfortably in the hegemonic layerings of our classrooms. Teaching is devalued except as it serves those who would learn mathematics (and other high-prestige disciplines). The emphasis on masculine contexts and symbols has been nearly invisible in the taken-for-granted world view presented in philosophical studies, economic arrangements, social traditions, biological routines, and anthropological rituals. Gender assignment is "culturally put in place" by ritual and behavioral manipulations in interaction with a social and/or one's own consciousness of possibilities for being.

To this point, women's studies scholars have been exploring the pervasiveness of gender as a foundational component within our reality construct. It should be no surprise to us that within the dichotomous frameworks of academia, women's studies and thus gender studies have been segregated from the traditional academic disciplines that do not promote or reward deliberate efforts to dislodge the encasements of patriarchal thought. By this implicit segregation, the traditional uninterrupted academic work that ignores or does not consider gender as a foundation is considered, in inference by some, as a continuation of segregated men's studies.[19] Not wishing to take anything away from the meaning, intention, and value of that inference, I do wish to shift the emphasis from men to patriarchy. If we consider the traditional organization of universities not to be men's studies, but rather hierarchical patriarchal studies, we will make it possible to look at that framework of value as well as the interactions among the gatekeepers who would keep some people out of privilege. Although almost all academic work is developed with examples drawn from the lives of men and is thus arranged hierarchically through perspectives from gender privilege, academics have not consciously studied men and men's lives as a part of an interactive condition of genderization in patriarchy.

Male persons are not born men, but are born with male privilege because they are born in patriarchy. The patriarchal language convention by which "masculine" reference is objectified and neutered has also twisted the meaning of being-in-the-world for one who is a gendered-male-person.

## TOWARD A COMMUNITY OF LEARNERS

If we are to risk a more thorough look at educational values, culture, and knowledge we must move away from the neutered-masculine and patriarchal frameworks of our earlier studies and participate with our students in an acknowledgment that we are "all 'forehaving' and that any human being should be able to follow the analyses."[20] We will recognize our failure to empower when we display a dependence on a group we have allowed to become objectified as "researchers."

Because of the sleeping consciousness about patriarchal ideology, gender characteristics, like groups, may at first appear to be objectifiable. Burdened with unexamined ideological views, some may continue to try to describe gender from an objectified world view. As such, those individuals may try to teach gender as a subject. Such an ideologically predictable performance is taking place in classrooms, but it is more evident in the work being done by those researchers who indulge in quantification methods and "scientized" activities. That type of research, while contributing a frozen section or a photograph done in a numerical medium, leaves off at the point where individuals interact and create meaning. It does not show individuals selecting or choosing the existential projects in their *owned* lives. All such efforts at objectification stop at the boundaries of existential meaning. Without breaking into or out of the ideological meaning of trying to be objective, we are caught in a nonconsciousness about the patriarchal values. Even ethnographers, who look at gender in contexts and cultural situations, are likely to be thwarted if they try to make their work apply to generalizable patterns. The overview denies and distorts both the context and the construct of individually owned lives.

Marie Lugones tells us:

> Through travelling to other people's "worlds" we discover that there are "worlds" in which those who are the victims of arrogant perceptions are really subjects, lively beings, resistors, constructors of visions even though in the mainstream construction they are animated only by the arrogant perceiver and are pliable and foldable, file-awayable, classifiable. . . . I always imagine the Aristotelian slave as pliable and foldable at night or after he or she cannot work anymore (when he or she dies as a tool). Aristotle tells us nothing about the slave *apart from the master.* We know the slave only through the master.[21]

Freeing ourselves from a need to be in control of objectivity and generalization does not leave us adrift. What we have in place of objectivity and hierarchical teacher-over-student power is the possibility for exploration of and co-disclosure about what we have in common. Finding the in-common becomes our pedagogical activity. When, for instance, in an "education and society" course we begin sharing and exploring our perceptions and experiences related to our genderization processes, we are likely to find ourselves overwhelmed by the dramatic dominance and constraints of the notion that there are only two sexes and that there is no way to get out of the one to which we have been assigned.

You may be one who knows intimately the urgency some people feel when they sense they are trapped in a category or locked in under a label. As a group pursues their in-common genderization stories it is likely (ideologically expected) that you will see two groups evolve, those who see themselves as, and who have been portrayed as, stereotypes of their gender and those who see themselves as exceptions to the in-common genderization process. At this juncture we have an opportunity to ask what it means to have something in common. Moving that sense of in common to the center of the discussion creates a possibility for community. In the context of a community of learners a meaningful examination of the foundations of education may take place. While on that common ground, we will ask, "Why do we need to classify people into groups? Why have we begun to compete over who came out best in the genderization process?" "For that matter," someone asks, "why are we competing with one another about who was the most controlled by the genderization process?" or "What does it mean to be socially controlled?"

Here, in discussions of these ideas, we as a community of learners begin to discover the long reach of the patriarchal ideology that has drawn us into a hierarchical structuring of knowledge. In community discussion it does not take long to notice that gender is not just an issue or a variable. Institutionally designated teachers are not experts in examining gender as a foundation within educational foundations; we are better recognized as "culprits," professors of the ideology and beginning now to be newly conscious co-learners.

In the necessary change in teacher/student role relations we will confront the presence of hierarchy and work to expand rather than contract variables that contribute to knowing and understanding. Teaching need not — in fact, must not — be a reductionism for the purpose of maintaining hierarchies by presenting an image of teacher simply as one who is more knowing. Reexamining foundational studies in teacher education involves reexamining schools as contexts in which teachers and students are bonded in a hierarchical power relationship. Looking at that power relationship is a most relevant and necessary part of a feminist critique and of gender studies in the foundations of education.

As the bearers of the designation "teachers of teachers," we may take a big step by coming to the community of learners with evidence of our own consciousness-raising as we describe the context and our uncomfortableness with that hierarchical title. As colleagues and students, we will do well to describe and express our sense of conflict as we work within the complex Euro-patriarchal-power-by-privilege ideologies that have defined us in relation to one another.

Rethinking what Marilyn Frye has called "arrogant perceptions," we open possibilities for understanding how learning to be a teacher, a researcher, and a leader has traditionally been a process of earning privilege through maintaining patriarchal ideology. Such consciousness-raising helps each of us to reconsider how being successful may have created barriers around our sense of what is possible and around our sense of our own possibilities for freedom.[22]

## Notes

1   For a videotaped statement of the contrast of women's issues with feminist structural analysis, see the videotape by Sonia Johnson, *Sonia Speaks: Going Farther Out of Our Minds* (Santa Cruz, Wolfe Video, March 1988).

2   Much of the literature prepared for preservice and in-service teachers has been directed to "issues of treatment" of students. These materials may imply, to those who read them, that sex equity can be attained by moving away from the differences in the way teachers treat males and females. Two excellent guides to issues in differential treatment are Bernice Sandler, *The Classroom Climate: A Chilly One for Women* (Pamphlet) (Washington, D.C.: Project on the Status and Education of Women, Association of American Colleges, 1982); and M. Gail Jones, "Gender Issues in Teacher Education," *Journal of Teacher Education*, January-February 1989, pp. 33–38.

Perhaps I am overly optimistic. Averil Evans McClelland reports in *Educational Foundations* (Summer 1988) that "our effort, over the past two years to assess the patterns of activity on gender issues in education suggests that there is a wide gap in both knowledge and action between those who have been and are doing substantial research in education and the majority of faculties in departments, schools and colleges of education who prepare new teachers and assist in the professional development of current teachers" (p. 16).

3    Carol Gilligan, *In a Different Voice* (Cambridge: Harvard University Press, 1982); Jane Roland Martin, *Reclaiming a Conversation* (New Haven: Yale University Press, 1985); Lois Weis, ed., *Class, Race and Gender in American Education* (Albany: State University of New York Press, 1988); Mary Field Belenky et al., *Women's Ways of Knowing* (New York: Basic Books, 1986); Evelyn Fox Keller, *Reflections on Gender and Science* (New Haven: Yale University Press, 1985); Joan Kelly, *Women, History and Theory* (Chicago: University of Chicago Press, 1984); and Christie Farnham, ed., *The Impact of Feminist Research in the Academy* (Bloomington: Indiana University Press, 1987).

4    Simone de Beauvoir, *The Second Sex,* trans. H. M. Parshley (New York: Alfred A. Knopf, 1952).

5    There are many descriptions of the genderization process in relation to patriarchal value, for example, Carolyn Steedman, Cathy Urwin, and Valerie Walkerdine, eds., *Language, Gender and Childhood* (London: Routledge & Kegan Paul, 1985).

6    For an excellent discussion of the concept of maverick and the way it is grounded in feminist pedagogy, see Janice G. Raymond, "Women's Studies: A Knowledge of One's Own," in *Gendered Subjects,* ed. Margo Culley and Catherine Portuges (Boston: Routledge & Kegan Paul, 1985).

7    I am not referring just to a liberal political notion of "free to" and "free from," related to human social arrangements. I would argue that patriarchy serves to limit even the freedom for creation of personal meaning and a sense of self-worth within a collectivity.

8    The argument that female beings should be valued over male beings may be reflective of a matriarchal view or may be a female chauvinist response to male chauvinism. It is not named a feminist view.

9    These categories of discriminators for types of minorities have been drawn from work by John Ogbu, "Variability in Minority School Performance: A Problem in Search of an Explanation," *Anthropology and Education Quarterly* 18 (1987): 312–34.

10    Kathy E. Ferguson, *The Feminist Case against Bureaucracy* (Philadelphia: Temple University Press, 1984), p. 211.

11    A common sign in women's offices these days is a mass-marketed plaque that reads "In order to succeed a woman must be twice as good as a man; fortunately that's not difficult." That motto serves as a message of awareness and resistance to the conversion while also displaying a willingness to gain from the system. "Cultural literacy" is a term recently popularized by E. B. Hirsch in his book *Cultural Literacy* (Boston: Houghton Mifflin, 1987). Hirsch's work is an excellent example of an effort to reestablish the values of patriarchy through what is learned in what contexts and by whom.

12    Martin, *Reclaiming a Conversation,* p. 104.

13    During much of the twentieth-century North American canonical discussion about women's education, special education, and the education of African-Americans, we have heard the debate about segregated and integrated schools. In the two decades prior to 1954 many people in the United States were humming the tune of "separate but equal" when it came to matters of African-American and Euro-American schooling opportunity. In the years immediately following the 1954 U.S. Supreme Court decision in Brown vs. the Topeka Board of Education, we were encouraged into a majority refrain that separate was not equal and could not be equal. The response to that chorus for equal opportunity was a government-enforced integration of schools. Now even after (and perhaps in part because of) attempts at integration by race, we know we must move deeper into the analysis of racial opportunity. Integration has

not sufficed to create equal opportunity.

14 See Sally Lubeck, "Nested Contexts," in *Class, Race and Gender in American Education,* ed. Weis, p. 54.

15 Mary O'Brien, *Reproducing the World: Essays in Feminist Theory* (Boulder: Westview Press, 1989), p. 224.

16 Dale Spender, "Education: The Patriarchal Paradigm and the Response to Feminism," in *Men's Studies Modified: The Impact of Feminism on the Academic Disciplines,* ed. Dale Spender (Oxford: Pergamon Press, 1981), p. 168.

17 E. F. Kaelin, *Heidegger's Being and Time* (Tallahassee: Florida State University Press, 1988), p. 42.

18 John Dewey, *The Quest for Certainty* (New York: Putnam, 1929); and Alan W. Watts, *The Wisdom of Insecurity* (New York: Vintage, 1951).

19 Spender, *Men's Studies Modified.*

20 Kaelin, *Heidegger's Being and Time,* p. 42.

21 Maria Lugones, "Playfulness, 'World' Travelling, and Loving Perception," *Hypatia* 2, no. 2 (Summer 1987): 18. The concept of "arrogant perceiver" is credited to Marilyn Frye, *The Politics of Reality: Essays in Feminist Theory* (Trumansburg, N.Y.: Crossing Press, 1983).

22 Maxine Greene has begun this work and it is ours to share in reading her *The Dialectic Freedom* (New York: Teachers College Press, 1988).

# Some Maxims for Learning and Instruction

RICHARD C. ANDERSON,
BONNIE B. ARMBRUSTER
*University of Illinois at Urbana-Champaign*

*This article describes some maxims derived from recent theory in learning and instruction and from reflection on excellent practice, explaining and illustrating them using examples from a successful literacy training program, Reading Recovery. Anderson and Armbruster speculate on how the maxims could be applied to teacher education — not only to improve the training of prospective teachers, but also to improve their ability to teach others.*

We use the word *maxim* instead of a term such as *principle* in order to convey a sense of informality and open-endedness. A maxim is a heuristic or rule of thumb, not a universal law. We intend the term to convey the idea of a proposition that is conditionally true and for which the relevant conditions cannot be completely specified. Maxims may overlap instead of being mutually exclusive. Creative tension among maxims is possible; completely satisfying one maxim may entail the risk of violating another. To our minds, maxims capture advice about teaching in a manner that felicitously represents what is currently possible and desirable in a theory of instruction.

The maxims we propose are partially derived from the work of cognitive scientists. Among those whose thinking has influenced us is our colleague Rand Spiro, who is investigating the acquisition of knowledge in complex, ill-structured fields such as biomedicine.[1] Especially influential in our thinking is the work of Collins and Brown and their colleagues,[2] who claim that knowledge is "situated," or a product of the activity and context in which it

*We are indebted to Jeanette Methven, who was the first author's Reading Recovery teacher leader, and who is a major source of our insights into Reading Recovery and its wider implications for teaching. The preparation of this article was supported in part by the Andrew W. Mellon Foundation and the U.S. Department of Education under Cooperative Agreement No. OEG 0087-C1001.*

develops. They argue for teaching through a "cognitive apprenticeship" that takes into account the situated nature of knowledge. We have been influenced by the Russian psychologist Vygotsky, who believed that cognitive development begins as a social process, usually between adults and children, and gradually becomes internalized.[3] The maxims are also based on our own experience with successful instruction.

The maxims proposed here are illustrated using features of one example of successful instruction, Reading Recovery.[4] This is a program intended to help first-graders who are failing to learn to read. Children in the lowest 20 percent in reading within a class are provided one-on-one thirty-minute lessons every day by a teacher trained in the strategies and techniques of the program. The typical lesson includes rereading books introduced in previous lessons, reading a new book at what is supposed to be just the right level of challenge, composing and writing a brief story, and word study and analysis. The teacher employs special techniques intended to help children develop fluency and use the strategies that are characteristic of successful readers.

The goal of Reading Recovery is to enable the very poorest readers to make accelerated progress until they read as well as or better than the average child in their class. When properly implemented, the program appears to achieve this ambitious goal. In New Zealand, where the program was pioneered, more than 95 percent of the children who receive the program are reported to make normal progress in reading after an average of twelve weeks of instruction.[5] The program was first introduced in this country in Ohio, where the success rate is currently reported to be 85 percent.[6] It should be stressed that the available data suggest that the gains produced by Reading Recovery persist over a period of years.

The consistent success Reading Recovery is able to achieve would almost certainly be impossible without excellent teacher training. Reading Recovery teachers are selected from among experienced elementary school teachers. They receive a year of intensive training in Reading Recovery methods and strategies. The goals are for teachers to become sensitive observers of children's reading and writing and to develop facility in making moment-by-moment diagnoses on which to base instructional decisions. The creators of Reading Recovery say that the program "does not come in a box"; they claim the program depends on carefully nurtured teacher expertise. A group of outside educators and scholars who evaluated Reading Recovery in Ohio concurred that the program would achieve uncertain results if teacher training were attenuated.[7]

Reading Recovery is educationally interesting at the level of educating children and at the level of teacher training. We will draw on both levels to exemplify maxims for learning and instruction.

## THE MAXIMS: DEFINITIONS AND EXAMPLES

1. *Whole to Part*   Generally, a major goal of instruction is for the student to acquire a conceptual model of how parts fit together. Therefore, instruction needs to be framed in terms of complete cases and tasks. Since a sense of the whole task facilitates the subsequent learning of subskills, subconcepts and subskills usually should be taught within the context of the whole. The whole-to-part approach runs counter to the part-to-whole approach of the behaviorist tradition, which holds that component skills need to be taught first.

The whole-to-part maxim is well illustrated by Reading Recovery. Children read several books during every session (including the very first session, with the help of scaffolding provided by the teacher; see Maxim 8), and write a brief story. The assumption is that children will make useful discoveries while reading books and writing stories that will advance their knowledge of component skills and concepts. For example, a whole task provides a context that frequently enables a child to decode words that would be impossible if they were encountered in isolation. In contrast, the conventional American reading program rests on the assumption that the component skills need to be taught first. Consequently, most American children learn letters, sound, and words that have been introduced in isolation and practiced thoroughly before they try to read whole sentences, let alone whole books.

2. *Authenticity*   Instruction is based as much as possible on "the real world." Learners work with rich, complex cases and engage in meaningful, functional tasks. Instruction that is not authentic often oversimplifies; such oversimplification impedes the development of useful representations of knowledge and makes transfer, or the ability to use knowledge in new situations, difficult. Training that employs authentic tasks instills more functional and flexible knowledge.

This maxim is exemplified in several ways by Reading Recovery. One is the use of live lessons in teacher training. At every session two of the teachers bring children whom they tutor regularly and conduct lessons with them behind a one-way window. Under the guidance of the "teacher leader," as the teacher trainer is called in Reading Recovery, the rest of the trainees observe and engage in what is usually a vigorous discussion of all aspects of the lessons. Over the course of a year each teacher will teach three or four lessons "behind the glass" and participate in a discussion of forty or so other lessons. This is far and away more exposure to authentic cases than most teacher training and staff development affords.

3. *Multiple Perspectives*   Like a good work of art, authentic cases and complex tasks can be interpreted at different levels and in different ways. Looking at authentic cases and tasks from multiple perspectives helps novices develop the requisite cognitive flexibility for coping with complexity and novelty.[8]

This maxim, too, is exemplified in several ways by Reading Recovery. One stems from the variety of different behind-the-glass lessons teachers see over the course of a year. The children taught in these lessons read at different levels and have different strengths and weaknesses. The teachers have different degrees of control over instructional strategies and, like the children, have different strengths and weaknesses. At each session, the teacher leader focuses the group's attention on different aspects of these variegated lessons.

4. *Developmental Progression*   The mastery of complex skills involves a typical, though not necessarily fixed, progression of stages, from novice to expert. Expertise in any skill is characterized by a high degree of conceptual knowledge ("knowledge that") and procedural knowledge ("knowledge how"). Experts also have "executive control" over the skill; that is, they have a "meta-understanding" of their conceptual and procedural knowledge. Experts understand the major elements of the skill, why it works, what it is good for, when and where it should be used, and how to adapt it to varying situations.

Teachers need a sense of the typical stages in the development of the skills they are teaching. Sensitivity to the developmental progression allows a teacher to intervene in ways that will be optimal for growth. There needs to be a delicate interplay between what a student is able to do and the help the teacher provides. In Reading Recovery, one of many examples of this maxim is the development of the ability to hear the sounds in spoken words and produce the associated letters — that is, to spell.[9] A typical progression is hearing and writing initial consonants, hearing and writing other consonants, hearing sounds in sequence, figuring out vowels, and producing letter clusters.

Spelling instruction is done in the context of writing stories. The teacher finds opportunities for teaching from among the words the child wants to include in stories. At the beginning, the teacher selects short words with a regular phonetic structure. Later, she expects the child to tackle words of several syllables and a less regular structure. The teacher tries to choose words that are in the child's zone of proximal development,[10] that is, words that are neither too easy nor too hard, words that are possible for the child but will require some useful work from which the child can learn something new. With words that are currently beyond the child, the teacher may be satisfied if the child can hear the first sound and write the letter associated with it. The teacher may then write the rest of word for the child.

As an aid to hearing the sounds in words, Reading Recovery teachers draw boxes on a sheet of paper, with one box for each sound in a word, like these:

The first string of boxes would be used for words such as *pig* or *car,* the second for ones such as *lion* or *train.*

First, the teacher models saying words slowly and deliberately, clearly articulating every sound and giving exaggerated emphasis to sounds the child is having trouble hearing. To get children to slow down and individuate sounds, they are taught to push markers into the boxes while saying a word. Later, this step is attenuated and then dropped altogether. The teacher asks questions about the words being analyzed to promote careful sound analysis, such as "What do you hear?" "Where do you write that?" Children are encouraged to work out as much as they can with questions like these: "What else do you hear?" "What do you hear at the beginning?" "What do you hear at the end?" "What do you hear in the middle?" The child writes the letters he can hear and knows how to write. The teacher ensures that the letters are recorded in the right boxes, supplies letters the child cannot hear, and may write letters for sounds the child can hear but not yet write.

Responsibility shifts to the child as soon as the child is able. The teacher must avoid doing for the child what the child can do for himself or herself, and this sometimes means keeping abreast of surges in the child's ability. For example, the teacher should stop saying words for the child when the child can say them with deliberate articulation. At this point, the teacher needs to watch the child closely for evidence that he or she continues to articulate deliberately. Questions occasionally asked, such as, "Did you say it slowly and clearly to yourself?" help the child assume responsibility and remind the child to monitor his or her actions.

5. *Action Orientation*   Learners must be active participants in their own learning, not passive recipients of information. Learning and acting must be intimately related in order to develop procedural knowledge and link it to conceptual knowledge. Therefore, throughout training, novices must attempt to perform authentic tasks. They must repeatedly perform the tasks expected of expert practitioners.

We have already commented on the fact that from the very beginning children in Reading Recovery actively read and write. Likewise, from the beginning teachers learning Reading Recovery are actively involved in teaching and, for instance, spend very little time listening to lectures on pedagogy. The Reading Recovery teacher is an "active teacher" when working with children, as well as an active learner when in the role of Reading Recovery student. At one Reading Recovery training session, several minutes into a lesson one of the teachers was conducting behind the glass, the teacher leader abruptly said, "That woman is not teaching! She's just sitting there listening to the child read. I hope the rest of you are teaching. These children will not make accelerated progress unless you teach them."

It would be natural enough to expect poor readers to make slow progress, but Reading Recovery teachers are taught to expect the opposite. Accelerated progress is due to more than the diffuse, cumulative effect of a good program. It depends on the child's making noticeable progress in some particular aspects of reading and writing almost every day. This, in turn, will happen reliably only when the teacher can specify steps the child is ready to take and have good control of the technique required to help the child take these steps.

6. *Modeling* Instruction may begin with the observation of a master or expert, who models the target skill. By reflectively "thinking aloud," the expert may make explicit invisible mental processes that might otherwise remain mysterious to novices. Observation of an expert helps a beginner develop a conceptual model of the task before attempting to execute it. At a later stage of development, observation of an expert can help the learner further refine his or her conceptual model.

Modeling is used with both children and teachers in Reading Recovery. Usually it takes place in a brief moment rather than in the form of a lengthy demonstration. An example is the use of modeling to promote phrasing and fluency. The teacher selects a story to which the child has already been introduced. The story should lend itself to fluent reading; one that has rhyme, a considerable amount of dialogue, or a repeated pattern would be suitable. First, the child reads the story. The teacher comments approvingly and then says something like, "But I want you to read it fast and make it sound like the animals are really talking. Let me show you." The teacher then reads the story with good expression. Merely exposing the child to a model of fluent reading is not enough, however. The lesson cannot be counted a success until the child is able to read the story with a distinct improvement in fluency, so the child reads the story again and maybe yet another time.

7. *Coaching* Coaching involves observing and helping students while they attempt to perform a task. The teacher directs students to particular aspects of the task, reminds them about a part of the task they may have overlooked, provides hints and feedback, and designs and sequences new tasks aimed at bringing the students' performance closer to expert performance. Coaching has the flavor of collaboration rather than evaluation. It boosts students' confidence as they go through the frustrating early stages of skill development. It is also the best way to help those who are expert or near expert refine their techniques.

Coaching is at the heart of Reading Recovery procedures, which is only to be expected from a program that features whole, authentic tasks. For a specific illustration, we will summarize some of the coaching Reading Recovery teachers do while a child is reading. When a child comes to a problem word in a text, the teacher tries to give a prompt that will help the child get the problem word, and more important, will help the child gain control over generally useful strategies for attacking words.

Reading Recovery teachers seldom simply tell a child a problem word. Instead, they may suggest the word in a question: "Could it be *sea*?" The idea behind using a question is to encourage the child to check the suggestion against the printed word. If children are simply given problem words, they typically plunge forward having learned little or nothing. Of course, for this strategy to work well, sometimes the teacher has to suggest incorrect words, usually semantically plausible ones. Imagine that the word *sea* appears on a page displaying a picture of a small boat on a large body of water. In this context, the teacher might say, "Could it be *lake*?" The child may say no and, with the clue that the problem word refers to a body of water, may now be able to say "sea." However, if the child agrees that the problem word could be *lake*, the teacher ought to point to the water in the picture and say, "Yes, this could be a lake." Then, the teacher ought to point to the word and add, "But does this look like *lake*?" At this point, the teacher sometimes may suggest other incorrect words, such as *ocean* and *river*, or can say, "Could it be *sea*?" Notice that this routine encourages close analysis of the print, attention to meaning, and cross-checking of print information and information available about meaning.

Alternatively, depending on the child and the circumstance, the teacher may reread the phrase leading up to the word and then provide its first sound, or may say, "Get your mouth ready to say the first sound." If the child has good control of individual letter-to-sound relationships, but is not yet able to do much independent analysis of words in text, the teacher may write the word letter-by-letter on the chalkboard, getting the child to articulate the sound for the first letter, the first two letters, and so on, until a word that fits the context comes into his mind: for instance *c, cr, cra, crash.*[11]

Still another strategy is to encourage the child to think of words he or she knows that have spellings and sound patterns similar to the problem word, employing questions such as these: "Do you know a word that looks like that?" "Think of a word that starts like that." "Can you think of a word that ends like that?" To illustrate, suppose a child stops at *then*. The teacher might say, "You know *the*, don't you? If this is *the* (displays *the* in magnetic letters), what is this (points to *then*)?" Or, more indirectly, the teacher might ask, "Do you know a word that begins like that (indicating *then*)?" If the child is unable to think of a word, she might ask him or her to reread a line containing *the*, and then say, "You just read a word that looks like this (indicating *then*). Can you find it?" and once the word is found, "Now can you get this one (indicating *then*)?" When the child has solved a problem word, the Reading Recovery teacher will often not indicate whether the word is right or wrong, but will ask, "Do you have it right now?" or "Does it look right and sound right?" Questions such as these promote cross-checking and self-monitoring.

8. *Scaffolding*  Scaffolding is closely related to the maxims of developmental progression and coaching. Scaffolding means providing teacher support and regulating task difficulty so that the level of challenge is optimum for growth toward expertise. Effective scaffolding thus requires sensitivity to the students' skill level and developmental progress. Appropriate scaffolding

entails the ability to provide just the right amount of coaching or support so that students will succeed at performing the target task, but only by stretching their competence. With too little challenge, students will not achieve maximum growth; with too much challenge, they will become discouraged and dependent.

The scaffolding maxim can be illustrated by the means Reading Recovery teachers use to regulate the difficulty of the books children read. For the child whose text reading level is very low, appropriate first books are those with a regular, predictable pattern books in which the pictures illustrate most of the ideas, and books containing mostly easy, frequently repeated words. The following excerpt from *My Home* by June Melser is an example of a story for beginners.[12] The story is also lavishly illustrated.

> My home is here,
> said the bird.
>
> My home is here,
> said the frog.
>
> My home is here,
> said the pig.

Another means Reading Recovery teachers use to regulate difficulty is by varying their orientation, or introduction, to a book. The teacher's orientation can be lean if the book is likely to be easy for a child. A richer orientation is desirable if the book is likely to be difficult. A rich orientation may include looking through the book with the child, commenting on what is significant in the pictures, and discussing the story line. The teacher will use potentially troublesome words in the oral orientation and may ask the child to locate a few of these words in the text. For instance, if *snake* is likely to be a problem word, the teacher might say, "What letter would you expect to see at the beginning of *snake*?" Assuming the child knows, the teacher would next ask, "Can you find *snake* on this page?"

Too little scaffolding and a child may flounder. Too much scaffolding and the child will not have enough productive "reading work." A lesson at just the right level of challenge affords substantial teaching opportunities. It is one of the keys to accelerated progress. Providing just the right amount of scaffolding depends on comprehensive, up-to-date, accurate information about children's reading. In addition to informal impressions based on close observation during lessons, Reading Recovery teachers make a daily objective assessment of every child's reading level, using a procedure called the "Running Record."[13]

9. *Reflection and Articulation* Over the course of instruction, external scaf-

folding is gradually withdrawn as an internalized model of expertise develops. In moving from other-regulation to self-regulation, reflection and articulation are important processes. Both processes help students gain consciousness of and control over basic conceptual and procedural knowledge.

Reflection involves thinking about one's own conceptual and procedural understandings and comparing them with those of an expert or another student. The goal is to develop reflective thinkers who can monitor their own performance and bring it more in line with expert performance. Articulation refers to the verbalization of reflective thinking. It is reciprocal reflection, the sharing of knowledge and cognition with others. Articulation may include describing plans and intentions, explaining reasons underlying decisions and actions, checking perceptions, responding to the questions of others, and acknowledging frustrations and successes. The instructor's "thinking aloud" while modeling serves as a model of reflection and articulation as well as a model for the skill itself.

Behind-the-glass sessions are designed to promote reflection and articulation. While one teacher and a child work together on the lesson on one side of the glass, on the other side, the rest of the trainees discuss the lesson in detail. The teacher leader prods the group with rapid-fire, Socratic-style questions about the child's behavior and what can be inferred from the behavior about the child's reading strategies, the appropriateness of the books, the pacing of the lesson, the teacher's decisions at choice points, the teacher's control of key techniques, and whether opportunities were seized or lost. Trainees can be heard to applaud the teacher who has managed to convey a "powerful example." At other times, they can be heard to frankly challenge ill-considered decisions. A discussion exemplifying articulation and reflection continues when the two teachers who have taught behind the glass rejoin the group.

## TEACHER EDUCATION: THE MAXIMS IGNORED

The great irony of teacher education is that prospective teachers are taught in ways that are inconsistent with these maxims of effective learning and instruction. Instead of whole-to-part, prospective teachers are often prepared in an assembly-line fashion. They take discrete courses in various foundations and methods specialties. The culminating activity is an all-too-brief student teaching experience that typically bears little relationship to what students have learned in course work. Preservice teachers have little opportunity to observe or practice the whole teaching act, yet they are expected to be able to perform this extremely complex task solo — usually without coaching, monitoring, or support — on receiving their teaching credential.

Traditional teacher training lacks authenticity. Courses often present theories and principles that are far removed from the realities of classrooms.

Any cases prospective teachers observe or tasks they engage in are likely to be contrived and to lack the complexity and richness of authentic teaching situations. Skills are taught in the abstract, decontextualized from their uses in the real world.

Prospective teachers are rarely treated to multiple perspectives, at least in a manner conducive to growth. Courses are typically taught by individual instructors with their own idiosyncratic perspectives. Much content is delivered by lecture, with little opportunity for shared viewpoints. The student-teaching experience offers an opportunity for a different perspective — that of the cooperating teacher — but Doyle (see this issue) cites a study by McDiarmid suggesting that students are often so brainwashed by their methods courses that they are effectively inoculated against the perspective of the classroom teacher. In our experience, the opposite can also happen: Students adopt the perspective of the cooperating teacher and dismiss most of what was taught in their university classes. Either way, a singular perspective dominates. Since there are seldom opportunities for discussing and learning from multiple perspectives, there is limited potential for developing cognitive flexibility.

Current teacher education typically ignores the developmental progression of stages from novice to expert teachers. Few would claim that teacher certification marks the attainment of truly expert status; rather, it is recognized that teachers need years of classroom experience to become experts. One reason is that preservice teacher education tends to be heavy on the side of conceptual knowledge and light on the side of procedural knowledge. There is insufficient opportunity for prospective teachers to develop the knowledge and the executive control that characterize true expertise. Instead of offering an action orientation, preservice teacher education is largely passive. Students are told how to teach rather than shown and coached how to teach. They receive plenty of preaching but little practice. As a result, their knowledge remains inert and inaccessible.

Teacher education offers several opportunities for modeling. The first possibility is the way the university professors conduct their courses. Unfortunately, many professors are not living examples of the theories and methods they advocate. For example, a professor may deliver a boring lecture about the limitations of lecturing and alternatives to lecturing! A second modeling opportunity is for instructors to model how to do the particular skills they are teaching. For example, in a unit of measurement and evaluation, the instructor could model how to go about constructing a teacher-made test. It is our impression that this type of modeling is rarely done in foundations courses. Modeling does happen in methods courses, we hope, but even there the modeling is probably not ideal. Instructors probably do not "think aloud" about the planning, problem solving, monitoring, and evaluation involved in performing the skill. As a result, the cognition involved in the skill remains invisible to students. A third potential model is the cooperating teacher for the student-teaching experience. The cooperating teacher may be a wonderful model. On the other hand, he or she may not be a very expert teacher or may not be willing or able to introspect with the student about teaching.

Prospective teachers infrequently receive coaching or scaffolding. In education courses, feedback usually comes in the form of summative evaluations of completed products, with negligible opportunity for improvement or growth. Fortunate students may receive some coaching from their cooperating teachers or supervisors during student teaching, but the coaching often will be too little, too late. Preservice teachers see little modeling of reflection or articulation by their instructors; it is rare for professors to talk about their own teaching. For students, articulation is largely limited to writing papers and exams used for evaluation purposes. Students may receive little, if any, feedback about their reflections and articulations. By limiting reflection and articulation, teacher education fails to foster the development of an internalized model of expertise. Ironically, therefore, typical teacher education violates the very maxims of learning and instruction that should be its foundation. In our opinion, teacher education fails to prepare teachers as well as it might if these maxims were followed.

## APPLYING THE MAXIMS TO TEACHER EDUCATION: AN EXAMPLE

In order to illustrate on a small scale how these maxims might be applied to teacher education, we describe our own attempt to embody them in an experimental preservice education course at the University of Illinois. (We do so with all due hesitancy and appropriate qualifiers, since at the time of writing, this course is in its first trial semester.) The course is part of an experimental field-based teacher education program resulting from collaboration between the College of Education at the University of Illinois and the Urbana, Illinois, Public Schools. The program is our response to the consensus recommendation from the current educational reform movement that colleges of education should work collaboratively with school districts in planning and implementing teacher education.

Essentially, the program entails the joint implementation of a full-year experience for seniors in elementary education. Students are assigned to classrooms to work under teachers for an entire academic year. In addition, students complete required methods courses in blocks taught by small teams of university faculty and Urbana teachers. Because students are concurrently assigned to classrooms, they also have the opportunity to practice what they are learning in their methods courses under the guidance of classroom teachers.

The block for which we have a major responsibility is called Language and Literacy. It encompasses the domains of long-standing courses in reading, language arts, and children's literature. Our Language and Literacy course reflects the maxims we are espousing.

The course adopts a whole-to-part approach in two senses of the concept. The first is reflected in the course title: The course approaches literacy as a holistic concept, an integration of various language abilities, rather than as the sum of reading, writing, speaking, and listening skills. Second, students will observe and perform whole acts of teaching from the very beginning of the course. For example, they will teach a guided reading lesson beginning about the third week of the semester. As the course proceeds, they will be refining the subskills within each of these whole teaching acts.

The course highlights authenticity in several ways. Four teachers are heavily involved in the planning and teaching of the course. Instruction features professional-quality videotapes of real teaching situations. Students are in classrooms concurrently with taking the course, participating in authentic teaching episodes.

Multiple perspectives are a foregone conclusion in a team-taught course, especially with a team composed of both university professors and classroom teachers. In addition, content issues are discussed from various theoretical perspectives, and students are encouraged to share their own developing viewpoints. Finally, students observe multiple approaches to teaching assignments as they observe each others' videotaped lessons, as will be discussed further below.

Sensitivity to developmental progression is evident primarily in the type of coaching and scaffolding provided. For example, students teach several reading lessons throughout the semester. As the semester progresses, the preparation and support for, and feedback about, the lessons will change as required by the developmental level of individual students.

An action orientation is a hallmark of our Language and Literacy course. We have already described the students' active participation in classrooms and in actual teaching. Students are also actively involved in observing and coaching each other. Students videotape each other teaching; these videotapes then become the focus of three-hour discussion sessions that take place each Friday.

Modeling is accomplished in several ways. First, the course itself exemplifies the very maxims we are attempting to impart. Second, course instructors (especially the teachers) and cooperating teachers model specific skills throughout the semester. Third, as previously mentioned, we use several videotapes of lessons by expert teachers to model exemplary teaching practices. Finally, students observe each other as models (in varying stages of development, of course) during the Friday videotape-discussion sessions.

Coaching comes from several sources. Most coaching is done by course instructors before and after classroom teaching assignments. However, as the semester progresses and their expertise develops, the students increasingly assume responsibility for coaching each other. Most coaching takes place around the students' videotaped lessons. Lesson segments are targeted for analysis and discussion by the whole class.

The course features ample opportunity for reflection and articulation. Students keep a "dialogue journal" (a written exchange between individual students and the instructors); the journal not only provides a medium for reflection and articulation but also enables students to try out one type of writing experience we discuss in the course. The Friday discussion sessions, of course, are devoted to reflection and articulation about videotaped student lessons.

Our Language and Literacy course is a modest beginning, but we believe it exemplifies, in some crude form at least, the maxims of learning and instruction that we maintain should be the very foundation of all teacher education.

## Notes

1   R. J. Spiro et al., "Multiple Analogies for Complex Concepts: Antidotes for Analogy-induced Misconception in *Advanced Knowledge Acquisition,*" in *Similarity and Analogical Reasoning,* ed. S. Vosniadou and A. Ortony (New York and Cambridge: Cambridge University Press, 1989); and idem, "Cognitive Flexibility Theory: Advanced Knowledge Acquisition in Ill-structured Domains," in *Tenth Annual Conference of the Cognitive Science Society* (Hillsdale, N.J.: Erlbaum, 1988), pp. 375–83.

2   Allan Collins, John Seely Brown, and Susan E. Newman, "Cognitive Apprenticeship: Teaching the Craft of Reading, Writing, and Mathematics," in *Knowing, Learning, and Instruction: Essays in Honor of Robert Glaser,* ed. Lauren B. Resnick (Hillsdale, N.J.: Erlbaum, 1989); John Seeley Brown, Allan Collins, and Paul Duguid, "Situated Cognition and the Culture of Learning," *Educational Researcher* 18 (1989): 32–42; and idem, "Situated Cognition and the Culture of Learning" (Technical Report No. 481; University of Illinois at Urbana-Champaign, Center for the Study of Reading, 1989).

3   L. S. Vygotsky, *Mind in Society: The Development of Higher Psychological Processes* (Cambridge: Harvard University Press, 1978).

4   The first author received one year's training as a Reading Recovery teacher under the expert guidance of Jeanette Methven, a Reading Recovery teacher trainer from New Zealand.

5   Marie Clay, *The Early Detection of Reading Difficulties: A Diagnostic Survey with Recovery Procedures* (Auckland, New Zealand: Heinemann Educational Books, 1985).

6   Gay Su Pinnell, Diane E. DeFord, and Carol A. Lyons, *Reading Recovery: Early Intervention for At-Risk First Graders* (Arlington, Va.: Educational Research Service, 1988).

7   Ibid.

8   Spiro et al., "Multiple Analogies for Complex Concepts"; and idem, "Cognitive Flexibility Theory."

9   See Clay, *The Early Detection of Reading Difficulties* pp. 64–67.

10   Vygotsky, *Mind in Society.*

11   See Clay, *The Early Detection of Reading Difficulties,* p. 76.

12   June Melser, *My Home* (Auckland, New Zealand: Shortland Publications, 1981), pp. 2–4.

13   Clay, *The Early Detection of Reading Difficulties,* pp. 16–22.

# Motivation: What Teachers Need to Know

CAROLE A. AMES

*University of Illinois at Urbana-Champaign*

*Motivation, one of the foremost problems in education, is often inadequately addressed in typical foundational (educational psychology) courses. In this article, Ames clarifies the complex construct of motivation as it relates to learning and offers a revamped curriculum that applies motivation theory and research to practice. She recommends instruction in how motivation constructs relate to each other, to developmental changes, to individual and culturally related differences, and to the classroom context.*

There are three things to remember about education. The first one is motivation. The second one is motivation. The third one is motivation.
— Terrell H. Bell

What is it about the academic motivation of students that teachers should know? Certainly, knowledge of motivation concepts, principles, and theories should be basic elements in a foundations course in educational psychology, but this is not really what educational psychology should be about. Teachers need to know how this conceptual knowledge relates to the classroom and to their instructional role in the classroom. Teachers also need to know how to rely on this knowledge when dealing with issues that involve motivational concerns and when making instructional decisions.

For example, consider a not very unusual problem facing a teacher about homework. How can a teacher set homework policy so that students complete the homework and still maintain their interest in the material? Teacher A's policy states that all homework must be turned in daily, that all homework will be graded daily with letter or percentage grades, and that homework counts for 30 percent of the quarter grade. Teacher B's policy states that students are to spend no more than thirty minutes per night on homework, that homework will be graded satisfactory or unsatisfactory, that students can redo and correct their work, and that homework counts for 10 percent of the quarter grade. We may think the stringency of Teacher A's policy might be more effective, but research on motivation would suggest that Teacher B's policy is more likely to fulfill both objectives. At the classroom level, teachers are often faced with a child who continually avoids challenge. At the building level, teachers must come together and decide how to structure a reading program so that students will read more but also enjoy reading more. These are simple examples of everyday problems and decisions that involve motivation questions.

Student motivation has, for some time, been described as one of the foremost problems in education.[1] It is certainly one of the problems most commonly cited by teachers. Motivation is important because it contributes to achievement, but it is also important itself as an outcome.

Motivation is not synonymous with achievement, and student motivation cannot necessarily be inferred by looking at achievement test scores. Immediate achievement and test performance are determined by a variety of factors and may even be assured through a variety of ways, and some practices that serve to increase immediate achievement may actually have the effect of diminishing students' interest in learning as well as their long-term involvement in learning. When we talk about motivation as an outcome, we are concerned with students' "motivation to learn."[2] If we place a value on developing a motivation to learn in students, we are concerned with whether students initiate learning activities and maintain an involvement in learning as well as a commitment to the process of learning. Effective schools and effective teachers are those who develop goals, beliefs, and attitudes in students that will sustain a long-term involvement and that will contribute to quality involvement in learning.

If we evaluate our schools and classrooms strictly by how much students achieve, we can easily lose sight of these other educational goals and values. We not only want students to achieve, we want them to value the process of learning and the improvement of their skills, we want them to willingly put forth the necessary effort to develop and apply their skills and knowledge, and we want them to develop a long-term commitment to learning.[3] It is in this sense that motivation is an outcome of education. Students who elect to take advanced science classes because they want to learn more and not just because they think they can do well is an example of this outcome.

It is therefore a first priority to help teachers develop an understanding of why motivation is important. This, indeed, may be a challenge when educational psychology textbooks typically allot only one chapter to motivation, and this chapter usually provides little more than an overview of theories and concepts. Moreover, topics that are intricately related to motivation, such as classroom management, individual differences, testing and evaluation, grouping, and family, are often treated in separate chapters with little or no linkage to motivational concepts and without discussion of motivational processes. Educational psychology is about application; it is not enough to highlight theories or review basic constructs and dot these presentations with a few examples.

Motivation has often been characterized within what has been called a quantitative view of motivation,[4] in which motivation has been described as the *intensity* of behavior, the *direction* of behavior, and the *duration* of behavior.[5] The question for classroom teachers is how to get students to do what you want them to do and to do it consistently over time. This focus, however, does not help us in thinking about how to develop and nurture a motivation to learn in students.

Rather than the duration of behavior (or what has been called engaged time), we need to think about the quality of task engagement. Students need to develop motivational thought patterns that contribute to self-regulated learning. Observing students' time on task does not tell us about what they are attending to, how they are processing information, how they are reacting to their performance, and how they are interpreting feedback. What is critical is the quality of engaged time, not the duration of engaged time.

Rather than the direction of behavior, we need to think about students' goals or reasons for learning. Two students may choose to work on a science project or complete a math worksheet, but they may pursue quite different goals in doing so. A student who works for extrinsic rewards such as grades is likely to engage in very different thought processes and behaviors compared with the student who wants to learn something new about the subject matter or improve a skill. Students' reasons for learning have important consequences for how they approach and engage in learning.

Motivation is also not a matter of increasing the intensity of behavior. The task facing teachers is not one of maximizing or even optimizing the level of motivation; to suggest so perpetuates a view that motivation is a state of arousal or energy. What is assumed is that by increasing or optimizing this state, performance will be enhanced. What we often find, however, is that students can be equally motivated but for very different reasons. Often, it is not that the child is not motivated, but that the child is not motivated to do what *we* want him to do. Rather than focus on differentiating high, low, and optimally motivated students, we instead need to define adaptive and maladaptive or positive and negative motivation patterns and to understand how and why these patterns develop over time.

## MOTIVATION CONSTRUCTS

To teach quantitative concepts such as duration, intensity, and direction is not going to help teachers understand how or why students develop adaptive, positive, or effective thought patterns. At a very general level, these thought patterns include goals, beliefs, and attitudes that are involved in how students approach learning situations, engage in the process of learning, and respond to learning experiences. Some examples are self-worth or self-concept of ability, attributions, self-regulated learning, and achievement goals. We need to pay more attention to how teachers can become more successful in socializing these adaptive motivation patterns in students. To set the stage for some later points, let me briefly describe just a few of these constructs.

## SELF-WORTH

Students' self-worth is intricately tied to their self-concept of ability in school settings.[6] This self-concept of ability or self-efficacy has significant consequences for student achievement behavior. Self-efficacy is an expectation or belief that one is capable of performing a specific task, organizing and carrying out required behaviors in a situation.[7] Efficacy is not self-concept of ability in a general sense; it is task- or situation-specific. One's self-worth is implicated when the task is important and when one's ability is threatened. Clearly, in the classroom, all tasks can be made important through the use of external rewards and certain evaluation procedures. Indeed, it is very difficult to look in a classroom and determine what is or is not important to different children. As a consequence, self-efficacy is often a critical factor predicting children's task choices, willingness to try and persist on difficult tasks, and even actual performance in many classrooms.

At first glance, it may appear that increasing student's self-efficacy is merely a matter of increasing children's confidence that they can do well. This is not necessarily the case. Consider an example where a teacher tells all her students that everyone's story is going to become part of the class newspaper. Although all the children can expect success in getting their stories "published," a child may still harbor intense doubts about whether he or she can write a story. The child's self-confidence of ability to write the story has not been changed. Children's self-efficacy does respond positively when they learn to set short-term, realistic goals and are shown how to make progress toward these goals. It is not a matter of convincing them they can do well or even guaranteeing it; it is giving them the strategies to do so.

Children's understanding about their ability is responsive to developmental changes as well as situational influences, and this also has important implications for practice. Young children tend to have an optimistic view of their ability, high expectations for success, and a sort of resilience after failure.[8] Moreover, young children tend to equate effort with ability. To them, hard workers are smart and smart children work hard. As children progress through school, their perceptions of their ability decrease and tend to reflect the teacher's evaluation of their ability. Older children's self-evaluations are more responsive to failure or negative feedback, meaning that they are more likely to adjust their expectations downward after failing. Older children also develop a more differentiated view of effort and ability. While effort can increase the chance for success, ability sets the boundaries of what one's effort can achieve. Effort now becomes the "double-edged sword."[9] Trying hard and failing threatens one's self-concept of ability.

What does this mean to teachers? First, for young children, praising their effort may actually convey to them a sense of confidence in their ability. Because ability and effort are not well differentiated, praise for children's efforts can enhance their self-confidence. However, this does not work with older children. To them, effort and ability are not the same, and they are more concerned with being perceived as able. It is at this point that teachers' and students' preferences diverge. While teachers may value effort and hard work, students prefer to maximize their chances for success and at the same time minimize their effort expenditure. Ability is important in most classrooms; when students' self-concept of ability is threatened, they display failure-avoidance motivation.[10] They engage in failure-avoiding tactics such as not trying, procrastinating, false effort, and even the denial of effort. Why would they do this when these behaviors most assuredly will increase the likelihood of failure? What these behaviors accomplish is reducing the negative implications of failure. From the students' point of view, failure without effort does not negatively reflect on their ability. What they have achieved is "failure with honor."[11]

## ATTRIBUTIONS AND RELATED METACOGNITIVE BELIEFS

The consequences of students' attributions for success and failure for their subsequent achievement behavior have been well described in the research literature. Attributions are related to expectations about the likelihood of success, to judgments about one's own ability, to emotional reactions of pride or hopelessness, and to a willingness to engage in effort-driven cognitions as in self-regulated learning. Over time, children who believe that failure is caused by a lack of ability are likely to exhibit a sense of helplessness. Low expectations, negative affect, and ineffective strategies characterize these children. Children with this dysfunctional attribution pattern are less likely to develop or enact those metacognitive skills that will enable them to tackle a wide range of classroom tasks. By contrast, children who perceive a relationship between their own effort and success are likely to respond to failure or problem situations with a sense of hopefulness and engage in strategic task behavior.[12]

Related to attributional beliefs is students' use of learning strategies and other self-regulated thought processes. These are effort-driven processes, and in that sense, they are motivational. They include, for example, organizing and planning, goal-setting, self-monitoring, and self-instruction. These strategies have been called generic or general learning strategies in that they can be applied across situations and across domains. Of course, students have to have knowledge of the strategies and an awareness of their appro-

priateness to the situation, but beyond knowledge and awareness is the voli-
tional (motivational) question of whether students will apply the strategies.
Whether students choose to engage in such strategic thinking is largely dependent on whether they are willing to apply the necessary effort and
whether they believe effort will lead to success. Thus, there are two issues
concerning students' strategy use. The first issue concerns whether students
have and can apply the necessary skills or strategies. The second issue is
motivational: whether students believe that effort is linked to success and
that the outcome is worth the effort, and whether they are willing to expend
the effort.[13]

## ACHIEVEMENT GOALS

Related to attributions are students' reasons for learning and their achieve-
ment-related goals.[14] The issue here is *why* students engage in learning and
choose to engage in academic tasks rather than whether they choose to do
so. For example, students may choose to participate in specific activities to
gain external rewards, to develop their skills and ability, or to demonstrate
that they are smart by outperforming others or by trying to achieve success
with minimal effort.

Students who are interested in learning new things and developing their
skills and ability have been described as mastery-oriented. These students
are willing to expend the necessary effort to learn something new and confront challenging tasks. It is this mastery-goal orientation that is more likely
to produce independent learning and sustained involvement in achievement
activities. These students are motivated to learn.

Students who instead perceive that normative performance is important
and want to demonstrate that they have ability or to protect their ability
when threatened are labeled performance-oriented. Such students tend to
think more about their ability than about "how to do the task." Their strategies, such as memorizing facts or reading or studying only what they think
will be on a test, tend to serve their performance only over the short term.

Whether students adopt mastery or performance goals is, in part, dependent on their classroom experiences, essentially their perceptions of how
the teacher structures the classroom.[15] Many children enter school with
mastery or learning goals but many become socialized into a performance-
goal orientation.[16] When we consider the preponderance of public evaluation
practices, normative comparisons, extrinsic rewards, ability grouping, and
emphasis on production, speed, and perfection, it is no wonder that children
find it difficult to maintain a learning or mastery orientation.

## ENHANCING MOTIVATION

In most of our foundational courses, we stop once we have covered the basic theories or motivational constructs. We cannot assume, however, that teachers are prepared to translate these ideas into classroom practice. This is a major problem for foundations courses. We give too little attention to how motivation concepts interface with the instructional program, too little attention to how the social context of the classroom can undermine or facilitate the development of students' motivation to learn, and too little attention to how motivation principles relate to each other. What we do is cover the basics, highlight a few principles, maybe even review a case study or two, and then hope that the teacher's intuition has somehow been enlightened and that the teacher will be able to apply this knowledge. Many textbooks, when it comes to dealing with applications, rely on conventional wisdom. There are several major texts that present a problem (e.g., how to deal with a child who exhibits poor motivation) and then present teachers' solutions. These solutions are not linked to any conceptual framework. There is even an implicit endorsement of these ideas and solutions as credible, viable, and conceptually sound because the source is practicing teachers. Unfortunately, it is often the case that this is not so. The problem is that many strategies for enhancing student motivation involve the use of principles that are counterintuitive. Let me illustrate this point with examples that are related to the motivation constructs described in the preceding section.

1. If children lack confidence in their ability to succeed, we might infer that these low-confident children should receive a heavy dose of success experience. The considerable literature on learned helplessness and attribution retraining, however, has shown that success alone does not alleviate a helplessness syndrome.[17] In contrast to what we might surmise, providing or ensuring successful outcomes or feedback does not necessarily bolster children's confidence in their abilities. Such a prescription ignores the role of cognitive motivational factors in determining how children interpret their classroom experiences. For many children success is not sufficient to create or maintain a belief that they have the ability to reverse failure. Children who are convinced that they lack the necessary ability to do school tasks do not take responsibility for success and even underestimate their performance when they do well. Thus, it is not a matter of persuading them they can do well or even guaranteeing it; instead, practice should involve giving them short-term goals and strategies for making progress toward the goals.[18] Once students understand how to reach a goal and focus on strategies, rather than outcomes, they are more likely to "own" the outcome.

2. Related to an emphasis on success is the prescription "try to find *something* positive to say about a child's work." Reinforcing children's work even if it involves some small aspect of the total effort should be a step in the direction of giving the child more confidence. Unfortunately, for the very children who most need positive feedback, the "something positive" is often something unimportant and irrelevant to the task requirements. For example, if the task is to write a book report in a certain format, commenting positively on the

child's neat handwriting is not likely to have the intended effect.

On the one hand, the generous use of praise would seem to be an obvious and salient way of encouraging children who generally perform poorly, but as Brophy has shown, the way praise is often used in elementary school classrooms can undermine the achievement behavior of these children.[19] The praise children receive is often on irrelevant aspects of a task; in these instances, children discount the praise. Praise on easy tasks or praise that is noncontingent on children's effort or performance quality can be interpreted by children as evidence that they lack ability; it can, therefore, have unintended negative effects on children's self-confidence.

The effects of praise must also be considered from a developmental perspective. Praise can be interpreted quite differently by younger and older children. Praising young children's effort conveys to them a positive expectation that they can do the work and can enhance their perceptions of their competence. Because older children have differentiated concepts of ability and effort, praising their effort may actually be interpreted by them as low expectations for their ability. It is therefore important to understand how developmental changes in cognition mediate the effects of well-intended behaviors. The application of basic psychological principles requires more than just a casual understanding of how cognition gives meaning to actions and classroom events.

3. One of the seeming paradoxes of research on student learning concerns the effects of rewards and incentives on student motivation. We have been taught that, if we want to increase the probability of a behavior, the most efficient method is to apply reinforcement principles. In fact, it seems that we have been indoctrinated into this way of thinking so well that these extrinsic reinforcements are often overused. Recent research by Boggiano and her colleagues certainly supports this assertion.[20] They presented a number of scenarios that described children involved in both high- and low-interest activities to adults, college students, and parents and asked them to judge how well certain strategies would maintain or increase the child's interest over time. For example, they described one ten-year-old child as one "who really enjoys reading and particularly likes to read books to learn about new things." Another ten-year-old was described as a child who "does not enjoy reading and chooses the easiest books to read when asked to write a book report." What is particularly striking is that regardless of the child's interest level, extrinsic rewards (such as adding 50 percent extra to the child's allowance) were preferred over other strategies as a way of maintaining or increasing the child's interest. Reward was preferred to reasoning, punishment, and even noninterference. Moreover, Boggiano et al. found that adults consistently preferred large rewards over small rewards, which they interpreted as reflecting a belief that interest level would vary with the size of the reward.

Certainly programs involving extrinsic rewards tend to be pervasive in our schools as a mechanism for increasing achievement behavior. In many schools and classrooms, extrinsic incentives are seen as necessary to get children to spend time on various tasks and lessons. Over twenty years ago, Jackson suggested that many of children's schooling experiences involve a hidden curriculum of controls and social constraints.[21] As students progress through school, they become more and more extrinsically controlled.

What are the consequences of using extrinsic incentives to try to shape children's achievement behaviors, to get them to complete their work, to increase the quality of work, and to get them to spend more time on particular tasks? The evidence from considerable research converges in identifying the "hidden cost" of using extrinsic rewards to motivate children.[22] This is not to say that incentives cannot be effective in some situations and for some children. The fundamental problem is that when we look into classrooms, we see the same incentive system being used for all the children in the classroom.

I am not suggesting that we need to inculcate the idea that incentives are ineffective or motivationally detrimental. The use of extrinsic incentives can have multiple effects on children's motivation; predicting the specific effects requires an analysis of a number of component processes. For instance, it is important to consider the relationship of extrinsic incentives to other motivation variables. In certain instances, rewards may have the effect of increasing self-efficacy, which can positively influence students' motivation or willingness to learn. The relation of extrinsic rewards to individual differences is of critical importance. In the classroom, extrinsic incentives are often intended to motivate the least attentive students or those who typically perform poorly; however, the rewards are typically applied to the entire classroom or even the entire school population, as in many reading incentive programs. The hidden costs become most apparent when they are applied to these larger groups where individual differences in interest, performance, and ability are ignored.

4. From the work on intrinsic motivation comes the recommendation to give children choices and thus a sense of personal control in the classroom.[23] Choice of tasks or activities is viewed as fostering belief in personal control and increasing interest and involvement in learning. This is easy enough to endorse and gives us a nice, simple application of intrinsic motivation theory to the classroom. A problem arises when we consider the context or structure of many classrooms. When normative evaluation and public comparisons are expected, students' choices reflect an avoidance of challenge and a preference for tasks that ensure success. In other words, a choice is not an equal choice in some contexts. When evaluation is pending on one's final product, choices are not based on interest; they more likely reflect a protection of one's ability and concern for one's level of performance. In this case, motivation theory cannot be applied without considering the context of the classroom.

5. On the basis of attribution theory, we might infer that it is a good idea to try to persuade students that they are not working hard enough or that they need to work harder on occasions of failure or poor performance. The

implication is that students must perceive that outcome varies with effort expenditure and that increased effort will result in more positive outcomes.

The first consideration here is that the admonishment to try harder is to no avail to the student who believes he or she is already trying hard. This is a very likely scenario for young children, who believe they always try hard because it is not smart not to try. Telling these children that they did not work hard enough may actually decrease their sense of efficacy.

Second, problems arise when we put too much emphasis on effort. We do not want to impress on students that sustained maximal effort is what leads to success. Students may feel very satisfied when they have worked very hard and achieved success, but this is usually accompanied by the feeling that "I don't want to work that hard again." Conveying the expectation that a maximized effort is necessary may spark a child's investment once in a while, but over time students are more likely to become discouraged. In classrooms where the goal is to demonstrate one's ability over the long term, continuously maximizing one's effort is not desirable.

Finally, in most classrooms, students do not perceive the classroom hierarchy as effort-determined. As Nicholls suggests, students at the bottom of the hierarchy are not there because they are not effortful;[24] convincing students that this is, in fact, the case has little credence. If we want teachers to apply attribution theory to classroom practice, they need to know that whether they convey to students that effort is important depends on how they structure tasks, evaluate students, and give recognition and rewards.

These examples illustrate the complex nature of classroom learning and motivation. One of the major problems in our training of teachers is that we do not adequately address how motivation theory, constructs, and principles relate to practice: How can teachers develop in students a motivation to learn? As the preceding five examples illustrate, we currently rely on the wisdom of experience or derive applications without regard to the complexities involved. We need to consider how motivation constructs relate to each other, to developmental changes, to individual and culturally related differences, and to the context or structure of the classroom itself when we apply motivation theory and research to practice.

## CONTEXT OF MOTIVATION

Finally, if we want teachers to apply these constructs in order to develop these motivational patterns in students, it is important to recognize that motivation occurs within a context — the school, the classroom, and the family. We spend a great deal of time discussing individual differences in motivation, treating motivation as a trait, but not enough time attending to how the organization and structure of the classroom shapes and socializes adaptive and maladaptive motivation patterns. Moreover, developing a positive motivational orientation in students is necessarily a matter of dealing with diversity among students in the classroom.[25] Teachers need to know ways of dealing with this diversity, and these methods ought to involve a comprehensive look at the classroom.

Thus, the teacher must first be guided by goals that assign primary importance to developing in students a motivation to learn. Second, we need a framework for identifying those aspects or structures of the classroom that are manipulable. These structures must represent the classroom organization and must relate to instructional planning. Then we need to identify strategies that will serve to enhance the motivation of all students. These strategies or applications must be grounded in theory and research and evaluated in relation to developmental factors and in relation to other motivation constructs, as well as individual differences. Many educational psychology textbooks describe one or two ideas for application but do not provide a comprehensive view of classroom organization.

When we look at the classroom, there are six areas of organization that are manipulable and that involve motivational concerns: task, authority, recognition, grouping, evaluation, and time. These structures have been described in considerable detail by Epstein.[26] There is considerable research that relates to each area, and there are many motivational strategies that can be extracted from the research; the point is to apply appropriate strategies in all of these areas frequently and consistently. Preservice teachers often learn a great deal about only one area, and practicing teachers often focus on one or two areas but do little in the others. As a consequence, motivation becomes restricted to one area of the classroom. Often that area is reward or recognition (providing rewards and incentives), and even in that area inappropriate strategies are used.

This framework offers a starting point for extracting motivational strategies and applications from research and theory, and for relating them to all areas of classroom organization and instructional planning. This is important because motivation enhancement cannot be reserved for Friday afternoons, or be viewed as something to be used during free time or extra time or as superfluous to academic activities. Nor can motivational concerns surface only when a student does not do well. Motivation as an outcome is important to all students in the classroom all the time. This view gives student motivation a central place as an educational outcome, important in its own right. The emphasis is on identifying strategies that will foster a mastery-goal orientation in students and that relate to all aspects of classroom learning and organization. It requires a comprehensive approach to looking at how motivation theory and research interface with classroom learning.

*Notes*

1  See Lawrence A. Cremin, *The Transformation of the School* (New York: Random House, 1961).

2   See Carole Ames and Jennifer Archer, "Achievement Goals and Learning Strategies," *Journal of Educational Psychology* 80 (1989): 260-67; Jere Brophy, "Conceptualizing Student Motivation," *Educational Psychologist* 18 (1983): 200-15; Elaine S. Elliott and Carol S. Dweck, "Goals: An Approach to Motivation and Achievement," *Journal of Personality and Social Psychology* 54 (1988): 5-12; Martin L. Maehr, "Meaning and Motivation: Toward a Theory of Personal Investment," in *Research on Motivation in Education, Vol. 1: Student Motivation,* ed. Russell Ames and Carole Ames (Orlando: Academic Press, 1984), pp. 115-44; and John Nicholls, "Quality and Equality in Intellectual Development," *American Psychologist* 34 (1979): 1071-84.

3   Brophy, "Conceptualizing Student Motivation," pp. 200-15.

4   Carole Ames and Russell Ames, "Systems of Student and Teacher Motivation: Toward a Qualitative Definition," *Journal of Educational Psychology* 76 (1984): 535-56.

5   For example, Nathan Gage and David C. Berliner, *Educational Psychology* (Boston: Houghton-Mifflin, 1984).

6   See Martin Covington and Richard Beery, *Self-Worth and School Learning* (New York: Holt, Rinehart & Winston, 1976); and Martin Covington, "The Motive for Self-Worth," in *Research on Motivation in Education, Vol. 1,* pp. 77-113.

7   Dale Schunk, "Self-efficacy and Cognitive Skill Learning," in *Research on Motivation in Education, Vol. 3: Goals and Cognitions,* ed. Carole Ames and Russell Ames (San Diego: Academic Press, 1989), pp. 13-44.

8   Deborah Stipek, "The Development of Achievement Motivation," in *Research on Motivation in Education, Vol. 1,* pp. 145-74.

9   Martin Covington and Carol Omelich, "Effort: The Double-Edged Sword in School Achievement," *Journal of Educational Psychology* 71 (1979): 169-82.

10   Covington and Beery, *Self-Worth and School Learning.*

11   Ibid.

12   Ames and Archer, "Achievement Goals," pp. 260-67; and Carole Diener and Carol Dweck, "An Analysis of Learned Helplessness: Continuous Changes in Performance, Strategy, and Achievement Cognitions following Failure," *Journal of Personality and Social Psychology* 36 (1978): 451-62.

13   Ames and Archer, "Achievement Goals," pp. 260.

14   Ibid.; Elliott and Dweck, "Goals," pp. 5-12; Nicholls, "Quality and Equality," pp. 1071-84; and Maehr, "Meaning and Motivation," pp. 115-44.

15   Covington and Beery, *Self-Worth and School Learning;* Ames and Archer, "Achievement Goals," pp. 260-67; and Ames and Ames, "Systems of Student and Teacher Motivation," pp. 535-56.

16   John Nicholls, *The Competitive Ethos and Democratic Education* (Cambridge: Harvard University Press, 1989).

17   Carole Dweck, "Motivation," in *Handbook of Psychology and Education,* ed. R. Glaser and A. Lesgold (Hillsdale, N.J.: Erlbaum, 1985).

18   Schunk, "Self-efficacy and Cognitive Skill Learning."

19   Jere Brophy, "Teacher-Praise: A Functional Analysis," *Review of Educational Research* 51 (1981): 5-32.

20   Ann Boggiano et al., "Use of Manimal-Operant Principle to Motivate Childrens Intrinsic Interest," *Journal of Personality and Social Psychology* 53 (1987): 866-79.

21   Philip W. Jackson, *Life in Classrooms* (New York: Holt, Rinehart & Winston, 1968); see also Mark Lepper and Melinda Hodell, "Intrinsic Motivation in the Classroom," in *Research on Motivation in Education, Vol. 3,* pp. 73-105.

22   Mark Lepper, "Extrinsic Reward and Intrinsic Motivation: Implications for the Classroom," in *Teacher and Student Perceptions: Implications for Learning,* ed. J. Levine and M. Wang (Hillsdale, N.J.: Erlbaum, 1983a), pp. 281-317; and idem, "Social Control Processes and the

Internalization of Social Values: An Attributional Perspective," in *Developmental Social Cognition: A Sociocultural Perspective,* ed. E. Tory Higgins et al. (New York: Cambridge University Press, 1983), pp. 294–330.

23   See Richard deCharms, *Enhancing Motivation: Change in the Classroom* (New York: Irvington, 1976); Edward Deci and Richard Ryan, *Intrinsic Motivation and Self-determination in Human Behavior* (New York: Plenum, 1985); and Richard Ryan, James Connell, and Edward Deci, "A Motivational Analysis of Self-determination and Self-regulation in Education," in *Research on Motivation in Education, Vol. 2: The Classroom Milieu,* ed. Carole Ames and Russell Ames (Orlando: Academic Press, 1985), pp. 13–51.

24   Nicholls, *The Competitive Ethos and Democratic Education.*

25   Joyce Epstein, "Effective Schools or Effective Students: Dealing with Diversity," in *Policies for America's Public Schools: Teachers, Equity, Indicators,* ed. Ron Haskins and Duncan MacRae (Norwood, N.J.: Ablex, 1988).

26   Ibid.; and idem, "Family Structures and Student Motivation: A Developmental Perspective," in *Research on Motivation in Education, Vol. 3,* pp. 259–95.

# Essentials of Student Assessment: From Accountability to Instructional Aid

ROBERT L. LINN
*University of Colorado, Boulder*

*There is a growing consensus as to the need for revising instruction in assessment at the preservice and in-service levels. After discussing the mismatch between instructional priorities in measurement courses and the perceived needs of teachers, Linn proposes seven general assessment topics that need more attention in teacher education.*

I have been asked to address two basic questions: What should teachers of today and tomorrow know about measurement and evaluation in order to be effective teachers, and when and how should they learn this information? Since these questions are posed within the context of a reconsideration of foundational studies in teacher education, it should be noted that there is a difference between the question of what teachers need to know and the question of what should be included in foundational studies. Teachers need to know a great deal (e.g., subject matter content and pedagogy) that is not a part of traditional foundational studies.

The fact that measurement and evaluation are sometimes included in foundational studies is, in part, a historical accident owing to their psychological roots. Much of what is included under the measurement and evaluation rubric, or under the somewhat broader rubric of assessment, is more closely associated with technique than with foundations. In any event, the focus of this article will be on needed knowledge rather than on the inclusion or exclusion of student assessment issues in the foundational studies component of teacher education.

## THE DOMAIN OF MEASUREMENT AND EVALUATION

The mention of measurement and evaluation most commonly brings about an immediate image of paper-and-pencil tests—particularly standardized, multiple-choice tests. This image is hardly surprising. It is consistent with a good deal of what is emphasized in traditional courses in educational measurement. More importantly, it is consistent with the type of measurement that has come to play an increasingly critical role in educational policy. For, as Petrie has noted, it is not "too much of an exaggeration to say that evaluation and testing have become *the* engine for implementing educational policy."[1]

The growth in externally mandated testing and the increased sanctions that have been attached to test scores have been extraordinary. The expansion of high-stakes testing in the pursuit of accountability and educational reform has increased the salience of testing for teachers and students. Given the role of standardized tests in educational policy, it is essential that teachers have a better understanding of the technology and its uses and abuses. However, it would be unfortunate indeed if the vision of measurement and evaluation were limited to the immediate image of standardized paper-and-pencil tests.

Assessment of student learning is a central part of teaching. Paper-and-pencil tests, both standardized and teacher made, can contribute to assessment. Compared with the informal assessments made by teachers every day on a minute-by-minute basis, however, the contribution of tests is quite modest. Oral questioning and informal observation are much more central to the assessments that teachers rely on to make instructional decisions, particularly at the elementary grade levels.[2]

Students spend more time taking teacher-constructed tests than standardized tests and when other student activities that are evaluated (e.g., worksheets, homework assignments, and responses to oral questions) are included it is evident that standardized testing represents only a small fraction of the total time that is devoted to assessment.[3] Furthermore, "surveys of teachers and students have consistently indicated that they believe the educational and psychological effects of classroom evaluation are generally substantially greater than the corresponding effects of standardized testing."[4] Clearly, limiting one's conception of student assessment to standardized tests or even to all types of paper-and-pencil tests is to narrow the domain far too much. Indeed, it risks missing the most important aspects of measurement and evaluation that are crucial to effective teaching. Thus, a broader conception of assessment is needed.

## ASSESSMENT AND EFFECTIVE TEACHING

Given a broader conception, it is clear that student assessment is a critical aspect of effective teaching as it is envisioned by the Holmes Group.[5] Essential to that vision are "competent teachers empowered to make principled judgments and decisions on their students' behalf."[6] Principled judgments and instructional decisions require information about student learning, information that is obtained by a variety of approaches to student assessment. "Professional teachers," for example, are described as "skilled diagnosticians of children's learning needs."[7] They are expected to "interpret the understandings students bring to and develop during lessons . . . [and to] identify students' misconceptions, and question their surface responses that mask true learning."[8]

The view that teachers need to be skilled in assessing the learning needs of students is not new. A number of authors have emphasized the importance of assessment skills for effective teaching.[9] Darling-Hammond, for example, has argued that the diagnosis of student learning needs and the adaptation of instruction to those needs is an essential part of effective teaching.[10] Stiggens, Conklin, and Bridgeford claimed that all models of effective teaching require "that teachers base their instructional decisions on some knowledge of student characteristics."[11] They acknowledge, however, that "assessment is unquestionably one of teachers' most complex and important tasks."[12]

Student assessment is important not only because of its value to teachers in making instructional decisions, but because of its more direct effects on students. Based on his recent review of the impact of classroom evaluation practices on students, Crooks identified a number of important ways in which assessment affects students. For example, "it guides their judgment of what is important to learn, affects their motivation and self-perceptions of competence, structures their approaches to and timing of personal study (e.g., spaced practice), consolidates learning, and affects the development of enduring learning strategies and skills."[13] The evidence reviewed by Crooks provides a compelling case for these varied effects of assessment on students.

Professional teachers with the characteristics envisioned by the Holmes Group and authors such as Darling-Hammond and Stiggens, Conklin, and Bridgeford clearly need to be adept at assessing student learning. Moreover, the importance of effective assessment practices to effective teaching is all the more critical because the effects on students summarized by Crooks can be either positive or negative. Exemplary instructional goals can too easily be undermined by assessment techniques that are inconsistent with the goals. It is clear, for example, that the use of normative grading can conflict with some of the goals of a cooperative learning program. It is also evident that classroom tests that stress recognition of numerous factual details will quickly undermine plans and efforts to encourage deep understanding of concepts and critical thinking.

Recognizing the importance of assessment and the need for teachers to be highly skilled in the area does not answer the questions about what a teacher needs to know about measurement and evaluation or when they should learn it. The descriptions of professional teachers and the recognition of the varied effects of assessment on students expand the image of measurement and evaluation in ways that will be useful in considering these questions, however.

Teachers need to be able to interpret and evaluate standardized tests and results that are produced by externally imposed testing programs. They also need to be knowledgeable about a wide range of assessment techniques that they can use on a day-to-day basis in their classroom instruction. Improving the quality of classroom assessments can have a positive influence on the quality of learning.

## CURRENT INSTRUCTION IN MEASUREMENT

To provide a context for considering what should be, it is useful to consider briefly what is. A recent survey of the 707 colleges that are members of the American Association of Colleges of Teacher Education found that with the exception of the areas of school counseling and special education, formal coursework in measurement is a required part of slightly less than half of the certification programs offered.[14] Consistent results were obtained in a smaller survey of professors in twenty-eight midwestern colleges, which found that while most (71 percent) of the colleges offered a separate course in measurement and evaluation, such a course is required for preservice teachers in only about half of the colleges.[15] Since an assessment course is a requirement for certification in only four states, it is hardly surprising that roughly half the college programs do not include such a requirement. Indeed, given the extensive list of requirements in many states, one might expect even fewer programs to include such a requirement when it is not mandated by the state.

Where a separate course is not required, instruction in measurement and evaluation is generally provided as part of another required course. Overall, "roughly half the students receive measurement and evaluation as a separate course and half receive this instruction within the context of another course."[16]

Gullickson asked a sample of 24 professors who teach measurement courses to indicate the amount of emphasis they give to 67 topic areas on a five-point scale ranging from "very slight emphasis" to "very great emphasis." A sample of 360 teachers also rated the items with the same five-point scale in terms of the amount of emphasis they thought should be given to each topic. The 67 items were used to define 8 scales. Mean ratings on the 8 scales that were given by the two groups are plotted in Figure 1. The scales are arranged in descending order of the mean ratings of the emphasis that topics on the scale should be given according to the responses of the sample of teachers.[17]

As can be seen, only one of the six areas that teachers believe should be emphasized most is given relatively heavy emphasis according to the reports of the professors. Teachers believe that a good deal of attention should be given to the preparation of exams and professors indicate that this area is the second most heavily emphasized area in their courses. On the other hand,

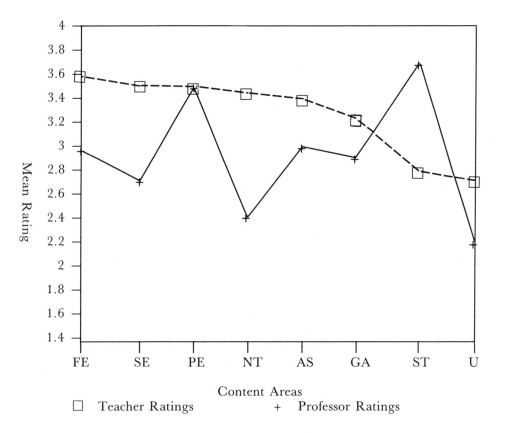

Figure 1.  **Mean Ratings of Content Emphases by Teachers and by Professors Teaching Courses in Educational Measurement**

*Note:*
FE: using test results for instructional planning and formative evaluation; SE: using test results for summative evaluation purposes; PE: preparing examinations; NT: using nontest assessment procedures; AS: administering and scoring tests; GA: general assessment information regarding selection and use of tests; ST: computing and interpreting statistical data; LI: legal issues, testing and the law. Based on Arlen R. Gullickson, "Teacher Education and Teacher Perceived Needs in Educational Measurement and Evaluation," *Journal of Educational Measurement* 23, no. 45 (1986): 347–54, Table 1.

three of the four areas that teachers believe should be most emphasized are given relatively little emphasis by professors. Those three areas are (1) using test results for instructional planning and formative evaluation, (2) using test results for summative evaluation purposes, and (3) employing nontest evaluation devices. In contrast, the topic that professors emphasize most, comparing and interpreting statistical data, is judged to deserve relatively little emphasis by the teachers.

A comparison of the results reported by Gullickson with those obtained in a survey conducted by Goehring in the early 1970s suggests that teachers' views regarding priorities for instruction in measurement and evaluation have remained fairly stable.[18] Goehring asked teachers to rate a list of 116 competencies that were identified as candidates for inclusion in courses on educational testing and measurement in terms of their value to a classroom teacher. Assessment competencies that were most clearly linked to classroom practice (e.g., the identification of student strengths and weaknesses, effective use of oral questions, communicating to parents) were rated as critical for effective teaching. The competencies receiving the lowest ratings, on the other hand, generally involved the calculation and use of statistics. Based on his survey, Goehring recommended that courses should give major emphasis to "those teacher competencies concerned with the work of a teacher as this work affects directly the pupil and parent, and the construction, application, administration, and interpretation of classroom tests and other instruments of measurement and evaluation."[19] This recommendation seems just as pertinent today as it was when it was made in 1973.

The apparent mismatch between current instructional priorities in measurement courses and the perceived needs of teachers is consistent with the overemphasis that seems to be given to standardized tests and the related reliance on statistical results in comparison with the type of assessment that is stressed by the Holmes Group and others as being an essential part of effective teaching. Formative evaluation based on teacher-constructed tests, written assignments, oral questions, and informal observations plays a much more important role in the day-to-day instructional decisions that a teacher needs to make than do standardized tests, statistical estimates of reliability, items analysis statistics, or the characteristics of scale scores.[20] Thus it is not surprising that teachers give high ratings to formative evaluation and the use of nontest evaluation devices.

As Stiggins et al. and Gullickson and Hopkins have suggested, the mismatch between course content and perceived needs in the area of assessment may partially explain the fact that somewhat less than half of the teacher preparation programs require a course in measurement and that such a course is a requirement for certification in only four states. They also suggest that it is time to rethink the instructional program that is provided for teachers in the area of assessment.

## NEEDED INSTRUCTION IN ASSESSMENT

The teacher ratings of the amount of emphasis that should be given to various content areas in measurement and evaluation that were obtained by Gullickson provide a reasonable starting place for identifying what teachers need to know.[21] As is shown in Figure 1, the six general content areas that teachers believe deserve the most emphasis in the order I will treat them are (1) the preparation of exams, (2) the use of nontest evaluation procedures, (3) the use of test results for instructional planning and formative evaluation, (4) the use of test results for summative evaluation, (5) the administration and scoring of tests, and (6) general assessment information regarding the selection and use of tests. The focus on "tests" in five of these six broad content areas may reflect, in part, teacher perceptions of what is included in a course in measurement and evaluation. The focus also reflects the set of more specific topics that defined the items on Gullickson's questionnaire. Hence, it should not be assumed that tests should necessarily be as pervasive as is suggested by the list. Nonetheless, tests do provide a reasonable starting place.

## 1.   *Planning and Constructing Classroom Tests*

Test preparation was the only content area that teachers identified as in need of emphasis and professors said they in fact emphasized in Gullickson's survey.[22] The fact that both groups judged this content area to be important is consistent with the belief that classroom tests have a major impact on students. There is ample evidence to support this belief. Tests provide signals to students about what teachers consider important to learn and thereby shape student learning.[23]

Information that is available regarding the characteristics and quality of classroom tests, while limited, suggests that considerable attention needs to be given to the improvement of classroom tests. Of particular concern is the frequent observation that "teacher-made tests tend to give greater emphasis to lower cognitive levels than the teachers' stated objectives would justify."[24] Such tests encourage the memorization of surface-level details at the expense of a deeper understanding of the subject matter. As Crooks has argued, "there is a need to make deep learning a central goal of education, and to foster development of this goal through the evaluation of students. . . . This requires that we place emphasis on understanding, transfer of learning to untaught problems or situations, and other thinking skills, evaluating the development of these skills through tasks that clearly must involve more than recognition or recall."[25]

Although many observers would agree with Crooks's plea for greater emphasis on deep understanding, there are many obstacles to achieving this end in classroom tests and other evaluation activities. Under the best of circumstances, it is difficult to prepare tests and other approaches to evaluation that assess deep understanding. Such procedures are apt to be more time consuming to construct, and since they often require the use of constructed responses (e.g., short-answer problems, essay exams) and other types of authentic performances (e.g., laboratory exercises, term papers) rather than multiple-choice or other objective testing formats, they also require more teacher time in evaluating student responses.

In stressing higher-order thinking skills, it is important not to confuse those skills with difficulty of the content. This point was well made by the National Academy of Education (NAE) committee that reviewed the Alexander-James report.[26] The NAE committee provided the following caution.

It is all too easy to think of higher-order skills as involving only difficult subject matter as, for example, learning calculus. Yet one can memorize the formulas for derivatives just as easily as those for computing areas of various geometric shapes, while remaining equally confused about the overall goals of both activities. All subjects have a basic knowledge component that can be taught by drill and practice. This basic knowledge, while prerequisite to competence, is also distinct from the intellectual skills of gathering relevant information, evaluating evidence, weighing alternative courses of action, and articulating reasoned arguments.[27]

Assessments need to be designed that probe the latter types of skills regardless of the content area or level of instruction. Materials and workshops provided by researchers at the Northwest Regional Educational Laboratory represent one significant effort to help teachers improve their assessment procedures, in general, and their assessment of thinking skills, in particular.[28] The materials and workshops provide a framework for planning oral, paper-and-pencil, and performance forms of assessment that include five defined levels of thinking skills: recall, analysis, comparison, inference, and evaluation. The simple creation of a chart with three rows for the forms of assessment and five columns for the levels of thinking skills encourages the planning of assessments that do more than cover the "recall" row of the matrix. Good examples are provided of questions that require the higher-level skills of analysis, comparison, inference, and evaluation. Together with the practice provided by the workshop, the program has been found to have a positive impact on teacher attitudes toward and self-reports of use of procedures for assessing higher-order thinking skills.

Some of the needed skills in constructing measures that emphasize deep understanding can be developed in preservice courses. Good discussion of the art of test construction and the strengths and weaknesses of approaches ranging from simple true-false questions to essays can be found in a number of widely used textbooks.[29] To be more effective, however, these materials need to be integrated with both subject matter content and instruction in methods.

Although an introduction to these concepts and the development of rudimentary skills in constructing a wide range of classroom tests that will emphasize deep understanding should begin in preservice teacher education programs, the importance of the quality of the assessments to effective teaching and the difficulty of constructing assessments that do justice to the higher-level goals of instruction suggest that continuing attention is needed as part in-service instructional programs. Crooks summarizes the need as follows: "A more professional approach to evaluation would demand regular and thoughtful analysis by teachers of their personal evaluation practices, greater use of peer review procedures, and considerable attention to the establishment of more consistent progressions of expectations and criteria within and among educational institutions."[30]

## 2.  *The Use of Nontest Evaluation Procedures*

Teachers recognize the need for better preparation in the use of a wide range of evaluation procedures other than traditional tests. However, as is shown in Figure 1, nontest evaluation procedures are given relatively little attention in measurement and evaluation courses. There is, as Gullickson and Hopkins have suggested, "a need for a shift toward greater emphasis on qualitative techniques."[31] The effective use of oral questioning and classroom observation techniques needs greater attention in preservice courses in measurement and evaluation and in in-service education and professional development.

Observational techniques and the use of ratings are considered in a number of textbooks designed to introduce prospective teachers to educational measurement. A useful addition to these traditional discussions is the notion of performance assessments that are designed specifically for the purpose of assessing a student's "ability to translate knowledge and understanding into action."[32] Stiggins has provided an instructional module on the design and development of such assessments for use by classroom teachers. It presents a systematic approach that stresses four critical components in the design of an assessment "through the specification of (a) reason(s) for assessment, (b) the type of performance to be evaluated, (c) the exercises that will elicit performance, and (d) systematic rating procedures."[33]

The performance assessments described by Stiggins have the characteristics of what Wiggins and others call "authentic" assessment.[34] Wiggins describes criteria for authentic assessments, which in his view "are contextualized, complex intellectual challenges, not fragmented and static bits or tasks."[35] They tend to be relatively unobtrusive and to involve "representative challenges within a discipline." They measure essentials and "must be scored in reference to authentic standards of performance, which students must understand to be inherent to successful performance."[36]

Because most professors who teach courses in measurement are less familiar with, and possibly less favorably disposed toward, nontest evaluation procedures, particularly the more qualitative procedures, increased emphasis on these techniques may require "a change in professors' attitudes toward qualitative evaluation techniques."[37] It may also require a closer integration of instruction in assessment with instruction in the pedagogy of specific subjects. This is so because a major purpose of assessment is to identify student learning needs and use this information in making instructional decisions. For a teacher to use assessment information to guide instruction, to facilitate learning, and to make "principled judgments and decisions on their students' behalf,"[38] much more than an understanding of assessment techniques is required. Knowledge about assessment principles needs to be integrated with an understanding of the subject matter, pedagogy, principles of learning, and children. As in the case of planning and constructing classroom tests, one cannot hope to accomplish these ends solely through preservice instruction. Continuing attention to the needed skills and understandings through professional development programs is needed.

### 3. Use of Assessment Results for Instructional Planning and Formative Evaluation

The content area that teachers in Gullickson's survey rated as deserving the most emphasis was the use of test results for instructional planning and formative evaluation.[39] Tests, however, are only one of the components of formative evaluation. Other types of assessment information are also needed for effective instructional planning and formative evaluation. Broadening the focus to include the full range of student assessment techniques makes this content category all the more important.

Much of the discussion of the two preceding content areas applies equally well to a consideration of the uses of assessment results in instructional planning and formative evaluation. Tests that will be useful for these purposes need to reflect the instructional priorities of the teacher. If the teacher hopes to foster, for example, the development of deep understanding, the ability to think critically about the subject matter, and the ability to apply concepts to solve new problems, then tests and other evaluative techniques need to match these goals. Tests and work assignments that require only factual recall of details will not help achieve these goals. Nor will they provide the teacher with information about the depth of student understanding or students' ability to apply concepts in other contexts that can be used in planning instruction. The same could be said about nontest assessment information.

The use of student assessment for purposes of formative evaluation should be a central theme in the education of prospective teachers and in their continuing professional development. As in the use of nontest assessment techniques, effective use of assessment information in planning instruction requires an integration of assessment with pedagogy in the subject matter. A closer cooperation between professors in the areas of assessment, professors in curriculum and instruction, and professional teachers is needed.

### 4. *The Use of Assessment Results for Summative Evaluation*

Although the use of assessment information for making instructional decisions, for planning, and for formative evaluation deserves first priority, teachers are also expected to make summative evaluations. Grading and reporting to pupils and parents can be onerous and frustrating. Reporting to both parents and pupils is an essential task, however, and, in many instances, grades will be a required part of the report.

Grades and other forms of summative evaluation obviously can have important implications for judgments and decisions concerning students that are made by school personnel, parents, and the students themselves. Grades are also important determinants of what students believe teachers consider important and of what and how students attend to. "Will it be on the test?" is a question that is all too familiar to teachers, and is easily understood in terms of Walker's observation that "the things that are *really* important, as every student knows, are the things that appear on tests and are used in grading."[40] It is essential, therefore, that teachers understand the potential positive and negative influences of their summative evaluations, whatever their form. They also need to understand the implications of different approaches to marking and combining marks so that the resulting summative evaluation validly and fairly reflects student accomplishments that are consistent with the teacher's instructional priorities and stated intentions. If students can obtain high grades based on memorization of surface-level facts they are not apt to perceive the importance that the teacher wishes to attach to deep understanding.

### 5. *Administration and Scoring of Tests*

Test administration and scoring, while clearly tasks that must be done well, appear on the surface to be relatively straightforward. That is true, however, only if one's vision of assessment is limited to traditional tests with fixed responses (e.g., multiple-choice tests). For assessments of more complex and authentic performances of the type discussed by Stiggins,[41] however, "administration" requires greater skill. Settings must be created that will elicit the desired performance or natural occurrences must be used in a way that provides all students with a fair opportunity to perform. Scoring is also more complex and needs to be adapted to the purposes of the assessment and the nature of the exercises.

Some general principles of administration and scoring of essay exams, class projects, and other types of performance assessments can be dealt with in introductory courses in measurement. Applications are apt to be more meaningful and have greater utility for teachers if they are considered within the context of particular subject areas and grade levels. In-service education in performance assessment and the evaluation of particular types of student products should be useful in this regard.

### 6. *General Assessment Information regarding the Selection and Use of Tests*

The last of the six content areas rated as needing emphasis by the teachers surveyed by Gullickson concerns general assessment issues, including the selection and use of tests.[42] It is here that information about standardized tests — their uses and potential misuses — and bases for evaluating such tests should be considered. Teachers need to be informed about the types of tests that may be used and their strengths and limitations for particular applications. They need to understand the various contexts in which standardized tests are used and the appropriate interpretation of results.

Although instruction about standardized testing is now commonly included in introductory courses in educational measurement and such inclusion is appropriate, this form of assessment probably receives more attention than it deserves at that level. Furthermore, issues related to the uses of standardized tests take on a different meaning for practicing teachers who have experienced the pressures for accountability, which commonly reduce to demands for higher test scores, than they are apt to have in a preservice context. Professional teachers not only have a need to be informed about standardized tests, but they need to be in a position to make professional judgments about the appropriate and inappropriate influences such tests can have on classroom instruction. For example, what constitutes appropriate and inappropriate preparation of students for taking a standardized test? To what extent, if any, should such tests influence curriculum and instructional emphases?

Ethical issues need to be addressed by all professionals and assessment, especially assessment that serves external accountability functions, is an area in which there are some complex ethical issues to consider. The question of what sort of preparation is appropriate to provide students prior to the administration of a high-stakes standardized test is a significant issue on which there are diverse opinions among practicing teachers. Gonzalez, for example, found that only 37 percent of the teachers and test administrators surveyed thought that it was definitely cheating for a teacher who remembers specific questions from a test to teach next year's students the same questions. Another 24 percent indicated that that was not cheating at all. Even when the question was whether it was cheating if copies of the actual test are made available to colleagues and the actual test items are taught in the classroom, 11 percent of those surveyed failed to respond "definitely."[43]

The range of instructional activities that might help students do better on a standardized achievement test is quite broad. Mehrens and Kaminski, for example, have identified seven types of activities, ranging from "general instruction on objectives not determined by looking at the objectives measured on standardized tests" to "practice (i.e., instruction)" on the actual form of the test that is used. Mehrens and Kaminski argue that while the first is always ethical, the latter never is. Clearly, the ethics of test administration and test preparation is a topic worthy of serious consideration by both preservice and in-service teachers.[44]

### 7. *Principles of Measurement*

Although not included in the content categories identified in Gullickson's survey,[45] there are some general principles of measurement that teachers should know. Concepts of validity and reliability are essential to the evaluation of any assessment procedure. These concepts are important to understand and can be taught with a minimum of statistics. They are guiding principles that can provide a perspective for evaluating assessments based on qualitative information obtained from informal classroom observations as well as the scores they compute on a weekly quiz or a final examination.

### STANDARDS

Before closing, it seems relevant to mention an ongoing effort involving four professional associations to develop standards for teacher competence in educational assessment.[46] The associations are the American Association of Colleges for Teacher Education, the American Federation of Teachers, the National Council on Measurement in Education, and the National Education Association. A joint committee with representatives from each association has developed a draft set of seven standards emphasizing knowledge and skills in areas closely linked to the classroom assessment of students that teachers are responsible for obtaining and interpreting. When published, these standards should provide a good indication of areas of high instructional priority.

### CONCLUSION

A number of people involved in the teaching of measurement have focused their attention on needed changes and improvements in the instruction that is provided for teachers.[47] Although the suggested changes vary in details and do not always correspond to the above suggestions, the various proposals have a good deal in common. In particular, there seems to be a growing consensus that there is a need for a substantial restructuring of the instruction we provide in assessment for both preservice and practicing teachers. There is also a growing consensus that less emphasis should be given to statistical aspects of measurement and more emphasis to informal and qualitative assessment procedures.

The content areas discussed above do not exhaust the domain of knowledge about student assessment needed by teachers. As with other aspects of the job of a professional teacher, there are ethical and legal issues that need to be considered. There are also specialized uses of tests, such as placing students in a wide range of special programs, the identification of learning disabilities, and making decisions regarding grade-to-grade promotion. An understanding of issues involved in such uses and, where relevant to the professional responsibilities of a teacher, an in-depth knowledge of technical, legal, and ethical considerations should be expected.

The general content areas described above, however, do provide an essential core. Improvements in test construction and the use of nontest assessment procedures such that assessments better reflected the instructional goals of professional teachers alone would represent a substantial advance.

## Notes

1  Hugh G. Petrie, "Introduction to 'Evaluation and Testing,' " *Educational Policy* 1, no. 2 (1987): 176.

2  Richard J. Stiggins, Nancy F. Conklin, and Nancy J. Bridgeford, "Classroom Assessment: A Key to Effective Education," *Educational Measurement: Issues and Practice* 5, no. 2 (Summer 1986): 5–17.

3  Terence J. Crooks, "The Impact of Classroom Evaluation Practices on Students," *Review of Educational Research* 58, no. 4 (1989): 438–81.

4  Ibid., p. 438.

5  *Tomorrow's Teachers: A Report of the Holmes Group* (East Lansing, Mich.: The Holmes Group, 1986).

6  Ibid., p. 28.

7  Ibid., p. 39.

8  Ibid., p. 29.

9  See, for example, William D. Schafer and Robert W. Lissitz, "Measurement Training for School Personnel: Recommendations and Reality," *Journal of Teacher Education* 38, no. 3 (1987): 57–63.

10  Linda Darling-Hammond, *Beyond the Commission Reports: The Coming Crisis in Teaching* (Santa Monica, Calif.: The Rand Corporation, 1984).

11  Stiggins et al., "Classroom Assessment," p. 10.

12  Ibid., p. 10.

13  Crooks, "The Impact of Classroom Evaluation Practices on Students," p. 467.

14  Schafer and Lissitz, "Measurement Training for School Personnel."

15  Arlen R. Gullickson and Kenneth D. Hopkins, "The Context of Educational Measurement Instruction for Preservice Teachers: Professors Perspectives," *Educational Measurement: Issues and Practice* 6, no. 3 (Fall 1987): 12–16.

16  Ibid., p. 13.

17  Arlen R. Gullickson, "Teacher Education and Teacher-Perceived Needs in Educational Measurement and Evaluation," *Journal of Educational Measurement* 23, no. 45 (1986): 347–54.

18  Harvey J. Goehring, Jr., "Course Competencies for Undergraduate Courses in Educational Tests and Measurement," *The Teacher Educator* 9, no. 1 (1973): 11–20.

19  Ibid., p. 20.

20  Stiggins et al., "Classroom Assessment."

21  Gullickson, "Teacher Education and Teacher-Perceived Needs."

22    Ibid.

23    Crooks, "The Impact of Classroom Evaluation Practices on Students."

24    Ibid., p. 442.

25    Ibid., p. 467.

26    Lamar Alexander and H. Thomas James, *Report of the Study Group* (Cambridge, Mass.: National Academy of Education, 1987).

27    National Academy of Education, "Commentary by the National Academy of Education on *The Nation's Report Card*"(Cambridge, Mass.: National Academy of Education, 1987), p. 54.

28    See Richard J. Stiggins, Evelyn Rubel, and Edys Quallmalz, *Measuring Thinking Skills in the Classroom* (Washington, D.C.: National Education Association, 1986).

29    See, for example, Norman E. Gronlund, *Measurement and Evaluation in Teaching,* 5th ed. (New York: Macmillan, 1985).

30    Crooks, "The Impact of Classroom Evaluation Practices on Students," p. 467.

31    Gullickson and Hopkins, "The Context of Educational Measurement," p. 15.

32    Richard J. Stiggins, "Design and Development of Performance Assessments," *Educational Measurement: Issues and Practices* 6, no. 3 (1987): 35.

33    Ibid., p. 33.

34    Grant Wiggins, "A True Test: Toward More Authentic and Equitable Assessment," *Kappan* 70, no. 9 (May 1989): 703–13.

35    Ibid., p. 711.

36    Ibid.

37    Gullickson and Hopkins, "The Context of Educational Measurement," p. 15.

38    *Tomorrow's Teachers: A Report of The Holmes Group,* p. 28.

39    Gullickson, "Teacher Education and Teacher-Perceived Needs."

40    Decker F. Walker, "What Constitutes Curricular Validity in a High-School-Leaving Examination?" in *The Courts, Validity, and Minimum Competency Testing,* ed. George F. Madaus (Boston: Kluwer-Nijhoff, 1982), p. 173.

41    Stiggins, "Design and Development of Performance Assessments."

42    Gullickson, "Teacher Education and Teacher-Perceived Needs.

43    M. Gonzalez, "Cheating on Standardized Tests: What Is It?" cited in William A. Mehrens and John Kaminski, "Methods for Improving Standardized Test Scores: Fruitful, Fruitless, or Fraudulent?" *Educational Measurement: Issues and Practice* 8, no. 1 (Spring 1989): 14–22.

44    Mehrens and Kaminski, "Methods for Improving Standardized Test Scores."

45    Gullickson, "Teacher Education and Teacher-Perceived Needs."

46    See James R. Sanders, "Standards for Teacher Competence in Educational Assessment of Students" (Paper delivered at the annual meeting of the National Council on Measurement in Education, San Francisco, March 28, 1989).

47    Peter W. Airasian, "Perspectives on Measurement Instruction for Pre-Service Teachers" (Paper delivered at the annual meeting of the National Council on Measurement in Education, San Francisco, March 28, 1989); Richard J. Stiggins, "Relevant Training for Teachers in Classroom Assessment" (Paper delivered at the annual meeting of the National Council on Measurement in Education, San Francisco, March 28, 1989); and William D. Schafer, "The 'Essentials' of Professional Education Characteristics of the Learner Assessment of Learners" (Unpublished paper, University of Maryland, October 1988).

# Inside the Classroom: Social Vision and Critical Pedagogy

WILLIAM BIGELOW

*Jefferson High School, Portland, Oregon*

*Bigelow, a secondary school teacher in Portland, Oregon, believes that public schooling in the United States serves social and economic class interests very unequally, and that one justifiable response for the educator is to help equip students to understand and critique the society in which they live. This article portrays students and teachers engaging in the kind of structured dialogue that Bigelow says is essential to the critical pedagogy he employs.*

There is a quotation from Paulo Freire that I like; he writes that teachers should attempt to "live part of their dreams within their educational space."[1] The implication is that teaching should be partisan. I agree. As a teacher I want to be an agent of transformation, with my classroom as a center of equality and democracy — an ongoing, if small, critique of the repressive social relations of the larger society. That does not mean holding a plebiscite on every homework assignment, or pretending I do not have any expertise, but I hope my classroom can become part of a protracted argument for the viability of a critical and participatory democracy.

I think this vision of teaching flies in the face of what has been and continues to be the primary function of public schooling in the United States: to reproduce a class society, where the benefits and sufferings are shared incredibly unequally. As much as possible I refuse to play my part in that process. This is easier said than done. How *can* classroom teachers move decisively away from a model of teaching that merely reproduces and legitimates inequality? I think Freire is on the right track when he calls for a "dialogical education."[2] To me, this is not just a plea for more classroom conversation. In my construction, a dialogical classroom means inviting students to critique the larger society through sharing their lives. As a teacher I help students locate their experiences socially; I involve students in probing the social factors that make and limit who they are and I try to help them reflect on who they *could* be.

## STUDENTS' LIVES AS CLASSROOM TEXT

In my Literature in U.S. History course, which I co-teach in Portland, Oregon, with Linda Christensen, we use historical concepts as points of departure to explore themes in students' lives and then, in turn, use students' lives to explore history and our society today. Earlier this year, for instance, we studied the Cherokee Indian Removal through role play. Students portrayed the Indians, plantation owners, bankers, and the Andrew Jackson administration and saw the forces that combined to push the Cherokees west of the Mississippi against their will. Following a discussion of how and why this happened, Linda and I asked students to write about a time when they had their rights violated. We asked students to write from inside these experiences and to recapture how they felt and what, if anything, they did about the injustice.

Seated in a circle, students shared their stories with one another in a "read-around" format. (To fracture the student/teacher dichotomy a bit, Linda and I also complete each assignment and take our turns reading.) Before we began, we suggested they listen for what we call the "collective text"—the group portrait that emerges from the read-around.[3] Specifically, we asked them to take notes on the kinds of rights people felt they possessed; what action they took after having their rights violated; and whatever other generalizations they could draw from the collective text. Here are a few examples: Rachel wrote on wetting her pants because a teacher would not let her go to the bathroom; Christie, on a lecherous teacher at a middle school; Rebecca, on a teacher who enclosed her in a solitary confinement cell; Gina, who is black, on a theater worker not believing that her mother, who is white, actually was her mother; Maryanne, on being sexually harassed while walking to school and her subsequent mistreatment by the school administration when she reported the incident; Clayton, on the dean's treatment when Clayton wore an anarchy symbol on his jacket; Bobby, on convenience store clerks who watched him more closely because he is black. Those are fewer than a quarter of the stories we heard.

To help students study this social text more carefully, we asked them to review their notes from the read-around and write about their discoveries. We then spent over a class period interpreting our experiences. Almost half the instances of rights violations took place in school. Christy said, "I thought about the school thing. The real point [of school] is to learn one concept: to be trained and obedient. That's what high school is. A diploma says this person came every day, sat in their seat. It's like going to dog school." A number of people, myself included, expressed surprise that so many of the stories involved sexual harassment. To most of the students with experiences of harassment, it had always seemed a very private oppression, but hearing how common this kind of abuse is allowed the young women to feel a new connection among themselves—and they said so. A number of white students were surprised at the varieties of subtle racism black students experienced.

We talked about the character of students' resistance to rights violations. From the collective text we saw that most people did not resist at all. What little resistance occurred was individual; there was not a single instance of collective resistance. Christie complained to a counselor, Rebecca told her mother, many complained to friends. This provoked a discussion about what in their lives and, in particular, in the school system encouraged looking for individual solutions to problems that are shared collectively. They identified competition for grades and for positions in sought-after classes as factors. They also criticized the fake democracy of student government for discouraging activism. No one shared a single experience of schools' encouraging groups of students to confront injustice. Moreover, students also listed ways — from advertising messages to television sitcoms — through which people are conditioned by the larger society to think in terms of individual problems requiring individual solutions.

The stories students wrote were moving, sometimes poetic, and later opportunities to rewrite allowed us to help sharpen their writing skills, but we wanted to do more than just encourage students to stage a literary show-and-tell. Our larger objective was to find social meaning in individual experience — to push students to use their stories as windows not only on their lives, but on society.

There were other objectives. We hoped that through building a collective text, our students — particularly working-class and minority students — would discover that their lives are important sources of learning, no less important than the lives of the generals and presidents, the Rockefellers and Carnegies, who inhabit their textbooks. One function of the school curriculum is to celebrate the culture of the dominant and to ignore or scorn the culture of subordinate groups. The personal writing, collective texts, and discussion circles in Linda's and my classes are an attempt to challenge students not to accept these judgments. We wanted students to grasp that they can *create* knowledge, not simply absorb it from higher authorities.[4]

All of this sounds a little neater than what actually occurs in a classroom. Some students rebel at taking their own lives seriously. A student in one of my classes said to me recently, "Why do we have to do all this personal stuff? Can't you just give us a book of a worksheet and leave us alone?" Another student says regularly, "This isn't an English class, ya know." Part of this resistance may come from not wanting to resurface or expose painful experiences; part may come from not feeling capable as writers; but I think the biggest factor is that they simply do not feel that their lives have anything *important* to teach them. Their lives are just their lives. Abraham Lincoln and Hitler are important. Students have internalized self-contempt from years of official neglect and denigration of their culture. When for example, African-

American or working-class history *is* taught it is generally as hero worship: extolling the accomplishments of a Martin Luther King, Jr., or a John L. Lewis, while ignoring the social movements that made their work possible. The message given is that great people make change, individual high school students do not. So it is not surprising that some students wonder what in the world they have to learn from each other's stories.

Apart from drawing on students' own lives as sources of knowledge and insight, an alternative curriculum also needs to focus on the struggle of oppressed groups for social justice. In my history classes, for example, we study Shay's Rebellion, the abolition movement, and alliances between blacks and poor whites during Reconstruction. In one lesson, students role-play Industrial Workers of the World organizers in the 1912 Lawrence, Massachusetts, textile strike as they try to overcome divisions between men and women and between workers speaking over a dozen different languages.

## STUDYING THE HIDDEN CURRICULUM

In my experience as a teacher, whether students write about inequality, resistance, or collective work, school is *the* most prominent setting. Therefore, in our effort to have the curriculum respond to students' real concerns, we enlist them as social researchers, investigating their own school lives. My co-teacher and I began one unit by reading an excerpt from the novel *Radcliffe*, by David Storey.[5] In the selection, a young boy, Leonard Radcliffe, arrives at a predominately working-class British school. The teacher prods Leonard, who is from an aristocratic background, to become her reluctant know-it-all—the better to reveal to others their own ignorance. The explicit curriculum appears to concern urban geography: "Why are roofs pointed and not flat like in the Bible?" the teacher asks. She humiliates a working-class youth, Victor, by demanding that he stand and listen to her harangue: "Well, come on then, Victor. Let us all hear." As he stands mute and helpless, she chides: "Perhaps there's no reason for Victor to think at all. We already know where he's going to end up, don't we?" She points to the factory chimneys outside. "There are places waiting for him out there already." No one says a word. She finally calls on little Leonard to give the correct answer, which he does.

Students in our class readily see that these British schoolchildren are learning much more than why roofs are pointed. They are being drilled to accept their lot at the bottom of a hierarchy with a boss on top. The teacher's successful effort to humiliate Victor, while the others sit watching, undercuts any sense the students might have of their power to act in solidarity with one another. A peer is left hanging in the wind and they do nothing about it. The teacher's tacit alliance with Leonard and her abuse of Victor legitimate class inequalities outside the classroom.[6]

We use this excerpt and the follow-up discussion as a preparatory exercise for students to research the curriculum — both explicit and "hidden"[7] — at their own school (Jefferson High School). The student body is mostly African-American and predominately working class. Linda and I assign students to observe their classes as if they were attending for the first time. We ask them to notice the design of the classroom, the teaching methodology, the class content, and the grading procedures. In their logs, we ask them to reflect on the character of thinking demanded and the classroom relationships: Does the teacher promote questioning and critique or obedience and conformity? What kind of knowledge and understandings are valued in the class? What relationships between students are encouraged?

In her log, Elan focused on sexism in the hidden curriculum:

In both biology and government, I noticed that not only do boys get more complete explanations to questions, they get asked more questions by the teacher than girls do. In government, even though our teacher is a feminist, boys are asked to define a word or to list the different parts of the legislative branch more often than the girls are. . . . I sat in on an advanced sophomore English class that was doing research in the library. The teacher, a male, was teaching the boys how to find research on their topic, while he was finding the research himself for the girls. Now, I know chivalry isn't dead, but we are competent of finding a book.

Linda and I were pleased as we watched students begin to gain a critical distance from their own schooling experiences. Unfortunately, Elan did not speculate much on the social outcomes of the unequal treatment she encountered, or on what it is in society that produces this kind of teaching. She did offer the observation that "boys are given much more freedom in the classroom than girls, and therefore the boys are used to getting power before the girls."

Here is an excerpt from Connie's log:

It always amazed me how teachers automatically assume that where you sit will determine your grade. It's funny how you can get an A in a class you don't even understand. As long as you follow the rules and play the game, you seem to get by. . . . On this particular day we happen to be taking a test on chapters 16 and 17. I've always liked classes such as algebra that you didn't have to think. You're given the facts, shown how to do it, and you do it. No questions, no theories, it's the solid, correct way to do it.

We asked students to reflect on who in our society they thought benefited from the methods of education to which they were subjected. Connie wrote:

I think that not only is it the teacher, but more importantly, it's the system. They purposely teach you using the "boring method." Just accept what they tell you, learn it and go on, no questions asked. It seems to me that the rich, powerful people benefit from it, because we don't want to think, we're kept ignorant, keeping them rich.

Connie's hunch that her classes benefit the rich and powerful is obviously incomplete, but it does put her on the road to understanding that the degrading character of her education is not simply accidental. She is positioned to explore the myriad ways schooling is shaped by the imperatives of a capitalist economy. Instead of being just more of the "boring method," as Connie puts it, this social and historical study would be a personal search for her, rooted in her desire to understand the nature of her *own* school experience.

In class, students struggled through a several-page excerpt from *Schooling in Capitalist America* by Samuel Bowles and Herbert Gintis. They read the Bowles and Gintis assertion that

major aspects of educational organization replicate the relationships of dominance and subordinancy in the economic sphere. The correspondence between the social relation of schooling and work accounts for the ability of the educational system to produce an amenable and fragmented labor force. The experience of schooling, and not merely the content of formal learning, is central to this process.[8]

If they are right, we should expect to find different hidden curricula at schools enrolling students of different social classes. We wanted our students to test this notion for themselves.[9] A friend who teaches at a suburban high school south of Portland, serving a relatively wealthy community, enlisted volunteers in her classes to host our students for a day. My students logged comparisons of Jefferson and the elite school, which I will call Ridgewood. Trisa wrote:

Now, we're both supposed to be publicly funded, equally funded, but not so. At Jefferson, the average class size is 20–25 students, at Ridgewood — 15. Jefferson's cafeteria food is half-cooked, stale and processed. Ridgewood — fresh food, wide variety, and no mile-long lines to wait in. Students are allowed to eat anywhere in the building as well as outside, and wear hats and listen to walkmen [both rule violations at Jefferson].

About teachers' attitudes at Ridgewood, Trisa noted: "Someone said, 'We don't ask if you're going to college, but what college are you going to.'"

In general, I was disappointed that students' observations tended to be more on atmosphere than on classroom dynamics. Still, what they noticed seemed to confirm the fact that their own school, serving a black and working-class community, was a much more rule-governed, closely supervised environment. The experience added evidence to the Bowles and Gintis contention that my students were being trained to occupy lower positions in an occupational hierarchy.

Students were excited by this sociological detective work, but intuitively they were uneasy with the determinism of Bowles and Gintis's correspondence theory. It was not enough to discover that the relations of schooling mirrored the relations of work. They demanded to know exactly who designed a curriculum that taught them subservience. Was there a committee somewhere, sitting around plotting to keep them poor and passive? "We're always saying 'they' want us to do this, and 'they' want us to do that," one student said angrily. "Who is this 'they'?" Students wanted villains with faces and we were urging that they find systemic explanations.

Omar's anger exploded after one discussion. He picked up his desk and threw it against the wall, yelling: "How much more of this shit do I have to put up with?" "This shit" was his entire educational experience, and while the outburst was not directed at our class in particular — thank heavens — we understood our culpability in his frustration.

We had made two important and related errors in our teaching. Implicitly, our search had encouraged students to see themselves as victims — powerless little cogs in a machine daily reproducing the inequities of the larger society. Though the correspondence theory was an analytical framework with a greater power to interpret their school lives than any other they had encountered, ultimately it was a model suggesting endless oppression and hopelessness. If schooling is always responsive to the needs of capitalism, then what point did our search have? Our observations seemed merely to underscore students' powerlessness.

I think the major problem was that although our class did discuss resistance by students, it was anecdotal and unsystematic, thereby depriving students of the opportunity to question their own roles in maintaining the status quo. The effect of this omission, entirely unintentional on our part, was to deny students the chance to see schools as sites of struggle and social change — places where they could have a role in determining the character of their own education. Unwittingly, the realizations students were drawing from our study of schools fueled a world view rooted in cynicism; they might learn about the nature and causes for their subordination, but they could have no role in resisting it.

## THE "ORGANIC GOODIE SIMULATION"

Still stinging from my own pedagogical carelessness, I have made efforts this year to draw students into a dialogue about the dynamics of power and resistance. One of the most effective means to carry on this dialogue is metaphorically, through role play and simulation.[10]

In one exercise, called the "Organic Goodie Simulation," I create a three-tiered society. Half the students are workers, half are unemployed,[11] and I am the third tier — the owner of a machine that produces organic goodies. I tell students that we will be in this classroom for the rest of our lives and that the machine produces the only sustenance. Workers can buy adequate goodies with their wages, but the unemployed will slowly starve to death on their meager dole of welfare-goodies. Everything proceeds smoothly until I begin to drive wages down by offering jobs to the unemployed at slightly less than what the workers earn. It is an auction, with jobs going to the lowest bidder. Eventually, all classes organize some kind of opposition, and usually try to take away my machine. One year, a group of students arrested me, took me to a jail in the corner of the room, put a squirt gun to my head, and threatened to "kill" me if I said another word. This year, before students took over the machine, I backed off, called a meeting to which only my workers were invited, raised their wages, and stressed to them how important it was that we stick together to resist the jealous unemployed people who wanted to drag all of us into the welfare hole they are in. Some workers defected to the unemployed, some vigorously defended my right to manage the machine, but most bought my plea that we had to talk it all out and reach unanimous agreement before any changes could be made. For an hour and a half they argued among themselves, egged on by me, without taking any effective action.

The simulation provided a common metaphor from which students could examine firsthand what we had not adequately addressed the previous year: To what extent are we complicit in our own oppression? Before we began our follow-up discussion, I asked students to write on who or what was to blame for the conflict and disruption of the previous day. In the discussion some students singled me out as the culprit. Stefani said, "I thought Bill was evil. I didn't know what he wanted." Rebecca concurred: "I don't agree with people who say Bill was not the root of the problem. Bill was management, and he made workers feel insecure that the unemployed were trying to take their jobs." Others agreed with Rebecca that it was a divisive structure that had been created, but saw how their own responses to that structure perpetuated the divisions and poverty. Christie said: "We were so divided that nothing got decided. It kept going back and forth. Our discouragement was the root of the problem." A number of people saw how their own attitudes kept them from acting decisively. Mira said: "I think that there was this large fear: We have to follow the law. And Sonia kept saying we weren't supposed to take over the machine. But if the law and property hurt people why should we go along with it?" Gina said: "I think Bill looked like the problem, but underneath it all was us. Look at when Bill hired unemployed and fired some workers. I was doin' it too. We can say it's a role play, but you have to look at how everything ended up feeling and learn something about ourselves, about how we handled it."

From our discussion students could see that their make-believe misery was indeed caused by the structure of the society: The number of jobs was held at an artificially low level, and workers and unemployed were pitted against each other for scarce goodies. As the owner I tried every trick I knew to drive wedges between workers and the unemployed, to encourage loyalty in my workers, and to promote uncertainty and bickering among the unemployed. However, by analyzing the experience, students could see that the system worked only because they let it work—they were much more than victims of my greed; they were my accomplices.

I should hasten to add—and emphasize—that it is not inherently empowering to understand one's own complicity in oppression. I think it is a start, because this understanding suggests that we can do something about it. A critical pedagogy, however, needs to do much more: It should highlight times, past and present, when people built alliances to challenge injustice. Students also need to encounter individuals and organizations active in working for a more egalitarian society, and students need to be encouraged to see themselves as capable of joining together with others, in and out of school, to make needed changes. I think that all of these are mandatory components of the curriculum. The danger of students' becoming terribly cynical as they come to understand the enormity of injustice in this society and in the world is just too great. They have to know that it is possible—even joyous, if I dare say so—to work toward a more humane society.

## TEACHERS AND TEACHER EDUCATORS AS POLITICAL AGENTS

At the outset I said that all teaching should be partisan. In fact, I think that all teaching *is* partisan. Whether or not we want to be, all teachers are political agents because we help shape students' understandings of the larger society. That is why it is so important for teachers to be clear about our social visions. Toward what kind of society are we aiming? Unless teachers answer this question with clarity we are reduced to performing as technicians, unwittingly participating in a political project but with no comprehension of its objectives or consequences. Hence teachers who claim "no politics" are inherently authoritarian because their pedagogical choices act on students, but students are denied a structured opportunity to critique or act on their teachers' choices. Nor are students equipped to reflect on the effectiveness of whatever resistance they may put up.

For a number of reasons, I do not think that our classrooms can ever be exact models of the kind of participatory democracy we would like to have characterize the larger society. If teachers' only power were to grade students, that would be sufficient to sabotage classroom democracy. However, as I have suggested, classrooms can offer students experiences and understandings that counter, and critique, the lack of democracy in the rest of their lives. In the character of student interactions the classroom can offer a glimpse of certain features of an egalitarian society. We can begin to encourage students to learn the analytic and strategic skills to help bring this new society into existence. As I indicated, by creating a collective text of student experience we can offer students practice in understanding personal problems in their social contexts. Instead of resorting to consumption, despair, or other forms of self-abuse, they can ask why these circumstances exist and what can they do about it. In this limited arena, students can begin to become the subjects of their lives.

When Steve Tozer of the University of Illinois asked me to prepare this article, he said I should discuss the implications of my classroom practice for people in social foundations of education programs. First, I would urge you who are teacher educators to model the participatory and exploratory pedagogy that you hope your students will employ as classroom teachers. Teachers-to-be should interrogate their own educational experiences as a basis for understanding the relationship between school and society. They need to be members of a dialogical community in which they can experience themselves as subjects and can learn the validity of critical pedagogy by doing it. If the primary aim of social foundations of education coursework is to equip teachers-to-be to understand and critically evaluate the origins of school content and processes in social context, then the foundations classroom should be a place for students to discuss how their own experiences as students are grounded in the larger society, with its assumptions, its inequities, its limits and possibilities.

As you know, a teacher's first job in a public school can be frightening. That fear mixed with the conservative pressures of the institution can overwhelm the liberatory inclinations of a new teacher. Having *experienced,* and not merely having read about, an alternative pedagogy can help new teachers preserve their democratic ideals. Part of this, I think, means inviting your students to join you in critiquing *your* pedagogy. You need to be a model of rigorous self-evaluation.

The kind of teaching I have been describing is demanding. The beginning teacher may be tempted to respond, "Sure, sure, I'll try all that when I've been in the classroom five or six years and when I've got a file cabinet full of lessons." I think you should encourage new teachers to overcome their isolation by linking up with colleagues to reflect on teaching problems and to share pedagogical aims and successes. I participated in a support group like this my first year as a teacher and our meetings helped maintain my courage and morale. After a long hiatus, two years ago I joined another group that meets bi-weekly to talk about everything from educational theory to confrontations with administrators to union organizing.[12] In groups such as this your students can come to see themselves as creators and evaluators of curriculum and not simply as executors of corporate- or administrative-packaged lesson plans.

It is also in groups like this that teachers can come to see themselves as activists in a broader struggle for social justice. The fact is that education will not be *the* engine of social change. No matter how successful we are as critical teachers in the classroom, our students' ability to use and extend the analytic skills they have acquired depends on the character of the society that confronts them. Until the economic system requires workers who are critical, cooperative, and deeply democratic, teachers' classroom efforts amount to a kind of low-intensity pedagogical war. Unfortunately, it is easy to cut ourselves off from outside movements for social change—and this is especially true for new teachers. As critical teachers, however, we depend on these movements to provide our students with living proof that fundamental change is both possible and desirable. It seems to me you cannot emphasize too strongly how teachers' attempts to teach humane and democratic values in the classroom should not be isolated from the social context in which schooling occurs.

In closing, let me return to Freire's encouragement that we live part of our dreams within our educational space. Teachers-to-be should not be ashamed or frightened of taking sides in favor of democracy and social justice. I hope *your* students learn to speak to *their* students in the language of possibility and hope and not of conformity and "realism." In sum, your students ought to learn that teaching is, in the best sense of the term, a subversive activity—and to be proud of it.

## Notes

1 Paulo Freire and Donaldo Macedo, *Literacy: Reading the Word and the World* (South Hadley, Mass.: Bergin and Garvey, 1987), p. 127.

2 See especially Ira Shor and Paulo Freire, *A Pedagogy for Liberation* (South Hadley, Mass.: Bergin and Garvey, 1983.)

3 See Linda Christensen, "Writing the Word and the World," *English Journal* 78, no. 2 (February 1989): 14–18.

4 See William Bigelow and Norman Diamond, *The Power in Our Hands: A Curriculum on the History of Work and Workers in the United States* (New York: Monthly Review Press, 1988), pp. 15–23.

5 David Storey, *Radcliffe* (New York: Avon, 1963), pp. 9–12. I am grateful to Doug Sherman for alerting me to this excerpt.

6 While most students are critical of the teacher, they should always be allowed an independent judgment. Recently, a boy in one of my classes who is severely hard of hearing defended the teacher's actions. He argued that because the students laughed at Leonard when he first entered the class they deserved whatever humiliation the teacher could dish out. He said the offending students ought to be taught not to make fun of people who are different.

7 See Henry Giroux, *Theory and Resistance in Education: A Pedagogy for the Opposition* (South Hadley, Mass.: Bergin and Garvey, 1983). See especially Chapter 2, "Schooling and the Politics of the Hidden Curriculum," pp. 42–71. Giroux defines the hidden curriculum as "those unstated norms, values, and beliefs embedded in and transmitted to students through the underlying rules that structure the routines and social relationships in school and classroom life"

and points out that the objective of critical theory is not merely to describe aspects of the hidden curriculum, but to analyze how it "functions to provide differential forms of schooling to different classes of students" (p. 47).

8    Samuel Bowles and Herbert Gintis, *Schooling in Capitalist America* (New York: Basic Books, 1976), p. 125.

9    See Jean Anyon, "Social Class and the Hidden Curriculum of Work," *Journal of Education* 162 (Winter 1980): 67–92, for a more systematic comparison of hidden curricula in schools serving students of different social classes.

10    There is an implication in many of the theoretical discussions defining critical pedagogy that the proper role of the teacher is to initiate group reflection on students' outside-of-class experiences. Critics consistently neglect to suggest that the teacher can also be an initiator of powerful in-class experiences, which can then serve as objects of student analysis.

11    Bigelow and Diamond, *The Power in Our Hands,* pp. 27–30 and pp. 92–94. See also Mike Messner, "Bubblegum and Surplus Value," *The Insurgent Sociologist* 6, no. 4 (Summer 1976): 51–56.

12    My study group gave valuable feedback on this article. Thanks to Linda Christensen, Jeff Edmundson, Tom McKenna, Karen Miller, Michele Miller, Doug Sherman, and Kent Spring.

# Case Studies — Why and How

## HARRY S. BROUDY
*University of Illinois at Urbana-Champaign*

*Harry Broudy argues that the persistent criticism of teachers and of teacher education programs is due in part to the absence of a "consensus of the learned" about how teachers should be educated. Broudy's position is that a working consensus could be established through a case-study method in teacher education if cases were developed to portray important problems identified by teachers as typical and recurrent in their professional practice. Such case study, in Broudy's view, would develop prospective teachers' abilities to bring educational theory and research to bear in interpreting perennial problems and exploring alternative solutions to them.*

The perennial reports on the status of schooling in the United States are dismal, but the reasons given for their sorry state run the gamut of socioeconomic conditions, drugs, lack of money, and political controls. One explanation they do have in common is the inadequacy of the teaching force, and most commonly blamed for the inadequacy is teacher training as conducted by schools of education. Replies to this charge range from frustrated silence to elaborate analyses of socioeconomic conditions, cultural diversity, research studies in instruction, and proposals for large-scale programs to improve teacher education.

An impressive example of the complexity of the issues was provided by Albert Shanker, president of the American Federation of Teachers, in his *New York Times* column "Where We Stand" of May 14, 1989, entitled "A Difference over Answers." He cites the research of Eric A. Hanushek, an economist at the University of Rochester, New York, that concludes from the findings of 187 research studies over 20 years that 75.4 percent of the studies showed that overall per pupil expenditures made no difference in scholastic performance; 82 percent showed that pupil/teacher ratio made no difference; and about 64 percent exhibited no difference with respect to teachers' experience. Similar findings were reported on teachers' level of education, teachers' salaries, administrative expenditures, and better school facilities.[1]

Shanker responded to these findings by asking what is meant by each of the variables. He argues that they are "basket terms" covering a wide variety of factors. For example, he notes that "It's hard to believe that money doesn't make a difference. It's easy to see why it might not in an educational system that isn't structured in ways that help most kids to learn."[2] Shanker's comment, in contrast with Hanushek's findings, suggests that understanding of a complex educational system and structure is not achieved by looking at single variables, such as pupil/teacher ratio or teachers' experience, removed from context. Similarly, educational critics who try to locate the cause of school problems primarily in the inadequacy of the teaching force, and in the college preparation of that teaching force, are substituting a short and inadequate answer for the complex analysis that such problems require. Shanker is right, but not convincing.

The persistent criticism of the schoolteacher is puzzling on several counts. The task teachers perform is acknowledged to be of prime importance: the foundation of everything valuable in the culture, from good jobs to the loftiest ideals of democracy. Partly for this reason, the nature and norms of good teaching have been the concern of scholars for centuries.

I cannot in this article go into all the reasons for the persistent criticisms of teacher education. Reams have been written on the subject; commissions by the dozen have examined and reexamined the causes and proposed remedies. One factor, however, has not received the attention it deserves, namely, the curious inability of teacher education to consolidate the gains that its history of scholarship, research, and service would warrant.

Why, for example, are there so many taxonomies of teaching, learning, curriculum design, objectives, and methodologies in the literature? Diversity of classification is characteristic of the early stages of a discipline. As scholarship in a field increases in scope and depth, a consensus on its concepts and modes of inquiry begins to emerge. This consensus, in turn, becomes the basis for the paradigms of induction of new generations of workers into the field.[3]

## THE NEED FOR A CONSENSUS OF THE LEARNED

Education for a profession professes a body of concepts that structures its field of practice. These it borrows from a variety of disciplines — for example, engineering depends on physics and mathematics; medicine on biology and physiology. Each professional field has its basic concepts, classifications, definitions, usages, and canonical literatures that at any given moment are not, except at the margins, in dispute. If at the frontier of its field or in its dependent disciplines new discoveries are made, this structure may have to be modified, but it is not the privilege of anyone or everyone in the field to invent paradigms at will. A new paradigm has to earn a place in the consensus of the learned. In education, however, the books or articles authors cite are likely to reflect those read while studying for the degree. Delightful and interesting as this diversity may be, it makes a shambles of the claim of teacher education to a consensus of the learned.

Why has the plethora of studies, analyses, and debates about schooling only served to deepen the mystery? What is it that prevents teacher education and teaching from becoming a profession in the accepted sense of that term? These queries may seem unrelated, but if teaching were regarded as a set of skills that could be identified and clearly analyzed, the causes of our educational problems should have been discovered and agreed on long ago. Complaints against the alleged incompetence of electricians, plumbers, and carpenters would not create commissions in virtually every decade that struggle with the search for the causes of their inadequacy. One obvious reason for this, of course, is that teaching is much more complicated than any of the skills mentioned and involves issues that touch on many factors in the community and society as a whole. This complexity, one would think, should increase the stature of the schooling enterprise and the public's concern that it be entrusted to the highest level of competence available in the population. Yet the guild of teachers cannot compare in status with those charged with the practice of law, engineering, medicine, or architecture, despite state requirements for qualification that in structure are not very different from those stipulated for these recognized professions. If teachers had genuinely professional status, would the criticism of the schools take its present form?

Why teaching is not yet regarded as a profession is still a relevant query because on most criteria it should be. I need not remind readers that colleges of education demand of their students and faculty qualifications generically similar to those required in schools of law, medicine, business, engineering, and so forth. Their faculties play the academic game according to the same rules—doctoral degrees, research, teaching, publishing, tenure. Why, then, has genuinely professional status eluded the public school teacher? A clue to an answer is suggested by an issue of the *Phi Delta Kappan* that offered four articles by scholars invited to comment on the effect of research on schools and schooling.[4] The articles cited more than fifty references, of which only two were mentioned more than once. Surely in a recognized profession a half-dozen "authorities" treating a common topic would cite a considerable body of common research literature. Either there is no such core or it is not recognized.

That there is a plenitude of educational research is witnessed by the number of journals and doctoral dissertations and the programs of the annual meetings of the American Educational Research Association (AERA). Dozens of subgroups meet to hear papers on every aspect of schooling. The corridors are filled for days with researchers talking to researchers about grants, projects, and prospects. How much of all this is "common" knowledge? With what books, articles, and issues can one assume all or most members of AERA are familiar? Presumably not many. Is this why, despite colleges of education doing what is commonly expected from a professional school, they do not produce a cadre of "professional" practitioners?

## CASES AS PARADIGMS

One dimension of the answer, and I believe a major one, is that teacher education has not developed paradigm cases, as have most of the learned professions. Why, for example, are there so many competing taxonomies of teaching, learning, curriculum design, objectives, and methodologies in the literature? Why is it so difficult to infer from what is going on in one third grade what one will find in another third grade five miles away? Why has not some consensus on concepts and modes of inquiry in teacher education—on paradigms—emerged?

Presumably teacher education has not developed a set of problems that can legitimately claim to be so general and important that all who are qualified to teach and to teach teachers should be familiar with them and their standard interpretations and solutions. Such cases in the recognized professions constitute the core of the clinical experience. The students under the tutelage of the clinical professor demonstrate that they can apply theory to a particular situation. Clinical experience need not and very often does not involve actual treatment of an actual patient by the student. It is rather a way of testing the student's understanding of theory. The clinical experience is not the same as a laboratory exercise. Internship introduces the student to actual practice, but still under supervision. Residency or apprenticeship in an actual enterprise, whether in the law office or a hospital or an engineering firm, provides practice with much less supervision. In the preparation of teachers, laboratory, clinical training, and internship tend to be collapsed under the rubric of practice teaching—but what does practice teaching in School A in Community X have in common with that undergone in School B in Community Y or even with School B in Community X? Not the theory necessarily; not a particular methodology, probably not even the textbook.

All of which does not mean that teacher training is unfamiliar with cases as a method of acquainting prospective teachers with some of the problems awaiting them.[5] For one thing, insofar as the schools come under the jurisdiction of government bodies, there have emerged cases in which legal and procedural precedents have been established. Such cases are eminently useful to students of educational law and administration. However, no such resources are available for the numerous problems that arise in the classroom or on the playground. There are case studies that describe and analyze real school situations. For example, in 1960, as part of a research project at the University of Illlinois, we investigated and described a number of such cases.

For several years these cases constituted a part of the required course readings in Social Foundations of American Education at the University of Illinois. The materials may have been used at other teacher training institutions, but at no time could it be taken for granted that a teacher in any particular public school classroom would be familiar with them. The same can be said about other and more recent case studies.[6]

Two sources of information on problem-based case study are the growing literature on teacher-identified problems and protocol materials.[7] However, for the development of a teaching profession, some cases have to be paradigmatic for nearly all schools of education, and the research literature for interpreting such cases should be common to all courses relevant to theory and practice. There is today no guarantee that *real* cases will be used widely or become standard parts of the teacher education curriculum. Indeed, who will come across which case is highly conjectural. In contrast, lawyers, doctors, and engineers, regardless of the university at which they received their training or where they are employed, are likely to use the same classifications and terminology to discuss the problems of their profession. Lawyers, doctors, and engineers read their professional journals, more or less secure in the knowledge that what they read has been validated or challenged by their peers. The same cannot easily be said about teachers or professors of education.

Paradigms of teacher education, however, cannot be commanded or legislated, albeit reform movements reflect beliefs to the contrary. Unless they grow out of the logic and scholarship of the disciplines that support the generic activities of teaching, nominal conformity is about all one can expect in response to such legislation. Furthermore, variety is essential to creativity and progress in any enterprise. It is a well-worn cliché to praise variety within unity — theme and variations, so to speak. However, a public school system, which has many diverse constituencies to serve, has a hard time avoiding two extremes: a theme with no variation and variations in search of a theme. Public education implies that all who are subjected to it will have faced some set, however limited, of similar tasks in similar ways and will have emerged with similar learnings.

That is why, in my view, the key to the improvement of teacher education lies in the identification of a set of problems that *legitimately* can claim to be so generic and so important that all who teach will be familiar with them. Because different professions treat different problems, cases vary in nature. In legal education, for example, case studies set forth the situation being litigated, the evidence presented, the edicts of the jury and the judge, actions on appeals, and so forth. They become part of the history of jurisprudence. In time they become models for legal argument and decision and an important component of legal studies. Case studies in medicine consist of careful descriptions of a disease entity, its history, symptoms, treatment and its effects. They may also include the theoretical explanation of the malady and evaluation of various modes of treatment.

Case studies in other professions approximate these models but understandably vary in the concepts used for their analysis and the degree of authority they invoke — but they are alike in that they portray a problem of practice. Whether they are chosen for the education of prospective practitioners depends on the degree to which they probe the principles or the theory on which the concepts of the profession rest and on the frequency with which they occur in practice.

Cases, therefore, consist of selected problems of professional practice and constitute the problemata of the professional curriculum. In the training of prospective professionals they form the core of clinical experience and test whether the student can apply theory. In teacher education, consensus on the professional education curriculum is not likely to be achieved without agreement on the nature and content of desirable clinical experiences for prospective teachers. Consensus on this clinical experience in turn must rely on the identification of paradigm cases of professional practice.

In the present state of scholarship in and about education, a consensus on what prospective teachers should know and experience is difficult to find, even though the potential for it exists. The consensus of the learned remains a remote hope in the presence of the volume and variety of research and textbooks, noted earlier.

For such reasons, it is more promising to seek a basis for consensus not in agreements on taxonomy or theory or modes of organizing in the training of teachers but, rather, in a standard set of problems, and perhaps most effectively, the videotape portrayal of such a set. What reason is there to believe, however, that such a set, however thoughtfully constructed, would constitute an acceptable consensus? The reason for acceptance would have to lie in the fact that the case selected would originate in the very constituency that is being trained to cope with them, namely, classroom teachers. It is to identify such a set of cases or problems that the project at the University of Illinois College of Education is directed.

## THE ILLINOIS PROJECT

The Illinois Project on Professional Knowledge in Teacher Education has three major components: the identification of standard problems in the teaching profession, the video representation of selected problems as cases for study, and the preparation of research-based instructional materials for studying the cases. Here, several points need clarification. First, this project is not the first to construct case studies for teacher education. Second, it is not claimed that this set will do for all phases of schooling. One could construct case studies in educational administration, law, and finance.[8] Finally, the aim of the project is not simply to construct a set of cases, but rather to construct a set that is validated by the procedures of selection. No doubt creative educators can *construct* interesting and useful cases and by assiduous research one could *find* situations in classrooms that occur with sufficient frequency to warrant their status as case studies. The Illinois Project depends on selection methods that will stand the scrutiny of two criteria — namely, frequency of occurrence and generic importance — as assessed by teachers themselves. These sets may not coincide. Dozens of annoyances plague or irritate teachers, but they may not be important problems. Their occurrence and treatment may be so familiar and routinized as not to warrant systematic study. Many housekeeping chores fall into this category, as do those gritty encounters between staff members up and down the chain of command.

Not all predicaments are problems and not all problems are generic. In order for a case to become standardized as a problem worthy of the study of all prospective teachers, it must involve principles, facts, and alternative treatment hypotheses.

Our project began with members of the faculty of the Educational Policy Studies Department recruiting teachers to take the summer course EPS 301 (a course in the Philosophy of Education) and in part relying on the normal load of schoolteachers and other graduate students who take the course. In addition to the teachers taking EPS 301, teachers enrolled in other summer session education courses in Champaign and two off-campus sites (Chicago and East St. Louis) participated in the project by completing written survey forms.[9]

The Champaign-area teachers, through a summer term's reading, writing, and dialogue, began the process of identifying what might be called "standard problems in teaching" — problems identified by teachers as frequent and important in their practice. To establish that such problems may legitimately be considered standard in the field, we conducted a national survey of schoolteachers at different grade levels in selected demographic settings. The national survey, the data from which are now being analyzed, asked teachers to identify the relative frequency and importance of over ninety specific instances of typically problematic situations in ten categories. The general categories, like the specific instances falling within those categories, were identified by the original population of teachers from three graduate classes. These general categories of professional problems are (1) low social and professional status, (2) low student motivation, (3) problems in parent-school relations, (4) problems with administrators and administration, (5) too many noninstructional duties, (6) time management, (7) student discipline, (8) tracking, labeling, and standardized testing, (9) problems with meeting the instructional needs of minority students, and (10) lack of funding for materials, salaries, and programs.

Our preliminary findings indicate distinct trends in teachers' regard for some specific instances as more recurrent and important than others. On the basis of our preliminary analysis, for example, we have developed two pilot cases, the first treating perceived problems of black male high school students and the second treating teachers' perceptions of their low professional status. Our aim is to develop, at first, fifteen of these typically problematic cases to be used in the professional preparation of teachers.

Prospective teachers will study each case in the context of accompanying research material (representing competing perspectives where appropriate) that contributes to our ability to interpret the case portrayed. In the case of the black male students' school problems, for example, one might rely on a broad range of foundational perspectives: historical, to understand the historically unique place of blacks in American culture; sociological, to understand the distinctive experience of blacks in contemporary institutions; sociolinguistic, to understand the significance of language and culture in different achievement outcomes in schools; psychological, to understand the role of students' sense of efficacy and self-esteem in school achievement; philosophical, to understand conceptions of "equality" and "opportunity" and how they are used in argument to justify and criticize the place of blacks in American schooling; and so on.

Although informed by these disciplinary perspectives, judgments about educational problems weave these perspectives together inseparably. The historical insights regarding the case of the black male student, for example, are full of economic, sociological, and normative dimensions. The purpose of the resource materials is not to make prospective teachers expert in history, sociology, or psychology of education, but to use the research such disciplines have provided so that students can exercise informed understandings in interpreting and diagnosing educational problems.

A distinctive dimension of the case-study approach we are developing is the use of video representation of the standard problems. We have produced video pilots for both of the above-mentioned cases and have found the tapes very effective in focusing research literature on problems of practice. It is our belief that the video format offers an unusually effective way to introduce and teach research-based resource materials to prospective teachers. If distributed nationally, a set of fifteen video case representations, together with the accompanying research materials, could provide a strong base for the codification of research knowledge about teaching practice. Such an effort could represent a significant step toward the "consensus of the learned" that is now absent from the teacher education profession.                    ·

Throughout the planning and production of such video cases, the primacy of a valid sample and the quality of the tapes themselves will have to be maintained. It cannot be repeated too often that to achieve the status of paradigms the cases cannot be idiosyncratic regionally or theoretically. It is essential that teacher training institutions in any state or region recognize them as portraying problems they are facing. Nor can the cases be slanted to reflect particular philosophies of education. The methods of selection that the project has employed are intended to provide assurance of this "neutrality" in the portrayal of the cases. It is expected, however, that one or another interpretive framework or educational philosophy may well be favored in the analysis and discussion of the cases in actual classroom use.

Such cases, properly produced, can become the focus for analysis, discussion, evaluation, and reading of relevant research in *every* course in the teacher education program. The sample videotape on the distinctive problems faced by black male students, for example, could be used in philosophical and social foundations, educational psychology, curriculum, administration, counseling, and methods courses. Every course in the teacher education curriculum could bring to bear its special disciplinary concepts, theoretical constructs, and research on its analysis and treatment. Above all, students and faculty, wherever they may be, could refer to Case X knowing that their fellow students and teachers, wherever they are, will be familiar with competing explanations and analyses of the problem portrayed.

## CASES AS CLINICAL SURROGATES

A primary use of case studies is to serve as a surrogate for clinical teaching, where theory is applied under the scrutiny of a clinical professor. In teacher training programs an analogue of this form of clinical teaching is hard to come by. It is not quite the sort of experience one gets in practice teaching — albeit as in all other educational matters it is risky to generalize. Not all practice teaching takes care to test theory under tutelage of the master teacher or the clinical teacher. The cases on videotape can serve as a useful substitute, for the technology allows the tape to be stopped and reversed as needed, to intersperse watching with discussion.

Indeed, this may well be one of the major advantages of the case study. Classroom teachers have been criticized for being allergic to theory. Publishers often report that texts and workbooks must be very specific about matters of curriculum and methodology. Careful directions for procedure at every step in the lesson, they say, are highly appreciated by all concerned. This overreliance on directions accounts for much of the reluctance to grant classroom teaching professional status. It is the mark of a craft, not a profession, merely to execute prescribed procedures with accuracy and skill. Given a predicament, the craftsperson needs only to identify the situation and apply the appropriate procedure. If that fails, another identification is made and its appropriate procedure applied. If all ploys fail, the predicament is turned over to a supervisor. The supervisor may have a wider repertory of situations, but if these also fail, there must be recourse to the engineer or architect or physician, who, in turn, can resort to a hypothesis based on theory and prescribe accordingly.

Assuming that the teachers of teachers correspond to theoreticians in other professions, the testing of theory on cases becomes a prime ingredient of "professional" teacher education. Many of the current proposals for the reform of teacher education tend to slur over this phase of instruction because an analogue of the clinical situation is not available.

## SUPPLEMENTARY MATERIALS

Unlike cases in other professional schools, the cases potentially identified for teacher education do not have a well-documented set of solutions in the form of court decisions or standard procedures. To be sure, there are problems in education that have been processed by the courts, and these are useful in the education of administrators, policymakers, and professors of school administration. The situations described by such cases, however, are not, as a rule, the point at which the classroom teacher directly intersects with pupils, parents, or colleagues.

The situations the Illinois sample has identified have no canonical descriptions or solutions. There is, no doubt, a considerable volume of research that bears on them, but rarely is there a manageable set of studies that the field accepts as definitive. What the textbooks in their courses on methods have to say about these situations depends, of course, on the text, and the course instructor who chose the text. The last phase of the project will provide the user with background materials for both the teacher of the course and the student. These will serve as a source of suggested solutions and critical discussion of them. Here, too, a wide range of materials is possible, from simple bibliographies to sophisticated analyses.

However, some professors will want to use the tapes without literature of any kind, preferring to choose their own study materials. Whatever approach the instructor chooses, this much can be expected as reasonable outcomes: a demonstrated ability to analyze the tape for the locus of the difficulty, to identify the causes of the difficulty and to give reasons for the identification, to supply analogous cases, to hypothesize as to treatments and defend them.

In conclusion, it should be noted that these or other case-study surrogates cannot take the place of a consensus of the learned. A genuine consensus awaits developments in the theory and research of educational problems that one hopes will emerge. Educational studies and research may one day be studied carefully, tested, discussed, and either survive to be read another day or be allowed to rest in oblivion. Educational research today has no systematic (formal or informal) way to do this, with the result that it does not face a scarcity of production, but rather a waste-disposal problem. If these cases

are no substitute for a genuine consensus of the learned, they may be a small
first step toward establishing one.

## Notes

1 Albert Shanker, "A Difference over Answers," *New York Times,* May 14, 1989.

2 Ibid.

3 The term *paradigm* was made popular by Thomas Kuhn in his *The Structure of Scientific Revolutions* (Chicago: The University of Chicago Press, 1962). It takes a revolution in science to bring about a change in the standard problems and categories that occupy the energies of the scientific community.

4 See the following articles in *Phi Delta Kappan* 65, no. 7 (March 1984): Eva L. Baker, "Can Educational Research Inform Educational Practice? Yes," pp. 453–55; Elliot W. Eisner, "Can Educational Research Inform Educational Practice?", pp. 447–52; Arthur R. Jensen, "Political Ideologies and Educational Research," pp. 460–62; and Mark G. Yudof, "Educational Policy Research and the New Consensus of the 1980's," pp. 446–59.

5 Amy McAninch has brought to my attention, for example, the remarkable early volume by Henryetta Sperle, *The Case Method Technique in Professional Training* (New York: Teachers College, Columbia University, 1933). An important later volume often cited in the case-study and protocol literature on problem situations in teaching is B. O. Smith, S. Cohen, and A. Pearl, *Teachers for the Real World* (Washington, D.C.: American Association of Colleges for Teacher Education, 1969). Sustained attention has been given to a case-study approach to problems in teaching by Donald Cruickshank, who employs the term *protocol* for what is referred to in other professions as case study. See, for example, his *Models for the Preparation of America's Teachers* (Bloomington, Ind.: Phi Delta Kappa Educational Foundation, 1985). Finally, this approach is applied in a teacher education text by Gordon E. Greenwood, Thomas L. Good, and Betty L. Siegel, *Problem Situations in Teaching* (New York: Harper & Row, 1971).

6 See, for example, *Case Studies in Educational Management,* ed. S. Gould et al. (London: Harper & Row, 1984). Some of the studies are based on published materials, others were commissioned. Some rely on data derived from interviews, while others incorporate documentary evidence, data from questionnaires, diary records, or observation of meetings.

7 See, for example, the extensive bibliography in Simon Veenman, "Perceived Problems of Beginning Teachers," *Review of Educational Research* 54, no. 2 (Summer 1984): 143–78. A good bibliography on the protocol materials movement, which has made extensive use of case-study techniques, can be found in Willis D. Copeland, "Laboratory Experiences in Teacher Education," *Encyclopedia of Education,* ed. H. Mitzel (New York: The Free Press, 1982). See also D. R. Cruickshank, "Instructional Alternatives Available for Use in Professional Education," in *Simulation and Clinical Knowledge in Teacher Education,* ed. E. Dale Doak, Ted Hipple, and Marcia Keith (Proceedings for a National Invitational Symposium, University of Tennessee, Knoxville, November 13-14, 1986).

8 Cruickshank notes that a problem with the case-study or protocol approach has been the difficulty of achieving consensus on which problems in teaching are most worthy of study *(Models for the Preparation of America's Teachers,* p. 96), and this problem extends to other educational spheres as well (educational administration, finance, law, etc.). However, in these other areas, case-study models from law, business, finance, etc., can prove immediately instructive. See Arch R. Dooley and Wickham Skinner, "Casing Casemethod Methods," *Academy of Management Review,* no. 2 (April 1977): 277–89.

9 Harry S. Broudy, Steve Tozer, and William T. Trent, "The Illinois Project on Professional Knowledge in Teacher Education: A Pilot Study of Core Problems in Teaching" (Report, University of Illinois College of Education, Champaign, 1986).

# CONTRIBUTORS

CAROLE A. AMES is professor of educational psychology at the University of Illinois at Urbana-Champaign. She has authored many articles on the subject of student motivation and is coeditor, with Russ Ames, of the series Research on Motivation in Education published by Academic Press.

RICHARD C. ANDERSON is professor of psychology, educational psychology, and elementary and early childhood education, and director of the Center for the Study of Reading, University of Illinois at Urbana-Champaign. He has published on the topics of psycholinguistics, human learning and memory, and reading instruction.

THOMAS H. ANDERSON is associate professor of educational psychology and a senior scientist at the Center for the Study of Reading, University of Illinois at Urbana-Champaign. His major research areas are content area reading and the diagrammatical representation of knowledge.

BONNIE B. ARMBRUSTER is associate professor in the department of curriculum and instruction, and the Center for the Study of Reading, University of Illinois at Urbana-Champaign. Her interests include content area reading and teacher education for literacy.

WILLIAM BIGELOW teaches at Jefferson High School in Portland, Oregon. He is author of *Strangers in Their Own Country: A Curriculum Guide on South Africa* (Africa World Press) and coauthor of *The Power in Our Hands: A Curriculum on the History of World and Workers in the United States* (Monthly Review Press).

HARRY S. BROUDY is professor emeritus of philosophy and education at the University of Illinois at Urbana-Champaign. He is author of *The Uses of Schooling* (Routledge, 1988).

CHRISTOPHER M. CLARK is professor of education at Michigan State University and professor in residence at Whitehills Elementary School. His professional interests include research on teacher thinking, teacher professional development, and the relationships between research and practice.

W. PATRICK DICKSON is professor and chair, department of counseling, educational psychology, and special education at Michigan State University. His scholarly interests focus on the study and practice of the use of technology in teacher education and in schools.

WALTER DOYLE is professor in the division of teaching and teacher education at the University of Arizona, Tucson. He specializes in research on academic tasks in classrooms and the development of knowledge structures in teaching. He is a former editor of the *Elementary School Journal* and past vice president of Division K (Teaching and Teacher Education) of the American Educational Research Association.

GLORIANNE M. LECK is a professor of foundations of education at Youngstown State University (Ohio) and is the current president of the American Educational Studies Association.

ROBERT L. LINN is professor of education and co-director of the Center for Research on Evaluation, Standards, and Student Testing, University of Colorado, Boulder. His primary area of interest is educational measurement.

PENELOPE PETERSON is co-director, Institute for Research on Teaching, and co-director of the Center for the Learning and Teaching of Elementary Subjects at Michigan State University. Her current research interests include the study of teachers' knowledge and thinking and research on the teaching and learning of mathematics in elementary schools.

LEE S. SHULMAN is the Charles Ducommun Professor of Education at Stanford University. His research is on the relationships between knowledge and teaching, on the development of teachers, and on the assessment of quality in teaching. He is a past president of the American Educational Research Association and is currently president of the National Academy of Education.

JONAS F. SOLTIS is William Heard Kilpatrick Professor of Philosophy and Education at Teachers College, Columbia University, and editor, *Teachers College Record*. He is a past president of the Philosophy of Education Society and is currently president of the John Dewey Society.

STEVEN TOZER is associate professor of philosophy of education, department of educational policy studies, University of Illinois at Urbana-Champaign. His primary research areas are in social foundations of education and teacher education.

WILLIAM T. TRENT is associate professor of educational policy studies and sociology at the University of Illinois at Urbana-Champaign. His current research interests include, equity issues in higher education; desegregated schooling experience; race, class and cultural implications for educational attainment; and core problems in teaching.

PAUL C. VIOLAS is a professor of history of education at the University of Illinois at Urbana-Champaign. He is author of *The Training or the Urban Working-Class* and a coauthor of *Roots of Crisis*.

# Index

Academic disciplines, 4, 59-60
Achievement, 56, 58, 112, 114-15, 116, 118-19
Action orientation, 102-3, 109
Activities, 52-54
Aims of education, 18-19, 75-76, 112
Articulation, 105-6, 108, 110
Assessment, 124-37
Attribution theory, 115-16, 119-20
Authenticity, 100, 106-7, 109

Blacks, 63-70

Case studies: and classroom knowledge, 58-59; as clinical surrogates, 159-60; and a consensus of the learned, 152-54, 156, 158, 160-61; and criticism of teachers/teacher education programs, 151-61; and educational psychology, 40-42, 43; and foundation studies, 10, 11, 17-20; as paradigms, 154-56; and supplementary materials, 160-61
Case Western Reserve University, 4
Certification, 107, 127
Civil rights, 63-70
Class issues, 139-49
Classroom knowledge, 52-60
Coaching, 103-4, 108, 109-10
Cognition. See Cognitive psychology; Educational psychology; Learning
Cognitive psychology, 8-10, 38, 50
Collective text, 140, 141
Colleges of education, 51, 108-10
Community of learners, 93-95
Community of practice, 20-21
Competency, of teachers, 67, 68-69, 81-82
Comprehension, of text, 8-10
Consensus of the learned, 152-54, 156, 158, 160-61
Constructivist theories of learning, 32, 33-37, 43
Content, 11, 17-20, 40, 130-36, 137
Context: and educational psychology, 33-37, 40-41; of gender oppression and interpretation, 90-93; and history, 74; and knowledge, 30, 57, 59, 98-99; of motivation, 120-21

Control of teaching, 51-52, 56, 57, 58-59
Critical pedagogy, 139-49
Cultural literacy, 16, 17, 22-23
Curriculum, 54-55, 58, 59, 142-45

Developmental perspective, 30, 38, 43, 101-2, 107, 109, 118
Dewey, John, 5-6, 11, 13-14, 20, 22, 92
Dialogical community/education, 139, 148
Disciplines, academic, 4, 59-60

Educated person concept, 15-17, 22-23
Educational psychology: and beliefs about knowledge, 33-37; and case studies, 40-42, 43; challenges for, 43-45; and constructivists, 32-37, 43; content of, 40; and context, 33-37, 40-41; and development, 30, 43; dilemmas in, 26-43, 44-45; domain of, 32, 38-40, 45; and instruction, 45; and learning hierarchies, 28-30; methods of, 27, 40; and motivation, 111; and prior knowledge, 28, 29, 30-31, 33-37, 42; rethinking, 26; and subject matter, 42; and teachers' knowledge of learning, 30-32; and teachers' learning, 37-40; and transferability, 27, 28-30, 40, 42-43; and unquestioned assumptions, 27-29
Effectiveness, 51-52, 55-56, 57, 59, 125-27
Equality, 64-65, 89-90
Ethnicity, 63-70
Evaluation. See Assessment Experience, history as a substitute for, 73, 74-76, 79-80

Feminism, 85-86, 88, 89, 91, 92
Flexner, Abraham, 2-3, 4, 5
Foundation studies: criticisms of, 14-17; and metaphors, 11-12, 14-15; purpose of, 21, 148; a reconceptualization of, 13-23; and schools, 19; and shared understanding/communication, 13-23
Freire, Paulo, 139, 149

Gender/Genderization, 67, 68-69, 84-97

Hidden curriculum, 142-45
Hierarchy, and gender, 89-90, 92, 95
Hispanics, 63-70